THE ART OF MEDIATION

Mark D. Bennett
Michele S.G. Hermann

Reproduction Permission
National Institute for Trial Advocacy
Notre Dame Law School
Notre Dame, Indiana 46556
(800) 225-6482
Fax (219) 282-1263
E-mail nita.1@nd.edu

Bennett, Mark and Michele Hermann, *The Art of Mediation* (NITA, 1996).

ISBN 1-55681-483-6

4/99 printing

DEDICATION

To my Father, Lyman Bennett, who provided a quiet,
eloquent example of personal integrity

and

To my Mother, Dorothy Bennett, who nurtured my
love of the written word.

M.B.

I had learnt the true practice of law. I had learnt to find out the better side of human nature and to enter men's hearts. I realized that the true function of a lawyer was to unite parties riven asunder.

Mohandas K. Gandhi

THE ART OF MEDIATION

Table of Contents

Table of Illustrations

ACKNOWLEDGMENTS

This book developed as an integral part of the basic and family mediation trainings we have co-led during the past ten years at the University of New Mexico School of Law. We wish to acknowledge the many people who have supported and assisted us in this work. In particular, we want to thank the participants in our trainings whose enthusiasm for learning the mediation process has provided questions, feedback, and suggestions that shaped every section of this book.

PREFACE

This is both an exciting and a troubling time for the mediation process in the United States. Our society needs tools to deal with the many conflicts that exist in our institutions and communities, and mediation has been recognized as an effective process to handle disputes. As mediation becomes popular and fashionable, many interest groups want to claim it and turn it to their use. We support the resultant expansion of the use of mediation. We are concerned, however, about some trends in the field that deserve the attention of practitioners, consumers, and academicians.

The benevolent face of mediation shows it to be a helpful way for people to retain power and control over their lives while dealing with conflict productively and economically. The darker side of mediation shows it to be a private process, insulated from scrutiny, in which people who are vulnerable can be overpowered, treated with bias or prejudice, and pressured into unjust agreements.

We believe that there are no simple answers that will help us realize the potential of mediation while mitigating the impact of the risky side of the process. We are skeptical of the efforts to legislate who can be a mediator and fear they apply arbitrary training and professional standards to control entry into the profession. We believe that the most powerful predictor of the quality of service received by mediation participants is the heart and intention of the mediator. We have trained many people who are already gifted at mediation. Their basic values, life experiences, and ability to be present in the midst of conflict qualify them as mediators far more than any degree or training certificate ever could. We also have trained respected professionals with advanced academic degrees who have found that they lacked the capacity to act as mediators and have willingly left the field for others.

We intend that these materials underscore the importance of personal style, self-awareness, and openness of spirit in mediator competence. Mediators have an obligation to acknowledge and monitor their values, cultural identity, potential biases, and blind spots. We do not believe that the assumption of a neutral and impartial role confers these qualities, nor that mediators can automatically check their personal baggage at the door. Therefore, it is incumbent on those who wish to mediate to undertake a rigorous and continuing path of honest self-examination.

This emphasis on personal responsibility and the mediator's inner qualities gave us our title, *The Art of Mediation*. By art, we mean the sum total of techniques, intuitions, inspirations, and insights that constitute skillful mediation. This book attempts to dissect mediation as a process, a set of skills, and a subject. We do not believe, however, that it is a reductionist process. As we take mediation apart and put it back together, we hope that the reader will share our conviction that the whole is far more than the sum of the parts.

The primary audience for this book is comprised of people taking basic mediation training. We assume that this audience will be as diverse as ours have been: practicing attorneys; second and third year law students; trial and appellate court judges; mental health professionals; administrators and managers; primary, secondary, and university teachers; realtors; planners; architects; accountants; human resource personnel; engineers; and even a well digger.

Section One contains six chapters that set the mediation process in context for the reader. It provides basic definitions, contrasts mediation with other forms of dispute resolution, describes varieties of mediation, lays out the roles and functions of the mediator, and identifies practical issues.

Section Two has eight chapters that analyze the specific stages of mediation. In each chapter, there is a summary of the stage, a list of the goals to be achieved, a description of the main tasks of the mediator, examples of common procedures, and cautions of possible challenges for the mediators during the stage. This approach to teaching mediation as a process with a series of discrete stages requires a caution to the reader that mediation as experienced by the mediators and the participants is far more circular than linear. Stages may be repeated or temporarily bypassed. Someone once said, *Mediation has three stages . . . a beginning, a middle, and an end, not necessarily in that order!*

Section Three takes substantive topics that either cut across the mediation process, e.g. communication skills, or raise issues and concerns that merit additional reflection by the reader, e.g. power and power balancing.

Section Four identifies commonly asked questions about mediation as a profession, a process, and a business, and discusses them with a practical and common-sense approach.

Section Five, the Appendices, contains four sections of practical applications. The first section replicates ethical standards. The second section includes worksheets for mediators to use as templates with disputants. The third section contains forms which illustrate both sample agreements to mediate and final mediation agreements. The final section is an annotated bibliography of dispute resolution books to help in the further study of mediation.

Section Six contains the role plays which form a major basis for experiential learning.

Although this book represents the fruits of our collaboration and our thinking at this point, we see it as a work in progress. As we believe that mediation is a way, a path of personal and professional growth for those who practice this art, we know that teachers of mediation can and must grow in their ability to share this knowledge in ways that respond to the needs of the learner. We welcome your comments and suggestions for improvement. Please contact us at the University of New Mexico School of Law, 1117 Stanford NE, Albuquerque, NM 87131.

Mark D. Bennett

Michele S.G. Hermann

April 15, 1996

SECTION ONE: INTRODUCTION TO MEDIATION

I. INTRODUCTION

This workbook is a brief and practical guide to the mediation process. It is intended to be used as an adjunct to a 40-hour training; a summary of the key points in lectures and discussions. The book permits the mediation student to reduce note-taking and focus on interactive learning, using the workbook as an annotated map of the course and of the mediation process. This book deals with classic mediation, where the disputants work with mediators to explore their conflict and seek a satisfactory resolution to their dispute. This book does not deal with the process of settlement facilitation, where the parties are accompanied by their attorneys who take the lead in working with the facilitator to negotiate a settlement. It will help you to keep this distinction in mind: mediators work directly with the disputants, teaching them communication and problem solving skills so that they may resolve their conflict themselves, while settlement facilitators work primarily in the context of litigation, helping attorneys to settle cases which are awaiting trial. The two processes, and the skills they employ, are not mutually exclusive, and the term mediation may be used at times to describe settlement facilitation. The major distinction is between a process where the parties are assisted in finding their own resolution and one where the parties' attorneys are assisted in achieving settlement.

We see mediation skills as fluid and responsive. There are no formulas or rituals of behavior which will guarantee a successful mediation. Because mediation skills focus so contextually on the interactions and reactions of the people involved, both disputants and mediators, they can best be taught experientially. Neither reading about mediation nor watching other people mediate can compare with participating in a mediation as a method of learning mediation skills. Thus, the focus of a successful mediation training will be on simulated mediation exercises with intensive feedback from experienced coaches.

You will participate in a series of role plays during mediation training. Initially, the simulations will be divided into stages, allowing you to focus on the separate sequences of the mediation process. You will then progress from simple to more complex complete mediations. You will play three roles in these exercises: mediator, disputant, and observer. Each offers you the opportunity for a different type of learning experience. As a mediator, you will apply your skills and receive feedback from coaches, disputants, and observers. As a disputant, you will act as a consumer of the process, learning what the mediators can do to help you come to resolution and also which of their interventions do not work for you. As an observer, you will focus on the interactions between mediators and disputants, and think about how you might handle situations as they arise.

Figure 1. Getting the Most Out of the Role Play Process

Context

** Role playing offers the learner the opportunity to try out mediator skills in an environment that is forgiving of errors.
** Each function within the role play offers the opportunity to learn:
  - the co-mediators can learn by doing;
  - a backup mediator can learn by thinking as if he or she must step in;
  - the observer can learn by watching for patterns, skills and behaviors that work and don't work; and
  - the disputant can experience which mediator behaviors help and hinder.

Tasks During the Role Play
Mediators ** Let the coach know if you have not had the opportunity to act as a mediator. ** When you are assigned your function (1. co-mediator, 2. backup mediator/ observer) study the appropriate materials in advance so you can get the most out of the role play experience. ** Co-mediators meet before the role play to plan how to work together. ** If you have questions, ask your coach. ** Take the mediator role seriously and stay in role until directed otherwise. **Disputants** ** Read your background information and role carefully. If you have questions, ask your coach. ** Stay in role until directed otherwise by your coach. ** Give the mediator a robust but reasonable level of difficulty to deal with. Make it interesting, not impossible. ** Don't make up information or motivations that are not in the script. You may need to invent a little bit in order to remain in role and respond to the dynamics of the role play. That is okay so long as it is truly consistent with your role and the case facts. If necessary, check with your coach in a quick "time-out." **Observer** ** Some people learn best by watching. ** There is a checklist of things to watch for at the beginning of the role play section. ** You may be asked to step in to one of the co-mediator roles. Watch the role play as if this is so. Ask yourself, *What would I do next? What is going well? What are the issues? How are the parties communicating?*

The workbook can serve as your mediation companion — a compilation of tips and suggestions to help you identify and execute options. It can be used both as a quick reference during mediation and as a guide to reflection and analysis after a mediation session is over.

Learning mediation skills is a journey of introspection. You cannot understand the actions and reactions of other people unless you understand yourself. You cannot assist disputants to think clearly and wisely unless you are clear within yourself. Obviously, such self-knowledge is a lifetime's work, not the product of a 40-hour skills training. We hope your initial mediation training will open some doors for you and invite you to walk on new and different pathways.

Because we believe that this kind of learning is particularly hard to undertake alone, we use the model of co-mediation in our classes. We also recommend that you associate with another mediator when you begin to practice. The other mediator ideally should be someone with more experience than you; someone who has a background complementary to yours. You can further broaden your learning environment by joining or forming a mediation discussion group comprised of other practicing mediators. This group can be a source of information, support, and insight as you develop your mediation skills.

II. MEDIATION AND ALTERNATIVE DISPUTE RESOLUTION

Alternative dispute resolution is both new and old. It is a recent and explosively growing movement which seeks to reduce litigation, increase participant satisfaction, and control court congestion. Many elements of modern ADR methods, however, have roots in ancient traditions of problem-solving valued for centuries in a variety of cultures throughout this country and around the world.

Dispute resolution alternatives run a broad gamut of forms and functions. At one end of the spectrum are different methods of adjudication which share reliance on a third-party decision maker. These include traditional, formal litigation in which courts make binding, public pronouncements of rights and responsibilities, as well as arbitration and rent-a-judge programs where the parties choose their decision makers and the rules which will govern their private, informal, speedy proceedings. At the other end of the ADR spectrum are applications of negotiation, in which the disputants, or their attorneys, work among themselves to settle their disputes. In the middle are processes of assisted negotiation, such as mediation and settlement facilitation, where a third-party neutral works to bring about a voluntary resolution.

Since more than 90 percent of cases filed in court can be predicted to settle, while less than ten percent proceed to trial, negotiation is by far the most pervasive dispute resolution process. Indeed, with the statistical success of negotiation, one might even question the need for other alternative dispute resolution processes. Negotiation, however, may not work efficiently, may not work fairly, or may not work at all. Thus, assisted negotiation processes, including mediation, have developed to meet these problems.

Assisted negotiation processes, which range from early neutral evaluation to summary jury trials, all share the characteristic of using a third party who is _not_ a decision maker, but whose role is to facilitate the disputants' efforts to reach a settlement. Unlike arbitration, where the parties are assured of a resolution through the arbitrator's decision, in all of the assisted negotiation processes the parties will achieve a resolution only if they, with the facilitator's assistance, agree to settle the case themselves.

In mediation as well, the mediators are not there to make a decision, nor to say who is right and who is wrong, nor to say what should happen to the parties or to the issues in dispute. The mediators are there to promote the disputants' use of constructive problem-solving skills. The mediators do this by guiding the parties through a structured process which has been developed to enhance their ability to achieve a resolution which is fair, satisfying, and durable. The ultimate success of the process, however, rests with the parties, not with the mediators. The mediators can only open doors for the parties; it is up to the parties to decide whether or not to walk through them.

Figure 2. Dispute Resolution Options

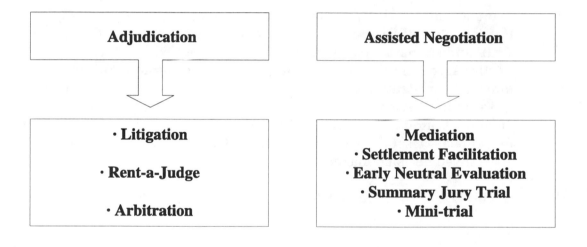

Adjudication	Assisted Negotiation
· Litigation · Rent-a-Judge · Arbitration	· Mediation · Settlement Facilitation · Early Neutral Evaluation · Summary Jury Trial · Mini-trial

III. DISPUTE RESOLUTION PROCESSES DEFINED

A. ADJUDICATION

1. Litigation:
Formal trial in a court of record which results in a binding decision. Useful in cases of public importance or where parties seek a decision of broad application. May be necessary where a just result requires one side to be compelled to pay or act.

2. Rent-a-Judge:
Statutory process in which parties hire decision maker to hear their case. Record is kept and decision is appealable as if it were made by a court. Useful in cases requiring fast, private resolutions within a court-like structure.

3. Arbitration:
Parties select decision maker, or panel of decision makers, often those with subject matter expertise rather than those with legal training. Parties agree on rules and procedures, which are normally relaxed and informal. Arbitration can be binding or non-binding, decisions in the latter being advisory. Usually there is no reasoned written decision. Judgment often can be perfected in court. Extremely limited grounds for appeal. Useful in cases requiring fast, private decisions and specialized decision makers.

B. ASSISTED NEGOTIATION

1. Mediation:
Neutral mediators (can be one, two, or a panel) help parties to engage in negotiation and cooperative problem solving. Lawyers typically not present, but counsel clients before and during process and review proposed agreements. Useful in cases with ongoing relationships, non-legal issues, emotional concerns.

2. Settlement Facilitation:
Third-party neutral, often a retired judge or experienced attorney, meets with parties and their lawyers, usually late in the litigation process as the case nears trial. Typically the neutral facilitator shuttles offers back and forth between sides after exploring the basis in reality of the parties' positions. Lawyers, after consulting with their clients, take lead role in the negotiating process. Useful in producing dollar settlements, breaking deadlocks.

3. Early Neutral Evaluation:
A court-annexed process where a respected neutral, often a retired judge or a lawyer with subject matter expertise, meets with both sides, usually after close of the pleadings but before discovery begins. Goal is to assess projected pretrial and trial costs, predict likely outcomes, and explore settlement. Limited discovery may be structured to assist ongoing negotiations. Useful in complex and protracted litigation.

4. Summary Jury Trial:
A court-annexed process used when long and complex cases are ready for trial. Involves each side presenting a case summary to a jury, usually in a single day, receiving an advisory decision, and using that decision as the basis for settlement negotiations which are facilitated by the judge who has presided over the summary trial. Useful in complex cases when value is uncertain.

5. Mini-trial:
Uses process similar to summary jury trial but is not court-annexed. Parties often choose a neutral to preside over the mini-trial who is an expert in the field and who can assist them with their negotiations afterward. Useful in complex cases where parties wish to retain process control.

C. COMBINED PROCESSES

1. Mediation — Arbitration:
Combines mediation and arbitration, beginning with mediation. If there is a determination by parties or mediators that negotiated settlement is not possible, the mediators act as arbitrators and issue a binding decision.

2. Special Mastering:
Court-appointed referee engages in conflict management, exercising some judicial powers while using negotiation skills and processes to promote settlement.

IV. SELECTING A DISPUTE RESOLUTION PROCESS

The development of alternative dispute resolution processes offers the opportunity to send disputes to the forums where they can best be resolved. Several things are necessary to achieve this goal. First, there must be a diversity of dispute resolution alternatives available so that a selection can be made on the basis of optimal choice rather than limited options. Second, there must be accurate dispute diagnosis so that the appropriate forum can be chosen. Third, there must be trained, competent providers of dispute resolution alternatives so that the chosen process can have the best opportunity to succeed. Fourth, there must be knowledgeable attorneys involved in the process, so that the parties can have effective legal support. Fifth, there must be educated disputants in the case so that they can have a sense of the advantages and disadvantages of the different alternatives as well as how to participate in them effectively. Sixth, there must be a real concern with the risks that participants of color, women, and other traditionally disadvantaged groups may face in alternative dispute resolution processes, so that appropriate protections can be utilized. Finally, there must be adequate funding available so that access to the alternative dispute resolution processes is not controlled by economic means, and so that the providers of dispute resolution services can be fairly compensated for their professional services.

At the moment, not all of these criteria can be met in all jurisdictions. The formal dispute resolution movement is relatively new and is still growing and developing. These criteria represent goals to strive for as dispute resolution programs expand, so that choices are made with a clear vision of the context as a whole. Nonetheless, it may be useful to consider the advantages and disadvantages of the various processes, paying particular attention to the unique attributes which mediation can contribute to dispute resolution. In selecting a dispute resolution process, there are a number of factors to consider. These include: goals, procedural status and outcome control, formality and cost, timing, relationships, and personalities.

The element of goals refers to what it is the participants would like to achieve as a resolution of their dispute. If a public pronouncement of rights and responsibilities in a formally written enforceable judgment is what is sought, then adjudication by a court of record will be most appropriate. Adjudication is also appropriate in disputes where one or more of the disputants seeks to have a public opportunity to take the witness stand and tell their story. On the other hand, goals which are outside the traditional reaches of the law, such as understanding, an apology, a change in attitude, or an offer of assistance, will not be brought about in the adjudicatory process of litigation or arbitration. Nor are the legally dominated applications of assisted negotiation such as settlement facilitation, early neutral evaluation, or summary jury trial likely to produce these results. Mediation is the process that works best for those cases where the parties desire more than damages or equitable relief, since both the issues which are explored and the resolutions which are crafted lie in the hands of the disputants.

Procedural status is another helpful guide to selecting a dispute resolution process. Processes which rely on the problem-solving abilities of the participants, such as mediation, often work best before any formal litigation is commenced in order to avoid the polarization and positional rigidity which is often generated by the filing and development of court cases. Arbitration is most economical if it takes place early in the process, so that resources are not expended on discovery and pretrial litigation. Early neutral evaluation, as its name implies, is best used shortly after the close of the pleadings, before substantial time and resources have been expended. Other negotiating processes such as settlement facilitation, summary jury trial, and mini-trial, are most effective after discovery is completed, so that everyone has the information necessary to evaluate the case fully, and close to trial, so that everyone experiences the pressure of an imminent setting. Summary jury trials cannot be held until all legal issues, including the charge to the jury, have been resolved, so that the parties are in agreement regarding the legal and evidentiary parameters of the trial. Interestingly, mediation can also work well late in the litigation process, particularly if the parties have become disillusioned by costs and delay, and have been shaken in their confidence that the verdict they desire will result at trial. This newly developed sense of reality can fuel their desire to engage in problem solving.

Outcome control refers to whether the disputants wish to place decision making power in the hands of a third party or retain it themselves. All of the assisted negotiation processes permit the parties to accept or reject a proposed solution. Mediation in particular allows the parties to create their own solution in whatever form, breadth and depth they can agree upon. The adjudication processes of litigation and binding arbitration, on the other hand, are characterized by third parties hearing presentations by the disputants or their lawyers and then deciding on the outcome. These processes give the disputants the certainty of a formal resolution. Non-binding arbitration straddles these options in that there is a decision by a third party, but it is advisory in nature and the disputants may choose to disregard it.

Within both the adjudication and the assisted negotiation modes there are more and less formal processes. In adjudication, litigation in a court of record will be strictly bound by rules and conventions, while arbitration will be a more relaxed, straightforward, and accessible forum. This will tend to make arbitration less expensive, with limited discovery and expeditious proceedings. Only in certain catagories of private arbitrations, for example, those where contractual agreements call for a panel of three arbitrators, each of whom may command a fee of several hundred dollars an hour, may arbitration appear to be prohibitively expensive to the participants. By contrast, court-annexed arbitration programs are often either free or supported by small supplemental filing fees.

Among the assisted negotiation processes, formality varies widely. Mediation is often the most flexible and least formal, since it rarely employs fixed rules or procedures. By contrast, summary jury trials and mini-trials are the most formal, as they mimic court procedures. Early neutral evaluation and settlement facilitation are less structured, but often reflect their legal domination and proximity to courtroom proceedings. The cost of assisted negotiations is based primarily on two factors: first, whether the process is private or court-annexed; and second, the complexity of the dispute. Often court-annexed processes are provided for free, under programs staffed by volunteers or funded by filing fees. Thus a disputant who wants to mediate a problem may receive the services of trained mediators upon payment of a filing fee and filing of a complaint. Private providers of assisted negotiation services normally charge on an hourly basis, the cost depending on their background, training, expertise, and experience, as well as the local market for such services. One economic advantage of mediation is that the parties typically attend sessions without their lawyers, so that they are only paying for the services of the mediator, not for the hourly costs of lawyers who are present as well.

One of the key factors in selecting a dispute resolution process is whether or not there is a potential for an ongoing relationship among the participants. The classic example of a dispute with an ongoing relationship is divorcing parents who will be connected to each other through their children for the rest of their lives even though their marriage has ended. Mediation's forte is to work with disputes involving future relationships, where there is real value in assisting the parties to expand their range of communication and problem-solving skills. In contrast, many tort lawsuits have no future relationship and indeed no past relationship other than the allegedly tortious contact forming the basis for litigation, for instance, an automobile accident or an injury from a defective product. In this kind of tort case, the need is for an acceptable resolution, typically one that is financially based. Thus the dispute resolution processes of adjudication and assisted negotiation, which do not focus on the possibility of cooperative relationships in the future, are appropriate.

Finally, in selecting a dispute resolution process one must look to the personalities involved: the disputants, their attorneys, and the potential providers. Some disputes and disputants require clear structure and firm control. They may fare best in adjudication or in a settlement process directed by a tough former judge or justice. Others may be unduly limited by such strictures and may fare better in a process where empathy is an integral part of the process and the emphasis is on creating integrative solutions. For these types of personalities, mediation is the process of choice.

In selecting a dispute resolution process, the greatest confusion arises in the choice between classic mediation and settlement facilitation. This confusion is exacerbated by the fact that some providers of settlement facilitation call themselves mediators. Figure 3 classifies disputes by subject matter and places them on the spectrum of subject matter and lawyers' roles. This chart can help distinguish between cases which are appropriate for mediation and those which will resolve more easily in settlement facilitation. While many of the subject matter areas overlap between processes, it is important to note that disputes with a primarily legal or financial focus normally should not be resolved in a mediation process where the parties do not have attorneys to advise them. On the other end of the spectrum, disputes where the primary focus is interpersonal may become more difficult to resolve when lawyers are involved. Because lawyers must translate the grievances into causes of action, the heart of the dispute is often lost. For example, a business partner who has hurt feelings and disappointment about another partner's actions and who seeks legal representation may end up with an attorney filing a securities fraud case. As the case progresses, the real issues between the partners become lost in the legal framework. In such interpersonal disputes the participants are more likely to be satisfied with a resolution achieved outside the formal legal arena, which can then be reviewed by counsel.

Figure 3. Comparing Mediation and Settlement Facilitation

Role of Lawyers (to the right) Subject Matter (below)	Settlement Facil. - Lawyers Involved and Present	Mediation- Lawyers Involved But Not Present	Mediation- No Lawyers Involved
Primarily Interpersonal & Relationship Focus	**Warning!** Lawyers may complicate resolution.	Some neighbor-neighbor disputes Some employee-employer problems Some organizational conflicts	
Mixed Focus (Interpersonal and Legal/$$)	• Medical malpractice, civil rights damage claims, sexual harassment, some products liability, construction • Some public policy issues, e.g. siting controversial facilities, "reg-neg" (regulatory negotiation) • Some complex multi-party disputes	• Divorce/Child custody • Probate and estates • Business dissolution, formation, and re-organization, family business problems • Special education and ADA (Americans With Disabilities Act) cases • Many commercial, construction & real estate • Victim-Offender • Many organizational conflicts and employee grievances • Many community public policy issues e.g. siting and zoning	• Small Claims Court cases (consumer problems, neighbor-neighbor issues) • School mediation • Gang mediation • FINS (families in need of supervision) issues • Lemon law/Better Business Bureau problems
Primarily Legal/$$ Focus	• Personal injury, major commercial, construction, public works, gov't-gov't cases, some products liability • Complex, multi-party litigation	• Some construction, commercial, and real estate • Some employment	**Warning!** Lawyers needed.

V.   THE MANY FACES OF MEDIATION

Although all forms of mediation share the common core of being delivered by neutral third parties who are not decision makers, there are tremendous variations in the ways that the mediation process takes place.

There may be one mediator, or a pair of co-mediators, or even a group of mediators who work together as a panel. The composition of co-mediator pairs or panels may be random, or it may be structured to bring in professional expertise. The makeup of the mediation team may also neutralize potential power imbalances by providing specific gender, ethnicity, or other diverse representation. There may be only two disputants, many individuals, or groups of disputants. The mediators may meet alone with the disputants one at a time, or may never speak separately with any disputant. The process may be highly structured, or completely fluid. The mediators may truly leave the outcome in the parties' hands, or may take a strong role in encouraging, influencing, or even coercing settlement. The mediators may, or may not, suggest to the parties what they ought to do. The mediators may encourage, permit, or forbid attorneys to be present. The mediators may work as a part of, or separate from, a court system. The mediators may write the parties' agreement as a legal document and may even file it with the court, or may draft an agreement in purely lay language. The parties' agreement may be written up after the mediation is completed by lawyers or others without direct mediator involvement.

The many variations in the mediation process reflect the relatively brief time within which the profession of mediation has developed, the lack of controls, norms, and standards, which might govern mediators, and the many different contexts within which the mediation process may be used. It is important for the student of mediation to recognize the power of this flexibility. It may be frustrating to find few definitive answers, but also it is exciting to know that there are so many tools and techniques with which to experiment. Experimentation and flexibility permit the process to be tailored to the needs of the participants. As a new mediator, you will want to remain open to the myriad ways in which you can work, explore applications, and remain aware of and reflective about the costs and benefits of each choice you make. It is important to remain clear that the primary axis of mediation styles ranges from open to directive. Figure 4 portrays this axis. While each style has its advantages, for many novice mediators the directive approach feels more comfortable because it allows them to tell the disputants what to do to fix their problems. Premature gravitation to this style deprives the disputants of the opportunity to create their own solutions, and deprives the mediator of the great sense of fulfillment which comes from assisting the disputants to solve their own problems.

Figure 4. Mediation Philosophies

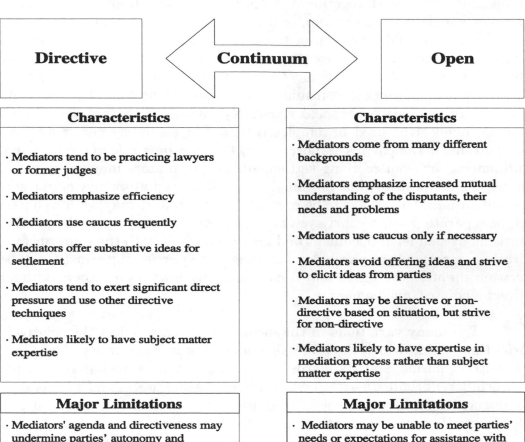

Directive ⟵ **Continuum** ⟶ **Open**

Characteristics	Characteristics
· Mediators tend to be practicing lawyers or former judges	· Mediators come from many different backgrounds
· Mediators emphasize efficiency	· Mediators emphasize increased mutual understanding of the disputants, their needs and problems
· Mediators use caucus frequently	· Mediators use caucus only if necessary
· Mediators offer substantive ideas for settlement	· Mediators avoid offering ideas and strive to elicit ideas from parties
· Mediators tend to exert significant direct pressure and use other directive techniques	· Mediators may be directive or non-directive based on situation, but strive for non-directive
· Mediators likely to have subject matter expertise	· Mediators likely to have expertise in mediation process rather than subject matter expertise

Major Limitations	Major Limitations
· Mediators' agenda and directiveness may undermine parties' autonomy and durability of agreement	· Mediators may be unable to meet parties' needs or expectations for assistance with substance
· Mediators' failure to pay attention to emotional and communication dynamics may result in unjust outcomes that hurt less powerful participants	· Mediators' focus on open communication may permit one party to be verbally abused or exploited by another
· Mediators leave unexplored the parties' potential for growth, change, and healing	· Mediators create a process which requires time and willingness to explore needs and feelings

VI. MEDIATOR ROLES AND FUNCTIONS

INTRODUCTION

Mediators perform a number of functions as they practice their art, sometimes simultaneously and sometimes sequentially. They manage the mediation process and assist the parties to move forward towards resolution. They create a safe environment within which power is balanced. Finally, they structure resolution as the parties are educated throughout the process. The following sections discuss these concepts in detail.

MANAGING THE PROCESS

The primary function of mediators is to manage the mediation process in order to provide a safe environment for the parties and a structure that leads them towards opportunities for resolution. Managing the process includes encouraging the parties to talk broadly about the issues that bring them to mediation. Talking broadly encompasses any information or feelings which the parties wish to express. One of the differences between mediation and other dispute resolution processes is that there are no limiting concepts of relevancy. Indeed, it is only by talking fully about the dispute that its roots and complexities are exposed. Often when the parties express their feelings and have them understood and acknowledged, this recognition enables them to move forward toward resolution.

CREATING A SAFE ENVIRONMENT

Creating a safe environment does not mean an environment that is free of acrimony, anger, or heated exchanges. Indeed, these common components of conflict are present at times in almost all mediations. Rather, the concept of safety is defined by the participants themselves, both in terms of what they say and in how they act and react. The mediators' job is to manage the expressions of conflict so that they do not damage any of the parties. This is work of great sensitivity, calling on the mediators to stay closely attuned with the parties both by empathetic engagement and by explicitly checking with them to see how they are doing. The mediators must be wary of substituting their own reactions for those of the parties and of assuming that because they are uncomfortable with the level of conflict, the parties must be uncomfortable as well, or vice versa. There is a delicate balance in mediation between the need to encourage a full range of emotional expression and the need to be ready to step in and protect a party who is being attacked.

BALANCING POWER

A key part of creating a safe environment is being alert to potential power imbalances between the parties. These power imbalances may be created by larger socioeconomic forces outside the mediation, for example, gender, ethnicity, age, sexual orientation, education, occupation, and financial status. They may be created by forces within the relationship itself, i.e., issues of control and submission. Power imbalances may also be created or fostered within the mediation if the mediator permits one of the disputants to dominate the process.

The mediators must be able to utilize a broad variety of techniques in order to address power imbalances. The mediators need to be aware of the ways that cultural differences may play a part in power imbalances in mediation, both in terms of actual lack of power and in terms of the ways that the dispute, the other disputants, the mediation process, and the mediators themselves may be perceived through the lens of another culture. Sections Three V and VI explore these issues of power and culture.

STRUCTURING RESOLUTION

When the mediators create a structure that leads to resolution, they are doing a variety of things. One is to understand and guide the parties through the steps of the mediation process. (See Section Two). A second is to understand and guide the parties through effective negotiation behaviors. A third is to understand and guide the parties through exploration of the interests and needs which they seek to meet in resolving their dispute rather than remaining fixed in defending the demands of their positions. A fourth is to understand and guide the parties through generating a range of possible solutions so that they may creatively expand their available options. A fifth is to understand and guide the parties through recognizing the costs of deadlock, that is, what may happen if they fail to achieve resolution. A sixth is to understand and guide the parties through measuring options and possible solutions against reality, both as known to the mediators and as described by the parties throughout the mediation. (See Section Three, III, for a fuller discussion of these topics).

SUMMARY OF MEDIATOR ROLES AND FUNCTIONS

- Facilitate the process of meeting and negotiating.
- Open and maintain communications pathways.
- Encourage full expression of information and emotion.
- Create a safe environment.

- Encourage exploration of the problem(s).
- Maintain balance in the process.
- Empower all parties.
- Expand resources available to the parties.
- Help the parties to generate options.
- Generate options for the parties to consider when they need help.
- Educate unskilled or unprepared parties to negotiate more effectively.
- Help the parties define and explore issues of fairness.
- Help explore procedural and substantive alternatives.
- Assist parties to get closure on the issues of the dispute.
- Memorialize the parties' agreements in a form which is useful to them.

MEDIATOR JOB DESCRIPTION

The heart of these functional elements of the mediators' role can be summed up by four major skills that are reflected in the mediators' work. These are portrayed in Figure 5.

Neutralize

Mediators work to de-escalate unproductive conduct that interferes with the negotiation and problem solving focus. Mediators help the parties to communicate and to hear each other better by neutralizing highly charged statements and antagonistic behaviors.

Party:	*Before I make a public apology I'll see you rot in hell!*
Mediator:	*So how others view this is extremely important to you.*

Mutualize

Mediators know that momentum for resolution can be generated if the parties recognize areas of shared concerns, interests, or benefits.

Mother:	*I want the kids with me so I can keep them in the same school where they are doing so well.*
Father:	*I want the kids with me so I can help them take advantage of better educational opportunities.*
Mediator:	*So you both care a lot about the quality and substance of your kids' education.*

Futurize

Mediators help the parties to let go of the past and focus on the present and future.

Business Partner: *It's a joke for you to talk about company finances — you've always been an idiot about numbers!*

Business Partner: *Well you've always manipulated the numbers so that they say whatever you want them to!*

Mediator: *It seems as if we will need to focus on a mutually satisfactory accounting system and / or person in order to work out the financial aspects of the company dissolution together.*

Clarify

Mediators help to make sure that they and the disputants clearly understand such things as what is being said, the options, and the consequences of impasse.

Neighbor: *There's the lawn and the noise and the bushes . . . those dogs . . . it's just a mess!*

Mediator: *Let me see if I understand your concerns about the dogs. One is that they come into your yard and damage your grass and your shrubs? A second is that they bark and make noise?* (Neighbor nods affirmatively). *Can you tell us first about the problems with the yard?*

Figure 5. Mediator Job Description

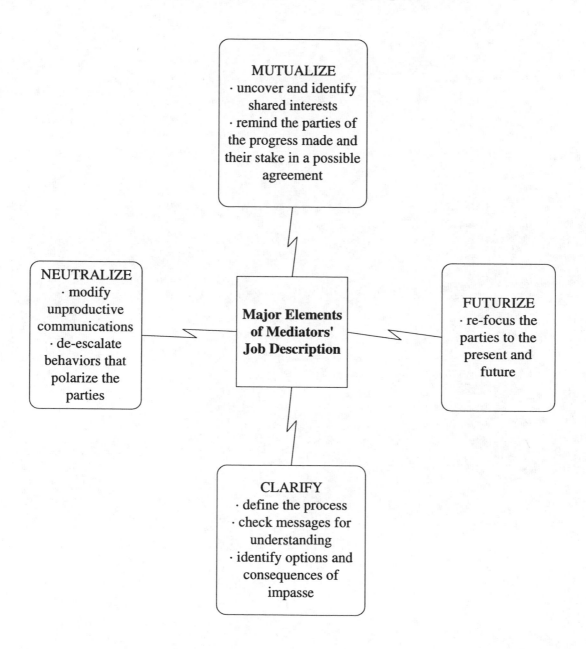

MUTUALIZE
· uncover and identify shared interests
· remind the parties of the progress made and their stake in a possible agreement

NEUTRALIZE
· modify unproductive communications
· de-escalate behaviors that polarize the parties

Major Elements of Mediators' Job Description

FUTURIZE
· re-focus the parties to the present and future

CLARIFY
· define the process
· check messages for understanding
· identify options and consequences of impasse

SECTION TWO: THE STAGES OF MEDIATION

I.   OVERVIEW OF THE STAGES OF MEDIATION

This section begins by briefly describing the stages of mediation. The following chapters then discuss each stage in detail. Figure 6 illustrates the stages that will be discussed.

Figure 6. Mediation Process in Stages

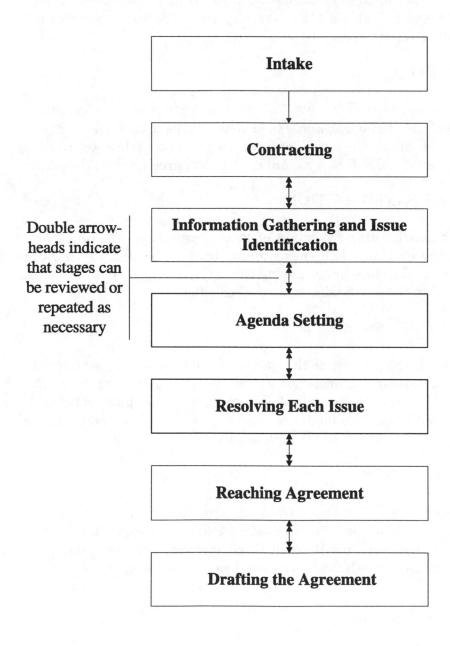

Double arrow-heads indicate that stages can be reviewed or repeated as necessary

Intake

Contracting

Information Gathering and Issue Identification

Agenda Setting

Resolving Each Issue

Reaching Agreement

Drafting the Agreement

The stages of mediation encompass the following activities and tasks. Although they are presented sequentially, in a linear fashion, the mediators should expect to move back and forth among stages, particularly as new issues are considered or unresolved feelings are expressed.

A. INTAKE

Parties contact mediators/mediation office. Initial discussions result in the scheduling of a first visit. Parties may be court referred, attorney referred, consumer referred, etc.

B. CONTRACTING

Mediators and parties review the goals and purposes of mediation, explore the role of the mediators, agree to mediate, agree to costs, fees, terms, and conditions of mediation, and commit to work together to resolve differences. Parties usually sign a formal mediation agreement at this time.

C. GATHERING INFORMATION

Mediators elicit full description of facts, perceptions, feelings, and reactions from the parties. The genesis and nature of the dispute and the parties' goals in resolution emerge during this work. Parties begin to listen to each other and to see all the dimensions of the dispute.

D. IDENTIFYING ISSUES

Mediators develop a list of the parties' issues, based on statements made by the parties during information gathering. The mediators frame the issues in neutral terms which define the problems that the parties bring to mediation for resolution. The mediators review the list of issues with the parties, checking for accuracy and completeness.

E. AGENDA SETTING

Mediators work with the parties to organize and, if necessary, prioritize the issues. The plan for proceeding usually includes the understanding that agreements on individual issues are tentative until all agreements can be put together and reviewed as a final package.

F.   RESOLVING EACH ISSUE

Mediators lead the parties through the exploration of the issues. The process for resolving each issue usually contains the following steps:

1.   Further information gathering — Parties describe facts/perceptions/feelings about this particular issue.

2.   Exploring needs and interests — Mediators help the parties to look at the interests and needs which must be met in relation to this issue.

3.   Generating options — Parties develop a list of possible options to deal with the issue. Process is creative, imaginative, free-flowing, with deferred reactions/judgments.

4.   Evaluating options — Parties critically review options, eliminating some, combining some, and focusing on developing those which are the most promising.

5.   Negotiating and selecting — Parties make choices and decisions based on the work they have done.

6.   Caucusing — Mediators may need to meet individually with the parties to help them consider their alternatives and to encourage them to make movement in order to reach agreement.

7.   Agreeing — Parties make tentative choices about how they will handle this issue.

Figure 7. Problem Solving in Mediation:
A Process of Expanding and Contracting

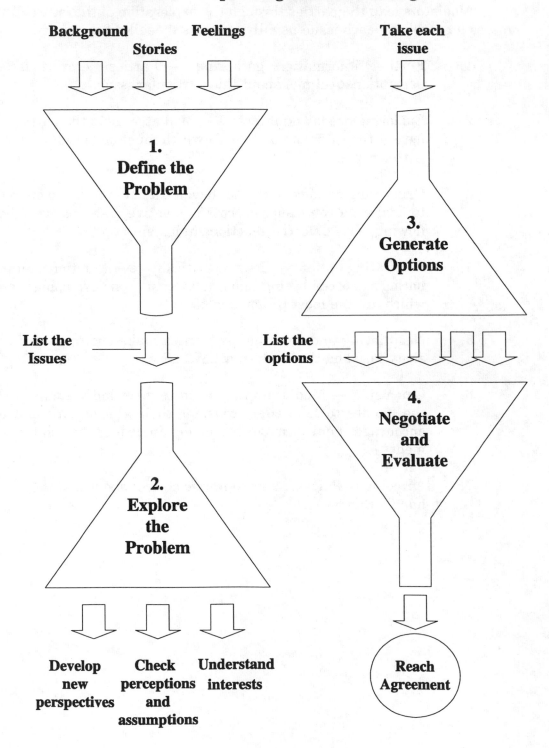

G. REVIEWING AND DRAFTING FINAL AGREEMENTS

Mediators help parties to review tentative agreements on all issues. Parties and mediators re-evaluate and adjust agreements as necessary for them to fit together as a final package. Mediators probe and challenge to help parties assess whether this is a realistic and durable agreement. Mediators may draft final agreement for review by the parties and their attorneys, or attorneys may draft final agreement based on mediators' memorandum.

II.   INTAKE

Mediators and potential clients have initial contact which results in scheduling the first session.

INTAKE OVERVIEW

The intake stage encompasses the first contacts between potential clients and the mediators or the mediation office. Intake may come from a court referral, often to a program which regularly conducts mediations for the court. Courts can also refer cases to individual private mediators, as can organizations, or the attorneys in the case. Frequently, referrals are based on satisfactory work which the mediators have performed in the past including referrals from satisfied former clients. Mediators also receive calls from people who have seen their advertisements in the phone book, or who have heard them make promotional presentations.

During the intake stage, the mediators must be aware of the pitfalls of discussing the subject matter of the dispute with potential clients. Any information received from one party alone puts the mediators' neutrality at risk, both by shaping the mediators' perceptions of the parties and their dispute, and by the improper appearance of having listened to only one side of the case.

The initial contacts with the parties offer the mediators opportunities to build a foundation for success. By providing clear information about the decision to mediate, the mediators enable the disputants to take responsibility for their choice. By avoiding a hard sell and encouraging the disputants to explore all their options, including meeting with other mediators, the mediators increase the chances for a strong commitment by the disputants to the process and the mediation team.

Mediators who have another profession, such as attorneys or therapists, need to be particularly careful in their intake process. It is critical that they establish what service the caller is seeking at the earliest possible moment, since ethical rules prohibit "switching hats", i.e., changing roles from adversary representation by the attorney to mediation by the attorney serving as a third-party neutral.

INTAKE GOALS

The mediators' goals at intake are to balance the need and desire for business against the risks of becoming enmeshed with one side of the dispute, bringing an inappropriate case into mediation, committing to deliver more than is reasonable in mediation, or confusing potential clients about mediators' roles. An organized structure created by mediators for the intake lessens the likelihood that they will get into difficulties. Offices that use a trained receptionist, mail clear pre-mediation materials, make introductory presentations, or conduct regular diagnostic intake sessions, tend to find the intake stage less problematic. See Appendix III, Part 1, Client Information Form, and Agreements to Mediate (A and B) for examples of the type of pre-mediation information that private mediators send to clients.

FIVE MAIN TASKS OF MEDIATORS AT THE INTAKE STAGE:

1. To develop procedures which will bring in potential clients, i.e., referrals, advertising, etc.

2. To use an intake procedure which does not risk mixing roles.

3. To avoid hearing too much or improper information from one side.

4. To give clear information about the mediation process used by these mediators.

5. To encourage the potential clients to come in for an initial session.

INTAKE PROCEDURES

- Verbal and/or written information is shared with the potential client and with other possible participants.
- The mediator asks questions about the dispute to perform an initial screen of the case:
  — Who are the parties and their attorneys?
  — Do the mediators have any relationships with the parties or their attorneys that raise concerns about a conflict of interest?
  — Is the case appropriate for mediation or is a settlement facilitation needed? (future relationship, non-legal problems, status of litigation, power balance)

— Do the parties need particular characteristics in a mediation team? (experience, subject matter expertise, culture, gender, ethnicity)

- If the person contacted is not the mediator, that person may coordinate the initial appointment with the necessary parties. In private mediation, it is often the responsibility of the person contacting the mediation-provider to bring the other parties to the table. Some institutional mediation-providers contact other parties and determine if they are willing to participate in the mediation. Clear, specific arrangements for the first joint meeting are communicated with thought given to the appropriateness of the place (size, comfort, privacy, acceptability to all participants).

- If basic information must be developed before the initial meeting, a decision must be made as to who should do this and how it can be done effectively and efficiently. Options include phone interviews, personal interviews, focus groups, questionnaires, and written submissions to the mediation team.

Figure 8. Summary of Intake Stage

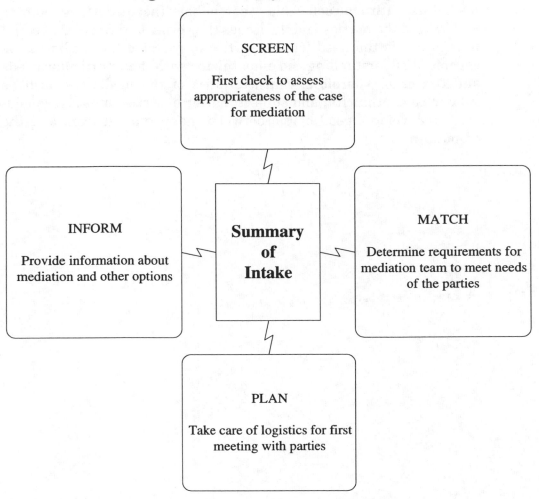

SCREEN

First check to assess appropriateness of the case for mediation

INFORM

Provide information about mediation and other options

Summary of Intake

MATCH

Determine requirements for mediation team to meet needs of the parties

PLAN

Take care of logistics for first meeting with parties

INTAKE CAUTIONS

- If the mediator is in direct contact with one or more parties at this stage, anticipate that parties may try to use this initial contact to give you their perception of the case and the other parties. This may create a problem with other parties who fear that the mediator has developed alliances and lost neutrality.

- If you wear more than one professional hat, e.g. lawyer and mediator, the party contacting you should be asked immediately if he or she is contacting you for legal services or mediation services. Failure to clarify your role may result in the inability to serve as a mediator due to a real or perceived conflict of interest.

- Even if mediation is the right process, a given case may require mediators with characteristics that enable the mediation team to understand the parties and the issues they bring to the table. Of equal importance is the need for the parties to perceive the mediators as capable of understanding and empathizing with their particular needs and concerns. Therefore, characteristics of the mediators such as gender, age, ethnicity, and subject matter expertise must be considered to develop a good match between the mediation team and the disputants.

III.   CONTRACTING

Mediators and the disputants agree to proceed and establish their intent to work together to resolve differences.

CONTRACTING OVERVIEW

The contracting stage lays the foundation upon which the rest of the mediation process builds. The mediators have their first opportunity to gain credibility with and trust from the parties. In contracting, the mediators and the parties agree on the structure, the rules, and the goals of the mediation.

The parameters of contracting vary greatly. In a court-annexed or community mediation, the contracting stage can be as brief as ten minutes spent explaining the mediation process. In a private mediation with substantial legal issues, such as a divorce case, it is not uncommon to spend one or two hours discussing such matters as fees, relationships with lawyers and therapists, the role of the children in the mediation, and privacy.

Unlike the rest of the mediation process, it is common for the mediators to talk most of the time during contracting. Some mediators refer to this as the "mediator monologue". If the mediators choose to be more interactive, they can play off questions they ask the parties and still cover the checklist of information appropriate to the contracting stage. Many mediators use advance information which they mail to the parties to sharpen the discussion during contracting and increase the parties' understanding of the process.

Contracting usually ends with the parties signing a written agreement to mediate which memorializes their understanding of the process, spells out the mediator's role, and details such matters as fees and costs. See Appendix III, Part 1, Client Information Form, and Agreements to Mediate (A and B) for examples.

CONTRACTING GOALS

Beyond providing clear and complete coverage of the basic information which the parties must assimilate before they can meaningfully agree to mediate, learning about why the parties are exploring mediation as a dispute resolution option, and beginning a solid relationship with the parties, there is another important goal in the contracting stage. The mediators need to make an initial tentative diagnosis of the parties and their dispute to assess whether the case is appropriate for mediation. Some conflicts are too new and raw to be ready for mediation. And, some disputants may be too disempowered, overwhelmed, or stressed to be able to represent themselves effectively in the process. Some parties may be addicted to conflict and lack motivation to achieve resolution. Some cases may work better with the additional structure and formality of arbitration or settlement facilitation. Some issues may call for the public forum and precedent-setting decisions of the court litigation process. These cases should either be weeded out of the mediation process at this point, or, alternatively, the parties should be alerted to the mediators' concerns. This will open the door to designing processes or procedures which are appropriate for these particular individuals if they are to continue in mediation.

SEVEN MAIN TASKS OF MEDIATORS AT THE CONTRACTING STAGE:

1.   To explain the process, including time, location, and fees, and ensure that all parties understand what will be taking place.

2.   To develop rapport with the parties and begin to build trust in the mediators and the process.

3.   To learn what brings the parties to mediation, in order to develop a foundation for later problem solving.

4.   To determine the suitability of the mediation process for the parties in this dispute.

5.   To establish clarity with the parties about the rules of mediation.

6.   To set a positive tone and establish a workable structure for the mediation.

7.   To obtain a signed agreement to mediate.

CONTRACTING PROCEDURES

- Make introductions, get everyone seated and comfortable. Determine how people will be addressed, e.g. first names, last names, or titles.
- Decide whether to begin by asking questions and play off the parties' answers to provide all of the information you need to cover or to start with a mediator monologue followed by the parties' questions.

- If you begin by asking questions, consider asking:
  Have you ever participated in a mediation before?
  Why did you decide to come to mediation?
  What would you like to know about the process?
  What questions do you have about the mediation agreement and the information we mailed you?
- If you begin with a monologue, consider covering the following areas:
  — Introductions.
    Let me tell you a little bit about my background.
  — Explain important aspects of the process.
    Mediation requires a willingness to consider the interests of the other party.
  — Description of mediation.
    Mediation is a negotiation process with the assistance of impartial people to help you stay on track.
  — Description of the role of mediator.
    We are here to help you negotiate and make good decisions. We will not make judgments about who is right and who is wrong.
  — The need for full disclosure of all necessary information.
    In order to make good decisions and find a fair way to resolve your issues, both of you need to have all necessary information about the issues.
  — Privacy/confidentiality limitations.
    Mediation is a private process. We will not talk to anyone about our work with you without your permission. There are two exceptions: (1) if we have reason to believe a child is being abused or neglected; and (2) if we have reason to believe a crime may be committed that will endanger someone.
  — Seek necessary waivers.
    It may be helpful for us to speak with your attorneys or therapists. May we have your permission to do so?
  — The parties remain in charge.
    This is your process. If you have a concern, please raise it with us so it can be addressed.
  — The parties are responsible for making their own decisions.
    We want you to make a good decision, but we will not tell you what to do, nor will we make recommendations.

— The possibility of a private meeting with each side (called a "caucus").

> *It may be useful to meet alone with us at some point. We call this a caucus. We may suggest this or you may request a caucus at any time.*

— Possible ground rules.

> *It will help us listen and understand if you will wait until the other is finished before you speak.*
>
> *If we begin to establish a sense of respect in the room, it increases the chance for a successful resolution. Would you agree to avoid comments about each others' character and integrity?*
>
> *How do you feel about agreeing not to use profanity?*
>
> *Please speak for yourself using statements that begin with "I," instead of speaking about others with statements beginning with "you."*
>
> *If I ask you to stop speaking, please cooperate by holding further comment at that time.*
>
> *Although we may need to discuss the past, will you agree to emphasize the present and the future in our discussions?*

— Fees.

> *It is most common for the parties to divide the mediators' fee with each paying some portion. How do you want to handle this?*

— Length of sessions.

> *We will usually meet for one or two hours. In longer sessions it is often hard for people to sustain their energy and attention.*

— Homework.

> *Your willingness to perform tasks outside the mediation session is essential (1) to build a sense that this is your process; (2) to make the best use of our time in mediation sessions; (3) to develop the information base you need to make good decisions.*

— Documents.

> *To be efficient, you will need to bring in necessary documentation as soon as we know it is required. For example, we may need deeds, financial statements, tax returns, school reports on children, medical bills, and insurance policies.*

— Role of Others in the Process.

It may be necessary to involve others in our work together, e.g. children, family, attorneys and other advocates, therapists, experts, or members of the community.

— Signing the Agreement.

Now that your questions have been answered, please take the agreement away, review it with your attorney, and interview some other mediators. If you decide you want to work with us, schedule another appointment. Then we can all sign the agreement and get started.

Figure 9. Summary of Contracting Stage

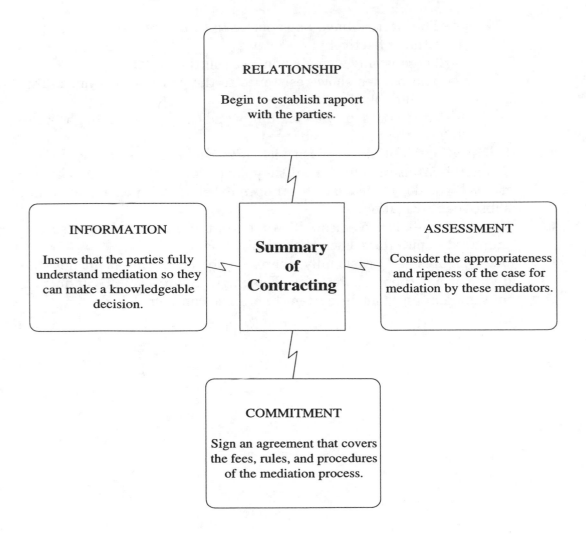

CONTRACTING CAUTIONS

- Suitability of a dispute for mediation.

    Yes, it is suitable if:
    — Ongoing relationship is present.
    — Future issues can be resolved
    — It involves non-legal problems.
    — There is potential for a mutually agreeable solution.
    — The parties have time to devote to the process to give it a chance to work.

    No, it is not suitable if:
    — There is a significant power imbalance, e.g. domestic violence.
    — The parties have no capacity to think, communicate, and negotiate effectively.
    — There is only a single win/lose solution available.
    — The parties show resistance to the concept of a mutually agreeable solution.
    — The parties are in a big hurry and there is not enough time to give the process a chance to work.

- Privacy/Confidentiality — Don't let them begin to talk in any detail about the issues involved until they have signed the privacy agreement. If you do, you leave the door open to being called as a witness in subsequent litigation.

- Impatience — The parties will want to jump into the issues so be prepared to pull them back to the task at hand.

- Fee Disputes — Occasionally, there may be a dispute about how to divide or pay the mediator's fee. This might require you to conduct a mini-mediation so an agreement to proceed can be reached.

IV. GATHERING INFORMATION

Parties have a full opportunity to discuss their problems, feelings and reactions.

GATHERING INFORMATION OVERVIEW

This is the stage when the parties talk. Usually the mediators begin by asking who would like to start, or explaining why one person, usually the complainant, is asked to begin. Then that party is asked the broadest possible question, such as, *What can you tell us about the situation?* While one party talks, the other usually is asked to remain quiet and make notes of any responses rather than interrupting. The mediators, as well, need to remain quiet and not jump in with questions and clarifications. Only after each party has spoken, and has had the opportunity to respond to the other, should the mediators ask questions. This is because the very process of questioning shapes the information which is received. Initially, mediators' questions should be topical, such as, *What should we know about the business?*; or *What about the children?* Only later in the process should the mediators press for details.

Exploration and expression of feelings are equally, if not more, important than fact development at this stage. It is vital that the mediators not only elicit the parties' emotional responses, but also acknowledge and validate those emotions using the techniques of active listening. The time that this stage takes depends on several variables: the complexity of the case, the need of the parties to air their feelings and concerns, and the number of participants in the mediation. In a simple, small claims court case, the initial information gathering might take 15 or 30 minutes. In a multiple issue divorce/child custody case, several two-hour sessions could be spent developing the information base that the parties need to identify the issues to be negotiated.

GATHERING INFORMATION GOALS

The key to success at this stage lies in the parties expressing their feelings and emotions honestly. The mediators must create an environment where feelings can be verbalized safely and where the parties feel that they are heard and understood. Throughout the information-gathering stage, the mediators should also be assisting the fact-gathering process by keeping a list of issues, either in their notes or on a flip chart in front of the parties. The mediators also need to keep their diagnostic skills attuned, thinking about the nature of the conflict, and how they may help the parties move towards resolution. They need to watch for stated positions, i.e., what the parties say they want, and for their underlying interests, i.e., why they say or imply they want it. These interests, particularly when they are overlapping or mutual, contain the keys to unlocking the potential for agreements between the parties. See also Section Three (I), Communication Skills and Section Three (II), Values and Feelings, for related information.

SIX MAIN TASKS OF THE MEDIATORS AT THE INFORMATION GATHERING STAGE:

1. To provide opportunities for the parties to express emotions and feelings.

2. To identify fully all the facts and other elements which influence each party's view of the various issues in the dispute.

3. To discover whether there are some areas and issues on which the parties agree.

4. To ask open-ended questions to produce additional information which may be useful later in the mediation process. Parties may also discuss their underlying needs and interests, and articulate principles and values that they believe are relevant to the dispute.

5. To make a tentative diagnosis of the causes of the parties' conflict and begin to develop a plan for the mediation, including strategies that may assist the parties in moving toward agreement.

6. To begin to identify the issues in the dispute.

Figure 10. Types of Information for Mediators to Gather

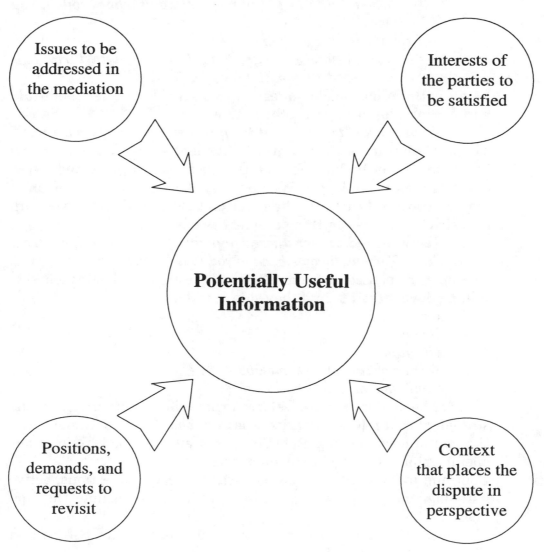

GATHERING INFORMATION PROCEDURES

●   Determine who will talk first.
             — Ask one side — the complainant or petitioner to start — and
             state the reason for your choice:
                     In small claims court mediation, we usually begin by
                     asking the person who filed the case to speak first.

— Ask the parties:

> *Who would like to begin by telling us what brought you here?*

— And, if one starts preemptively:

> *Jane, before you begin, I need to check with Terry. Is it all right with you if Jane goes first?*

- Begin with an open-ended question to each side and let them talk without interruption by the other party.

  > *What can you tell us about the problem that brings you here?*

- Three to five minutes of initial statement each is a reasonable estimate. It can be hard for the second person to wait and listen effectively for much longer. Be ready to ask a long-winded person to stop so you can hear from the other one. Assure him that you will come back to hear everything else he has to say.

  > *Terry, I need to stop there temporarily so we can hear from Jane. Then we'll come back to you to hear more from you.*

- Use open responses or open follow-up questions to keep each side talking during their turn if they stop quickly:

  > *I see.*
  > *Go on.*
  > *Uh-huh.*
  > *What else can you tell me about . . . ?*
  > *Could you give me an example?*

- If she or he pauses or stops, feel free to paraphrase. Otherwise let the statement continue; summarize what you heard from each person at the end of each opening statement; or, wait until both finish their opening statements and then summarize.

- Continue to guide the discussion with open-ended questions, active listening, and paraphrasing of significant facts and feelings that you hear.

- If necessary, reframe negative, unproductive statements. See Section Three (I), Communication Skills, for examples.

- Encourage constructive expression of feelings unless parties are incapable of refraining from destructive comments and personal attacks.

  > *Terry, it is clear that you are furious about what happened. Please tell me what you think the rest of the issues are that we need to work on today.*

- If one party is interrupting, in addition to invoking the ground rule, if you have made one, you can hand him a pad and pencil and ask him to make notes of anything he wants to ask/say so he can remember it when his turn comes.

  Toby, both of you agreed to wait until the speaker finished before commenting. Here's a pad to note your responses. When Sean finishes, we want to hear from you.

- Keep a balance between the parties. Make room for both to speak.
- Acknowledge and record mutualities and agreements, if any. If you have an easel and chart pad, this is an excellent way to keep the parties focused on agreement and shared goals.

  I think that I heard your first agreement. Let me write it up here so you can check my understanding.

Figure 11. Summary of Information Gathering Stage

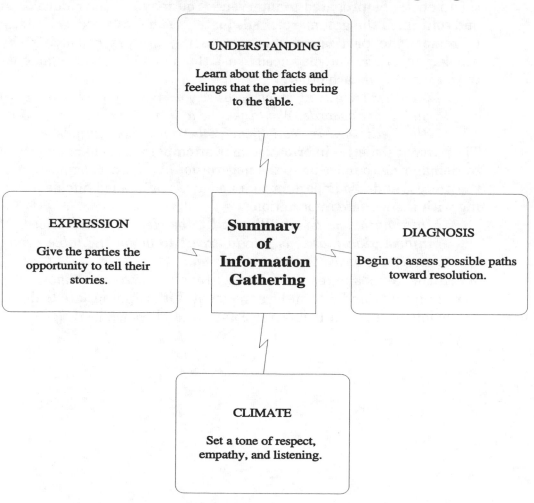

GATHERING INFORMATION CAUTIONS

- The parties often want to state their bottom lines, "cut to the chase," or move right to solutions. Be prepared to restrain them as you note their preferred solution or position, and ask them to say more about the topic.

    I know that you have given this a lot of thought. When we reach the point of developing options, we can use your idea as the first one on the list.

- If the parties treat each other with civility, acknowledge and encourage them to talk directly with each other instead of addressing their comments to you.

    Jane, instead of telling us, please turn and tell Terry directly about your concerns.

- If the parties are constantly sparring and trading verbal or non-verbal cheap shots, be prepared to intervene. You may not have developed and confirmed the ground rules adequately. You may need to back up to review the parties' commitment to the process of solving the problem together. You may need to ask them to direct their comments to you instead of each other.

    I sense we're getting stuck because you seem to react strongly to each other's words. Would you be willing to talk directly to us (the mediators) instead of each other for a few minutes?

- The party with better information may attempt to press her advantage by demanding to move on to the negotiation. You are the guardian of the process and it is important that no one be railroaded into negotiating with inadequate information.

    Information is power. We need to be clear about the level of information that it is fair to expect to be on the table before anyone is asked to make a decision.

- When the parties agree on anything, take the time to acknowledge their mutuality and record the agreement if it is appropriate to do so.

- Leave lots of room for feelings to come out and be acknowledged.

V.   IDENTIFYING ISSUES

Mediators review a list of potential issues to be addressed in the course of the mediation with the parties.

OVERVIEW OF IDENTIFYING ISSUES

During the information gathering stage, the mediators make a list of the issues raised by the parties. At the end of gathering information, the mediators review the issues they have identified with the parties. Often, especially in complex cases, the mediators will take a break between these two stages in order to consult with each other about the contents of the issue list. The formal step of identifying the issues can take as little as five minutes or as long as two hours. Some mediators choose to capture issues during information gathering and confirm them with the parties as they are expressed, rather than waiting until the information gathering stage has concluded.

It is critical that the issue list be reframed into neutral language. For example, in a workplace dispute, if one party says, *We need to talk about payment to me of $10,000 in lost compensation,* the mediators might reframe this as the issue, *compensation*. The mediators should also seek to mutualize as many issues as possible. For instance, if one party says, *You have to stop calling me names*, and the other says, *Well you have to stop talking about me behind my back,* the mediators might reframe these as the mutual issue *communication*. The mediators' list should include not only those issues specifically articulated by the parties, but also those which the mediators have inferred from their interactions, such as *future problem solving*.

Often mediators will create their issues list on a large flip chart to facilitate review by the parties. It is important that the parties have the opportunity to review the issues list for clarity, accuracy, and completeness during this stage of the mediation.

GOALS IN IDENTIFYING ISSUES

Beyond creating a neutral, accurate, and complete list of issues, the mediators have several other more subtle goals at this stage of the process. One is to help the parties feel heard because they see the concerns they have verbalized included in the list. A second is to help the parties feel optimistic about the mediation process. At last, they see in front of them a tangible task, a list of what must be accomplished in order to reach resolution. For many people, seeing their concerns expressed in a concrete, finite list reduces fear and anxiety and generates a hope that there may be manageable solutions to their problems. This creates a positive working environment for the mediation.

THREE MAIN TASKS OF MEDIATORS AT THE IDENTIFYING ISSUES STAGE:

1. Identify all issues raised by the parties.

2. Reframe the issues into neutral language and list them.

3. Check the issues list with the parties.

PROCEDURES IN IDENTIFYING ISSUES

*   Frame issues neutrally and list them on flip chart or your pad.
    I want to be reassigned to a different supervisor right away!
    Reframed issue: *Future supervision arrangements*
    The goal in framing issues neutrally is to be specific enough that the speaker feels the topic is captured and broad enough that there is room for more than a take it or leave it, Yes/No approach to resolving the issue.
*   Check to make sure you understand the issues correctly and that you have identified all of the issues and sub-issues to be explored during the mediation.
    Take a look at this list. Is anything missing? Do we need any changes in order to have a good road map?
*   Begin mentally to shape a mediation plan. Do you have a sense of what the big and small issues are? Where do you think you could begin and have some success?

Figure 12. Summary of Issue Identification Stage

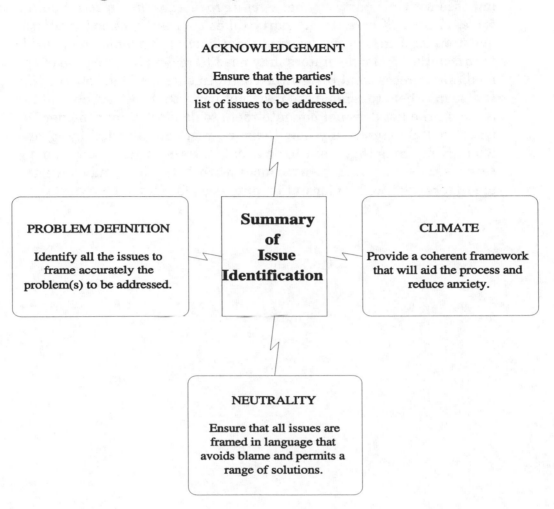

IDENTIFYING ISSUES CAUTIONS

- Don't get bogged down with lots of detailed sub-issues. Unless the dispute is complex, a set of clear topic headings should provide the necessary structure.
- Make sure your final issues list is clear, neutral, and acceptable to the parties.

- Some issues may not be shared. It is not uncommon to reach a mini-impasse with one party saying: *I refuse to discuss this. If that's on the table, I'm out of here.* If one party takes this tack, a good mediator question is: *What is your concern about having this topic on the table for discussion?* The mediators may need to review the purpose of the mediation process and review the commitments made in contracting. It also may help to remind the resistant party that the presence of the issue on the list does not obligate them to do more than consider the issue to understand fully how their interests are affected by it, and what, if anything they want to do about it. If these discussions do not resolve the concern, a short caucus with both sides may give the mediators additional information and ideas for moving forward.

VI. SETTING THE AGENDA

Mediators and the parties determine in what order to consider the issues.

SETTING THE AGENDA OVERVIEW

This is the stage of the mediation process where the work for the balance of the mediation gets organized. While it is possible to treat the issues as a topical checklist and proceed randomly, it is usually more useful to apply principles to organizing the order of resolution of the issues. There are several ways to approach organizing the issues:

- easy to hard
- most urgent to least urgent
- most important to least important
- least important to most important
- topical checklist (often followed in logical order)

Many mediators prefer the first organizational principle because it gives the parties the opportunity to learn problem-solving skills with a simpler issue. For instance, it is often easier to come up with a parenting schedule for the next week than it is for the next two years. Some issues are so critical, however, that the parties must address them immediately despite their difficulties. For instance, in dissolving a partnership there may be pressing contractual commitments which must be met by one or both of the parties immediately or the business will be lost. This may call for taking the urgent issue first.

However the agenda is organized, the parties must recognize that working on each issue is like putting together pieces of a jigsaw puzzle. Just as you can't be sure you have every piece of the puzzle in the right place until you see the whole picture, so should the parties treat agreements on each issue as tentative and revokable until they have worked through all the issues and put their tentative solutions together in a package.

Deciding on how to order the issues is a collaborative process between the mediators and the parties. Usually, the mediators will explain any preference they have on an approach and give the parties the benefit of their expertise before a decision is made. In many disputes, this stage is brief. In more complex cases, a full session may be spent negotiating and building an agenda.

GOALS IN SETTING THE AGENDA

Sometimes organizing the issues is a relatively straightforward task. At other times it represents a time of real struggle between the parties over whose issue will get covered first. This, of course, offers an opportunity for a mini-mediation. While it would be tempting for the mediators to step in and set the agenda, this could undermine efforts to teach the parties that they are responsible for decision making. Thus the major goal of the mediators at this stage of the process is to come up with a workable agenda that is collaboratively developed with the parties.

TWO MAIN TASKS OF MEDIATORS AT THE AGENDA SETTING STAGE:

1. To help the parties understand principles which may guide them in organizing the issues.

2. To elicit an agreement from the parties on the order in which the issues will be addressed.

PROCEDURES IN SETTING THE AGENDA

- Review and confirm the issues list, particularly if you are beginning a session.
- Obtain agreement on the approach to the list.
  Options:
  - Parties agree where to start.
  - Mediator picks a place to start.
  - Full agreement on the entire sequence.
  - Agreement only on the first one or two issues to start with.
- It helps to pick a place to start if you remind the parties that most disputants approach negotiations with the understanding that no agreement will be binding until there is agreement on everything, i.e. agreement on the first issue is conditioned on agreement on the last issue. This decreases the tactical considerations on where to start.
- Use the flip chart to help you by having a list of issues in front of everyone.
- Find out if there are standards, criteria, or principles for decision making that the parties can use in the next stage. If so, list them on the flip chart. They don't have to agree on the principles. The point is for each of them to be aware of the different ways to evaluate options, e.g. market value, precedent, or fairness.

Figure 13. Summary of Agenda Setting Stage

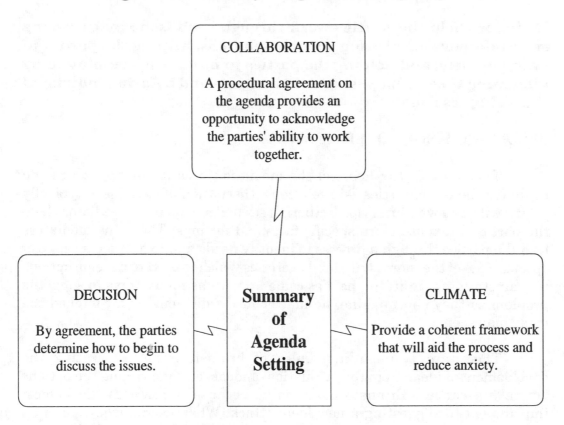

SETTING THE AGENDA CAUTIONS

- It is common for the parties to want to leap to demands and solutions. If you permit this, it is possible that they will select the biggest, thorniest issue to address first and then will promptly reach impasse. By breaking larger issues down into smaller pieces and by starting with less dramatic issues, it is possible to structure success by permitting the parties to develop confidence in the process and in you as you approach the more difficult parts of the conflict.

- Don't be too quick in imposing mediator choice in ordering the agenda. See if the parties can negotiate a selection. If they can, they have achieved an agreement that can be acknowledged.

- Don't let the parties flounder. It is very frustrating and they can lose confidence in the mediators and the process. If an agreement on where to begin is not forthcoming in a few minutes, you can ask the parties if they would like a recommendation from you.

VII. RESOLVING EACH ISSUE

Mediators help the parties work through each issue by gathering more information, eliciting possible solutions, helping the parties to evaluate them, and helping the parties to negotiate a resolution by refocusing them from positions to interests and by using individual caucusing sessions.

RESOLVING ISSUES OVERVIEW

This stage is the heart of the mediation process, during which the mediators help the parties find solutions. Discussion of each issue typically begins with a new information-gathering session in which the mediators help the parties to expose more specific facts and feelings. Then, the mediators lead the parties through a process to identify needs and to develop a range of options. One of the more structured exercises which is used to develop options is brainstorming. In it, the parties come up with as many ways to solve the problem as they can imagine, no matter how ridiculous or far-fetched the ideas may seem.

There are two cardinal rules of brainstorming: separating the development of ideas from the evaluation of ideas, and increasing the options before the parties. Brainstorming works because it removes the biggest impediment to suggesting a new idea: attack. When each suggestion of an idea meets with groans and criticism, new ideas are discouraged. The rules of brainstorming make it more likely that new ideas can emerge. It is far easier to go back and get rid of bad or unworkable ideas than it is to develop good ones.

To begin a brainstorming session, it is often useful for the mediators to review the rules with the parties: (1) no criticism; (2) wild, crazy ideas are okay; (3) it's okay to piggyback on another's idea with a variation; (4) quantity is desirable; and (5) everyone participates. Be prepared to capture the ideas with a flip chart and marker or pencil and paper.

Figure 14. Brainstorming

Do
Hold criticism
Freewheel
Piggyback
Get quantity

Don't
Judge
Dominate
Stop
Drop out

Once the parties have brainstormed a list of options, and, if necessary, been led to explore other options by the mediators, it is time to evaluate the options. The goal here is to weed out the ridiculous and focus on the possible. Often parties will see that combining several options will give them new and better alternatives.

The process of evaluating the options flows naturally into negotiating over the options. Sometimes, this will be an easy and natural transition, and the parties will work well without assistance. At other times, the parties will become stuck in advocating their preferred positions and the mediators will need to assist them with a variety of techniques. These include: using caucus with each side to explore settlement, discussing the costs and consequences of not settling, reviewing the parties' underlying needs and interests, and helping the parties explore whether their positions are realistic. The mediators may need to urge the parties to generate criteria about what is good and bad about each option, or ask them to stand in each other's shoes (put themselves in the other party's place), to help them consider the options. See Section Three (VII), The Caucus and Section Three (III), The Negotiation Process, for details on how mediators help the parties develop options. Appendix II, Worksheet 3, Evaluating Offers, provides a structured approach to assisting a party to evaluate a proposed offer before determining whether to accept, modify, or reject it.

RESOLVING ISSUES GOALS

The process of reaching resolution can sometimes be the easiest part of the mediation process. Everything which has taken place so far in the mediation has prepared the parties to take over and reach their own solutions. Thus, the goal of the mediators at this stage is to stay out of the way and let the parties work things out when they can, and to intervene and help them if they come to an impasse.

SEVEN MAIN TASKS OF MEDIATORS AT THE RESOLVING-ISSUES STAGE:

1. To elicit more facts and feelings about each issue, and to help the parties identify their underlying needs.

2. To assist the parties in generating and exploring a variety of solutions or options that might otherwise be missed or discarded. The mediators help the parties defer judgment on any option until the list is developed.

3. To reframe position statements into statements of underlying interests and needs and begin to move the parties from positional to interest-based bargaining. See Appendix II, Worksheet 2, Interest Analysis, for an analytical aid for mediators to use in identifying and comparing the parties' interests.

4. To focus continually on the importance of the ultimate outcome being acceptable to all parties and responsive to a basic sense of fairness. Developing a list of mutually acceptable criteria which the parties will use to evaluate options is often helpful. See Appendix II, Worksheets 4 and 5 for examples of structured ways to help parties look at criteria and options. These worksheets can be drawn on a flip chart pad for joint work, used as handouts with the individual parties in caucuses, or given as homework between sessions.

5. To help the parties understand the consequences and implications of each option once a number of different options have been identified and developed.

6. To continue to recognize and point out to the parties when their patterns of communication and interaction propel them into conflict. The mediators' overriding task during this stage is to help each party to understand his or her own and the other's perspective. It is important that the mediators facilitate efforts by each party to demonstrate to the other a genuine understanding of what the other person is saying.

7. To remember that it is the parties' ultimate responsibility to resolve their conflict. The mediators' job is to assist the parties in honestly and completely defining their conflict and in exploring the possible solutions that are available to them for resolving it.

RESOLVING ISSUES PROCEDURES

- Gather more information on the issue if necessary, using open-ended, fact-finding, and direct questions.
- Start with open questions:
  What else can you tell me about the house?
- Use digging questions (fact-finding, direct, leading) to pin down additional information:
  Exactly how many partners are there?
  Do you have a current appraisal on the property?
- Encourage direct dialogue and exchanges when the parties are capable of constructive, direct communication:
  Could you tell John how you see this issue?
  What did you understand Sherry to mean just now?

- Generate options/Brainstorming:

  Let's see how many different possibilities you can come up with in the next five minutes.

  Please don't comment or criticize any of the ideas now. After you come up with a list, you can shoot down any bad ideas. For now try to come up with quantity and variations. Far out ideas are okay.

- Explore needs and interests:

  Why is this important to you?

  How will your proposal meet your needs?

  What makes your proposal fair for them?

  What are you trying to accomplish with this approach?

- Evaluate options:

  Refer to the parties' stated goals or purpose in choosing to work in mediation:

  When we began, you said it was your intention to find a solution that enabled you to keep the property intact. How does this option fit with that purpose?

  Refer to or develop the parties' principles, criteria, and standards for decision making:

  You indicated that the precedent set by settlements with others is important to you as a measure of fairness. Using that measure, which options look better to you?

- Negotiate and select:

  Maximize satisfaction with three basic strategies:

  1. Build on shared interests—

  Find the things that both parties will benefit from and take every opportunity to nail these down. Search for scale economies, i.e. ways for the parties to save resources through cooperation that enable them to divide savings:

  You both stated that you want to structure the transaction to minimize taxes. How can you work together to accomplish this?

  2. Dovetail complementary interests—

  When one party values something and the other doesn't place as high a value on it, increase satisfaction by helping to structure an agreement in which the party who values something highly may receive it as her part of the settlement (low cost/high benefit trades):

  Freedom is most important to Terry and economic security is most important to Sean. Are there any options that give each of you a high level of satisfaction for these key interests?

3. Compromise, trade-off, package conflicting interests—
When both parties value a limited resource, split it, or allocate it so that one gets limited resource A and the other gets limited resource B. Compromises and trade-offs can be more palatable when they are packaged with other items that give more satisfaction:

> *Toby is asking for a compromise on the first issue. Is there some trade-off on another issue that could make this work for you?*

Use a flip chart or a handout that provides a simple decision making structure for the parties:

> *Here are the major elements of the proposal on the flip chart. What do you see as the advantages and disadvantages of each aspect of the proposal?*

A caucus can also be useful to find out if there is something going on that you don't know about.

> *Things seem pretty stuck. Is there anything we should know about what is going on?*

Figure 15. Summary of Resolving Each Issue Stage

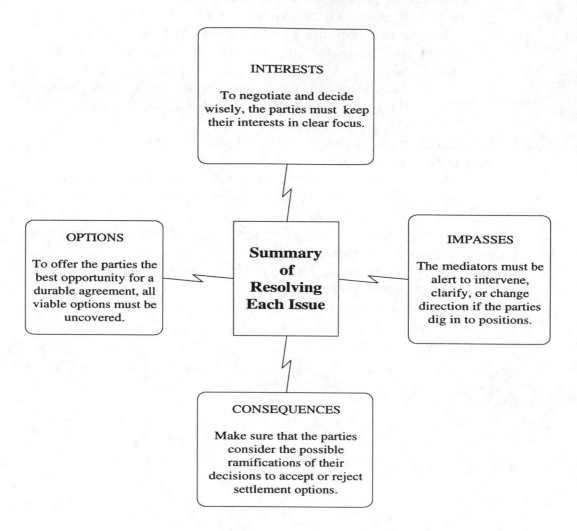

INTERESTS

To negotiate and decide wisely, the parties must keep their interests in clear focus.

OPTIONS

To offer the parties the best opportunity for a durable agreement, all viable options must be uncovered.

Summary of Resolving Each Issue

IMPASSES

The mediators must be alert to intervene, clarify, or change direction if the parties dig in to positions.

CONSEQUENCES

Make sure that the parties consider the possible ramifications of their decisions to accept or reject settlement options.

RESOLVING ISSUES CAUTIONS

- As a particular issue looms large in a party's mind, he or she may lose perspective, forgetting about agreements already reached and issues as yet undiscussed. Be prepared to remind the parties of how far they have come. This includes tentative agreements and concessions made by the other side.

- To explore carefully how far a party may be willing to go, a caucus can be very useful. If you don't know what someone's bottom line is, you can't help them compare it with their alternatives. This comparison is critical because it protects the party from making a foolish decision by walking away from an agreement that is better than what is available as an alternative.

- Look for growing impatience and frustration as the parties have trouble making progress. Be willing to suggest breaks, adjournments and other time/rhythm strategies.

- When parties say *No* or say they can't decide, probe to understand the reason(s), then act accordingly. For example, if information is deficient or in conflict, consider strategies to develop, enlarge or expand information, such as bringing in an expert or assigning additional homework.

- Take care so that you don't assume ultimate responsibility for the success of the mediation. Don't be afraid to have the parties take the weight.

  You both seem really stuck on this issue, what do you think it is going to take to move this mediation forward?

- If there is an impasse and the mediation is over, leave the door open for the parties to return in the future.

  Although no agreement seems possible at this time, keep in mind that this is a place to return in the future, if your other options don't produce the results you need.

BREAKING IMPASSES

There are times in some mediations when the parties get stuck. In order for the parties to have their best opportunity for a negotiated agreement, the mediators may need to become active. Some key questions for the mediators to ask themselves in order to choose a specific strategy for action are:

- What might I/we do differently?
- What do they want and do I/we fully understand what they want?
- Are there differences (culture, gender) that create barriers to understanding?
- Is the only way to get what they want to hold the position causing the impasse?
- Are some of the things they want in tension with each other? How do they prioritize these wants?
- What strategies are they using to get what they want that are not working? Is it in their interest to change their strategy and their behavior?

Based on the answers to these questions, the mediators may gather more information that guides the selection of intervention techniques. What follows is a list of techniques which may be used to help the parties achieve a settlement when they are at an impasse:

- Start over again.
- Caucus separately.
- Postpone discussion of the particular issue until later.
- Experiment with several options before reaching agreement.
- Shake up perspectives by approaching the issues from an entirely different direction.
- Review the mediation to remind them of progress.
- Help them to keep things in perspective by pointing out overall settlement possibilities versus the particular issue over which they are in conflict.
- Take short/long breaks.
- Find agreement on general principles, then refine details.
- Break issues into smaller fractionated problems and problem-solve on a smaller level.
- Use a flip chart and list what each party is giving and getting.
- Have in mind model solutions used in previous, similar situations and tailor them to respond to the parties' particular needs in this situation.
- Propose an option that is not totally acceptable to either party but provides a framework for jointly satisfying both parties.
- Turn to outside experts to develop new options.
- Bring in the parties' attorneys to help explore options and consequences.
- Develop a tentative proposal that is comprehensive and satisfies most of their interests, for the parties to critique.
- Discuss fairness, how to define it, whether there is more than one definition.
- Brainstorm additional solutions.
- Try short-term trial agreements.
- Refer the parties to therapy.

These impasse strategies are categorized in Figure 16.

Figure 16. Impasse Strategies

Strategy Category ➜	Perspective	Resources	Time/Rhythm/ Procedures
Overall Goal for Each Strategy Category ➜	Directly influence the way the parties see existing information, their choices, and each other.	Bring new elements to bear on the parties' situation that (1) change the dynamics, (2) provide new possibilities, or (3) help the parties view the situation differently.	Use the mediator's power to change something in the process of interaction between the participants.
Specific Strategies for Each Category ➜	• Ask them to consider what they will do if there is no agreement • Reality test the consequences of impasse (economic, social, time, emotional) • Review needs, interests, and desires and ask how their current non-negotiable position is satisfying them • Review a give and take worksheet listing the concessions made so far • Discuss fairness and objective standards (what benchmarks are they using, are others available) • Ask the parties what the roadblocks are and how they might get unstuck • Use perspective shifting tools such as reframing • Suggest that some issues must be decided because the cost of not deciding outweighs the cost of the undesirable decision • Use role switching technique (ask them to step into the shoes of the other person) • Use doubling technique (the mediator takes on the role of one of the parties)	• Bring in an independent expert • Get a second opinion from another attorney • Use an advisory attorney panel to review the pros and cons of each party's situation • Use advisory non-binding arbitration • Use therapeutic help (peers, family, professionals, support groups) • Offer mediator suggestions/ideas (solutions that have worked for others) • Assign homework so the parties develop additional information • Bring in the attorneys or other advocates • Develop additional options with techniques such as brainstorming. • Bring in other outside people (accountants, children, new spouses, appraisers) to surface hidden agendas, add knowledge at the table, and provide the parties with missing pieces of the puzzle	• Switch the focus area and come back to the sticky issue later • Start over (go back to mediation agreement) and check commitment to the process, understanding of ground rules • Caucus privately • Prepare a "one-text" proposal that each side can freely criticize and no one is committed to • Try trial periods • Take a break (walk, stretch) • Adjourn (with or without a time to reconvene) • Meet at a different time and place • Change the room configuration • Eat a meal together • Meet telephonically instead of in person • Have the attorneys in the room as observers • Use shuttle diplomacy (go back and forth between the parties with offers, ideas, and messages)

VIII. REVIEWING AND DRAFTING FINAL AGREEMENTS

Mediators help the parties reexamine and consolidate the agreements they have reached on all their different issues, then memorialize the final agreement for review by the parties and their lawyers.

REVIEWING AND DRAFTING FINAL AGREEMENTS OVERVIEW

Before actually drafting the final agreement, the mediators will often discuss its format and contents with the parties. This helps the parties to see the document as their own plan, and will give them guidance in carrying out the specifics of their agreement and in resolving future disputes. The mediators, in creating this document for the parties, will have to be wary of the pitfalls created by their prior professional experience. Often lawyers will write agreements which are jam-packed with legal jargon, and thus too technical to be useful to lay people. Lawyers may also deliberately exclude personal references, aspirations, and feelings from their mediation documents, leaving them too dry and impersonal. Mental health professionals, on the other hand, often focus on feelings and aspirations to the exclusion of specific detail and anticipation of contingencies.

The trick of agreement-writing is to be clear and concrete, while letting the concerns of the parties guide the contents. For instance, a parenting agreement which reads: *Joe and Mary agree to spend alternate weekends with their children* is loose and vague. It doesn't specify on what days the weekends begin and end (i.e. Friday to Monday or only Saturday and Sunday), nor what times the exchanges of responsibility will take place, nor where, nor who is responsible for driving, nor what will happen if a parent is late or needs to go out of town on an assigned weekend, etc. Not all agreements however, require this level of detail. The question is how much detail these particular individuals need to guide them, and in what areas. This means that the parties receive a document which is tailored to their situation, not taken wholesale from computerized forms.

Since the final agreement often forms the basis for a legal settlement as well, it is critical that it be reviewed by the parties' attorneys. Indeed, the mediation agreement often will serve as the basis for formal legal documents, prepared by the parties' attorneys, which will be filed with the court as the final agreement of the parties. This legal review will be most successful if the mediators have been sure to have the parties involve their lawyers throughout the mediation process, so that the lawyers have had input into and understanding of the issues from the start. Otherwise, the reviewing lawyer may be in an impossible position, lacking the background information necessary to evaluate the terms of the agreement. To the mediators, this attorney may appear to be picking apart the agreement and sabotaging the mediation. To the attorney, however, it may appear that she or he is being dragged into the mediation process at the last moment only to put a stamp of approval on a completed deal and to put his or her malpractice insurance on the line.

REVIEWING AND DRAFTING FINAL AGREEMENTS GOALS

The mediators' goal in drafting a final agreement for the parties is to create a document which is clear, concrete, balanced, and responsive to the parties' needs.

FOUR MAIN TASKS OF THE MEDIATOR AT THE REVIEWING AND DRAFTING OF THE FINAL AGREEMENT STAGE:

1. To draw up the agreement for the parties' review. This drafting task is one of the least dramatic, but most important functions of the mediation effort.

2. To write an agreement that works, in language the parties can understand. The language should be specific enough that the parties will not have future disagreements about the meaning of words or phrases.

3. To identify implementation steps and to lay these out in the agreement. It may also be appropriate to provide for some form of review and or revision of the agreement based on future performance or additional data not available at this time.

4. To encourage the parties to have the agreement reviewed by a lawyer of their choice before they sign it. The logistics of this review must be clarified and integrated into the closure process.

REVIEWING AND DRAFTING FINAL AGREEMENTS PROCEDURES

- Build in dimensions that produce strong settlement agreements:
  — Define specific exchanges.
  — Resolve all issues raised in the dispute.
  — Provide for a resolution of the dispute without future conditions.

      — Bind the parties to consequences in the event one of them does not follow through on their agreement.

      — Include a provision for handling future disputes.

      — Use balanced and reciprocal language.

      — Orient the parties toward the future.

- Review all conditional agreements and confirm them with the parties. Listing them on a flip chart in summary form is a good way to give everyone a visual as well as a verbal channel of communication.

- Combine issues into final agreement by asking if everything fits together.

- Reality-test the agreement with the parties jointly and/or in caucus.

- Check durability:

    Can anything go wrong that should be anticipated in the agreement?

    Should there be a mechanism for handling future disputes? If so, what should it look like?

- Check capability:

    Will you have any problems carrying out your responsibilities under the agreement?

    Do you have the authority you need to commit now?

    Are there any resources you will need to fulfill your obligations that you should confirm now?

- Check satisfaction level:

    Why is this agreement acceptable to you?

    Why is this agreement in your interest to sign?

    If you look back on this agreement three years from now, what will you think and feel?

    Is there anyone you will be explaining this agreement to (significant other, family, lawyer, banker, therapist, accountant)? What will you tell them about the agreement and why it is good/fair/wise?

- Determine whether you will prepare the final formal agreement or whether the parties' attorneys will do so.

- Verify that all aspects of the agreement are covered and that the language is clear.

- Ask the parties if they have reviewed (or will review) the agreement with appropriate advisors (attorneys, etc.).

- If the document needs to be reviewed or approved by others, determine the time-frame for the review. If there are issues raised during the review, discuss in advance how you and the parties will meet to address those concerns.

- Drafting suggestions:
    — Use personal, lay terms and avoid jargon and legalese if possible.

    Jay and Terry want to end their business partnership and fully resolve all legal and financial issues.

    — Include reciprocal obligations so the agreement is balanced.

    Terry will do 1.2.3., Jay will do a.b.c.

    — Include mutual obligations.

    Jay and Terry will make copies of documents in their possession and exchange them on 1/25/95 at their accountant's office.

    — Be specific.

    Terry will hand-deliver the original deed to the First Street Compound to Jay's residence on Friday, March 30, 1995 no later than 4:30 p.m. Jay will give Terry a cashier's check in the amount of twenty-five thousand dollars ($25,000) when he receives the deed.

Figure 17. Summary of Reviewing and Drafting Final Agreement Stage

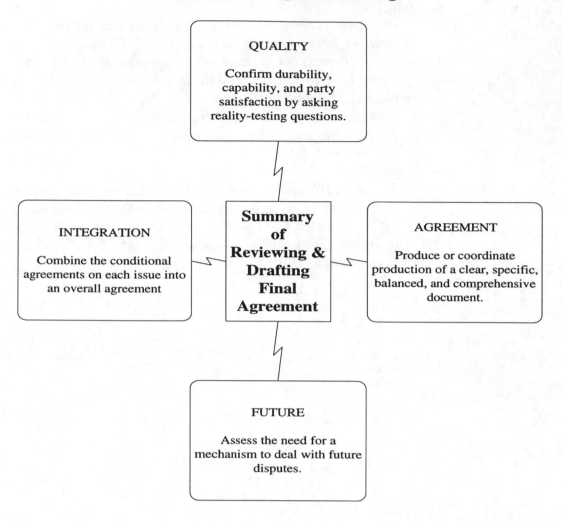

REVIEWING AND DRAFTING FINAL AGREEMENTS CAUTIONS

- Remember that weaker settlement agreements:
    — Do not include a resolution of all issues of the dispute;
    — Are provisional in nature and subject to future change;
    — Are contingent on additional information or future performance;
    — Are not binding; and
    — Lack consequences for failure to follow the agreement.

- In drafting the settlement agreement, precise language is important. Language that should be avoided in drafting settlement agreements includes such phrases and terms as:

  Adequate

  Reasonable

  Good faith effort

  As soon as possible

- Prepare people to go to their attorneys. If you know the agreement is unorthodox in some way or if it departs from legal norms, pay particular attention to the reasons the agreement is satisfactory to the party before he or she goes to the attorney.

- Don't be surprised by final bargaining on issues as they come together into a package. (Watch for "nibbles" and "oh by the ways" from more experienced, aggressive negotiators who try for last minute concessions.)

- If the parties get stuck on an issue at the end, beware of the entire agreement being jeopardized by take it or leave it stands. Remind the parties of the other aspects of the agreement and their investment in completing the negotiation successfully.

- Some parties are motivated to minimize expense and avoid contact with attorneys. As an attorney-mediator, beware of the trap of acting as the parties' attorney. If there is pending litigation, let attorneys prepare pleadings, formal settlement agreements, and dismissals. As a non-attorney mediator, beware of facilitating agreements by parties that miss important legal issues or of allowing parties to enter unknowingly into agreements that waive legal rights without the opportunity for independent legal advice.

- If a party indicates that his or her lawyer thinks the agreement is unacceptable, consider a separate meeting with the party to explore in detail the concerns that were raised. With the party's permission, it may be helpful to talk with the attorney.

- Sometimes, a party can play good guy-bad guy, at the end, using the attorney as the bad guy to attempt to gain final concessions.

- If both parties have attorneys and significant issues are raised regarding the draft agreement, consider a joint meeting with both attorneys and both parties to talk through concerns.

- Beware of letting the need to offer the parties reasonable opportunities for reflection so that no one feels pressured into signing. On the other hand, do not let delay dissipate the natural momentum of the process, with days turning into weeks. Be firm and clear with the parties about the importance of following through to gain closure.

- It may be possible to reach a partial or trial agreement that leaves other issues for the future. Trial agreements (written or unwritten) are common; don't be afraid to suggest them or use them to keep things moving.

SECTION THREE: THEMES IN MEDIATION

I. COMMUNICATION SKILLS

THE IMPORTANCE OF COMMUNICATION

The overall goal of mediation is to create the best opportunity for the parties to reach an agreement that satisfies their needs and meets their interests at an acceptable level. In order to achieve this goal, quality communication about the real issues is essential. Quality communication requires that the parties increase their actual knowledge of the conflict and the options for resolving it by sending and receiving messages accurately. Too often their attitudes and assumptions about each other, what each thinks and intends, get in the way of developing real knowledge.

It is usually the case that people who are in mediation have not been and are not now communicating well. Their communication patterns are often filled with dysfunctional elements. People in mediation are people in conflict and people in conflict are often under the influence of fear, anger, depression, and anxiety. These powerful emotions limit or eliminate quality communication.

Mediators must have the skills to manage the emotional climate of the mediation and to help parties strip away the illusions that they have about the dispute and about each other. The mediators must encourage a fresh, open approach to the issues, free of untested assumptions. To do this, the mediators will strive to apply three basic concepts. The first concept is that constructive communication is the foundation of conflict resolution. The goal of constructive communication is getting messages across with clarity and understanding. Therefore, establishing positive, clear communication between the parties is a top priority. The second concept is that messages must be translated between the foreign language of the message sender and the foreign language of the message receiver to assure actual understanding. Too often, people who speak erroneously assume that what they intended to say is the message which is heard. The third concept is that cultural and gender differences must be understood, considered, and factored into the mediators' communication approach to ensure clear communication. Not all groups speak, hear, and understand alike. Applying these three factors can foster an open communication climate in mediation.

Mediators must have a clear understanding of the way interpersonal communication works. All meaning intended to be sent from one person to another is coded in words, voice, and non-verbal signals. It then must be decoded by the intended receiver, whose biases, assumptions, and interpretation filter the incoming signals. Figure 18 sets forth an image of this model for understanding interpersonal communication.

Figure 18. Barriers to the Communication Process — Level I

The first layer of potential distortion in the communication process comes from the coding by the sender and the decoding by the receiver.

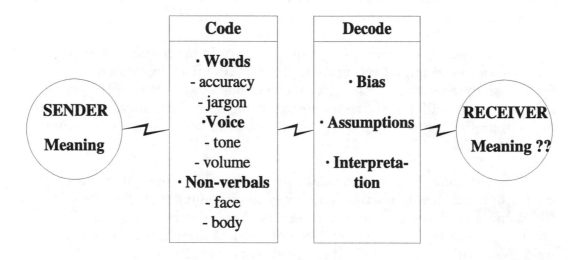

There are a number of techniques which mediators can master and apply to increase their own communication skills and those of the parties. These include skills which relate to creating a receptive environment, such as understanding the barriers to listening and using specific listening devices; skills which relate to eliciting information, such as inviting information flow with open responses and using specific guidelines for framing questions; and skills which relate to enhancing and clarifying communication, such as paraphrasing, summarizing, and reframing. The ability to apply these skills in mediation when appropriate is a critical element for successful mediations.

COMMUNICATION SKILLS FOR MEDIATORS AND PARTIES

1. LISTENING BARRIERS

A button that has circulated among mediators reads: *Mediator: When we listen, people talk!* Effective mediation is based on effective listening. Since the mediators have the most control over their own behavior, it is particularly critical that they eliminate any barriers to listening that lie within them. They must also be vigilant for evidence that listening barriers exist between the parties. Listening barriers can include the following:

- Lack of attention

    The mediation process and its parties deserve the complete, undivided attention of the mediators. This attention is certainly necessary for the mediators to learn about the dispute and to manage the process. It is also essential that the parties perceive the mediators giving them their full attention. Mediators must avoid excessive note-taking and ensure that their responses demonstrate concern and interest. Mediators must create an environment for the mediation session that is as free as possible of external distractions (ringing phones, loud answering machines, voices of others, etc.). The parties also need to pay attention. When a party does not appear to be paying attention, the mediators must be willing to stop the process and ask if the receiver understands what has been said.

- Internal chatter

    An active internal voice focused on matters unconnected to the speaker's message interferes with listening. Mediators must silence these voices in themselves. Messages like, *I wonder if someone is trying to reach me on the Johnson case this afternoon,* or *I hope my husband remembers to pick up the fish on the way home,* destroy concentration. If a party seems preoccupied, the mediators need to ask if something is impairing full attention to the process. Perhaps time to make a phone call could permit complete focus on the session.

- Talking too much

    If the mediators take too much air time, the process is harmed. It is impossible to learn from the parties when a mediator's mouth is open. A message may also be delivered to the parties that the mediators have most of the responsibility in the process. If one party talks endlessly or always interrupts the other, the mediators must intervene to permit the other party to have a fair opportunity to speak.

- Prejudice

     Stereotypical attitudes about the speakers based on their backgrounds, genders, cultures, orientations, or behaviors interfere with the listeners' ability to hear what any individual speaker seeks to communicate. If mediators have or develop stereotypical feelings about a party, *She's a woman, she can't understand these complex financial issues,* or *He's a man, he can't relate to the needs of a young child,* the mediators' effectiveness can be destroyed unless the feelings are resolved quickly. This is true of the parties as well. Confronting the prejudices of one party, however, can be a delicate and difficult task. Many mediators will work on prejudice issues in a caucus setting where they have more freedom to speak candidly.

- Premature judgment

     When mediators get ahead of the speakers in their thought processes and conclude that they know what the speaker means or intends before she or he finishes, their minds close and they stop listening. For example, *So this is really about the rights to the use of the business name,* or *There are only two ways to deal with this and one is too expensive.* With the parties, the mediators can exert influence and provide structure to avoid premature judgment. *John, I'm glad you have already given this some thought. Right now I need to hear more about the business operations. Once there is a good information base, let's take the two options you have, build on some others, and then critique them all at the same time.*

- Vocabulary and jargon

     The use of language that is unfamiliar or inappropriate to the cultural or educational background of listeners will interfere with their ability to understand messages. In addition to avoiding personal use of jargon, when the mediators hear jargon, they should check for understanding or stop the speaker and ask for an explanation.

Figure 19 offers a visual image of the complexity of communication which mediators must understand, building on the first layer of potential distortion, coding by the sender, and decoding by the receiver.

Figure 19. Barriers to the Communication Process — Level II

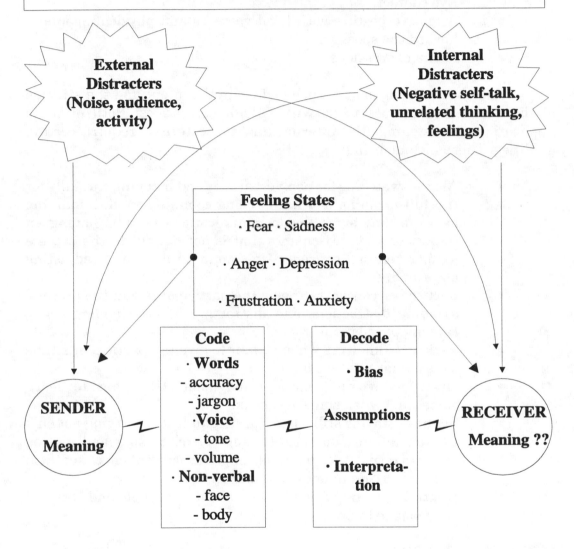

The second potential layer of distortion in the communication process comes from the internal and external distracters impacting both sender and receiver.

External Distracters (Noise, audience, activity)

Internal Distracters (Negative self-talk, unrelated thinking, feelings)

Feeling States
- · Fear · Sadness
- · Anger · Depression
- · Frustration · Anxiety

Code
- · **Words**
  - accuracy
  - jargon
- · **Voice**
  - tone
  - volume
- · **Non-verbal**
  - face
  - body

Decode
- · **Bias**
- Assumptions
- · **Interpreta-tion**

SENDER Meaning

RECEIVER Meaning ??

2. LISTENING SKILLS

Effective listening involves an internal mental state that permits accurate reception of the verbal and non-verbal messages of the speaker. It also requires external non-verbal signals, observable by the speaker, that indicate that he or she is being listened to. Research shows that about 65 percent of the social meaning in face-to-face encounters is communicated nonverbally. Thus, it is critical that the mediators be aware of all of the non-verbal communications in the room, including their own. Non-verbal communications indicating attention can encompass the use or absence of:

- Eye contact.
- Attentive posture with head gestures and physical openness toward the speaker.
- Facial expressions.

Effective listening has as much to do with the intent and the attitude of the listener as it does to do with specific techniques. Both of these applications of listening, the internal and the external, require certain qualities. These include being:

- Alert — watching for non-verbal cues and listening carefully for the full meaning of what is being communicated; remaining aware of any signs that communications may be having an impact on the participants that is not helpful to the process (defensiveness, reticence to communicate) and adjusting accordingly.
- Focused — concentrating on the participants and the process; avoiding distractions and distracting habits (jiggling coins, tapping pencils or feet, etc.).
- Patient — knowing when to wait to give the participants time to say what needs to be said.
- Open — avoiding passing judgment; expecting to learn something when someone speaks.
- Silent — staying still when it is helpful to do so; trying not only to stop talking, but also to stop (1) rehearsing and getting ready to respond, (2) using assumptions without checking them out, and (3) jumping to conclusions.
- Neutral — setting aside feelings about the people and personal reactions to them.

3. OPEN RESPONSES

Responses by the mediators can encourage continued communication. Responses can be non-verbal or verbal. Non-verbal responses include head-nodding, hand gestures, silence with eye contact and attentive body posture, and holding a pen or marker poised and ready to write.

Verbal responses include encouraging noises such as *mm hmmm,* as well as phrases such as:

Say more about . . . .
What else would you like to add?
Can you give me an example of . . . ?
I would like to hear more about . . . .
How would that work?

4. ELICITING, DISCOVERING, AND GUIDING

The mediators gain quality information and guide the communications in mediation by using skillful questions. There are some questions that encourage openness and dialogue, while others destroy it by causing the recipient of the question to feel pressed, defensive, challenged, or cut off. Skillful mediators are conscious of the effect of their questions, and ask questions for a purpose. Instead of jumping in and asking a question that occurs to him or her, the mediator could:

- Set context by stating the basis for the question.
  I'm troubled by your last statement conveying hopelessness about a resolution. What specific places do you see us getting bogged down?
- Forecast and indicate where the question is heading.
  I'd like to identify the most important concerns that each of you have before the end of today's session. Jan, what is significant to you about the appraised price of the property?
- Ask permission to question.
  Would it be all right if I ask you a few questions about your family and their perspective on this dispute?

Figure 20 illustrates a flow chart describing the process of skilled questioning for mediators.

Figure 20. Skillful Mediator Questioning

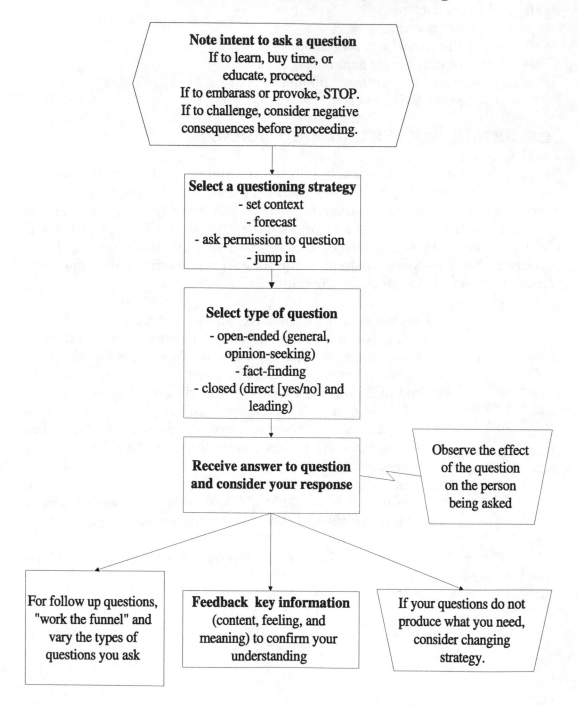

Note intent to ask a question
If to learn, buy time, or
educate, proceed.
If to embarass or provoke, STOP.
If to challenge, consider negative
consequences before proceeding.

Select a questioning strategy
- set context
- forecast
- ask permission to question
- jump in

Select type of question
- open-ended (general,
opinion-seeking)
- fact-finding
- closed (direct [yes/no] and
leading)

**Receive answer to question
and consider your response**

Observe the effect
of the question
on the person
being asked

For follow up questions,
"work the funnel" and
vary the types of
questions you ask

Feedback key information
(content, feeling, and
meaning) to confirm your
understanding

If your questions do not
produce what you need,
consider changing
strategy.

There are five major categories of questions. If questions are seen as a funnel that is designed to catch or receive information, each of these types of questions represents a different degree of openness in the funnel. It is important to use the most open-ended question appropriate to the situation. This gives the parties the most latitude in telling what they believe to be important without feeling that they are being interrogated or controlled.

- General — most open.
  What's on your mind?
  What can you tell me about this situation?
  What happened?
- Opinion Seeking — open.
  What do you think would be fair?
  What is most important to you?
  What is your reaction to his proposal?
- Fact Finding — somewhat open.
  Who needs to approve this?
  When is the deadline?
  Where, What, When, How?
- Narrow Direct or Forced Choice — mostly closed.
  Did you tell him before it happened?
  Will you be there before 5 o'clock?
  Will you accept her version of the agreement without any changes?
- Leading — closed.
  Isn't it true that there is no alternative?
  Didn't you say that it would be done without fail by Tuesday?
  Isn't it a fact that he cannot go to another school?

Figure 21 illustrates the funnel of questions moving from general at the open end to leading at the narrow end.

Figure 21. Question Funnel

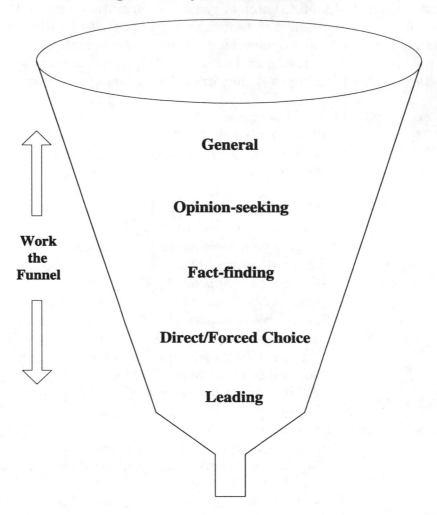

Work
the
Funnel

General

Opinion-seeking

Fact-finding

Direct/Forced Choice

Leading

5. PARAPHRASING

The paraphrase is a major tool of mediator communication skills. A paraphrase briefly focuses on the experience of the speaker. A paraphrase sums up the key elements of the speaker's message, whether they are directly or indirectly expressed. The focus of a specific paraphrase may be on the information content (the literal meaning of the words), the emotional tone (the feelings expressed or implied), or the meaning (the significance) that has been heard and understood by the receiver.

When a party speaks in mediation there are at least three potential receivers: the other party (in a two person mediation) and the two co-mediators. Paraphrasing is important for several reasons: (1) The receiver lets the speaker know she or he has been heard and understood; (2) The receiver makes sure he or she gets it right; (3) The receiver gives the speaker an opportunity to assess the message she or he is communicating and modify it; (4) The receiver gives the other party to the mediation a second opportunity to hear and understand the speaker's message.

The flow chart diagram in Figure 22 provides a graphic view of the steps in the process of paraphrasing the speaker's message.

Not only is it essential for the mediators to use paraphrasing techniques but it is also useful and constructive for the parties to paraphrase and confirm the information they are receiving from each other. Mediators can encourage parties to paraphrase each other:

Could you tell him what you understood from his last statement?

What did you just hear her say that was important to her?

Before you respond, please sum up his key points in your own words.

Such an exchange can be completed by then turning to the speaker and asking for acceptance or rejection of the paraphrase.

Did he understand the important parts of your message?

If not . . . What did he miss that you want him to understand?

There are a number of different ways to paraphrase or feed back messages.

Let me make sure I understand. You're saying that . . . .

So what I'm hearing is a concern that you reach an interim plan for the next month by the end of today's session.

You're most upset about the way other people in the office are speculating about the relationship between the two of you.

You seem very angry about receiving partial information.

It sounds as if you are anxious about the choice you must make.

So there are two things that are very important to you. First, you want to stay in the house. Second, you want to be assured that he talks respectfully about you with mutual friends.

If you really aren't sure, paraphrase and check your perception out in the form of a question:

Are you saying that there is only one person who has any knowledge of the situation?

Do you mean that you are more angry about the misinformation you received than the money that was lost?

Figure 22. Paraphrasing in the Communication Process

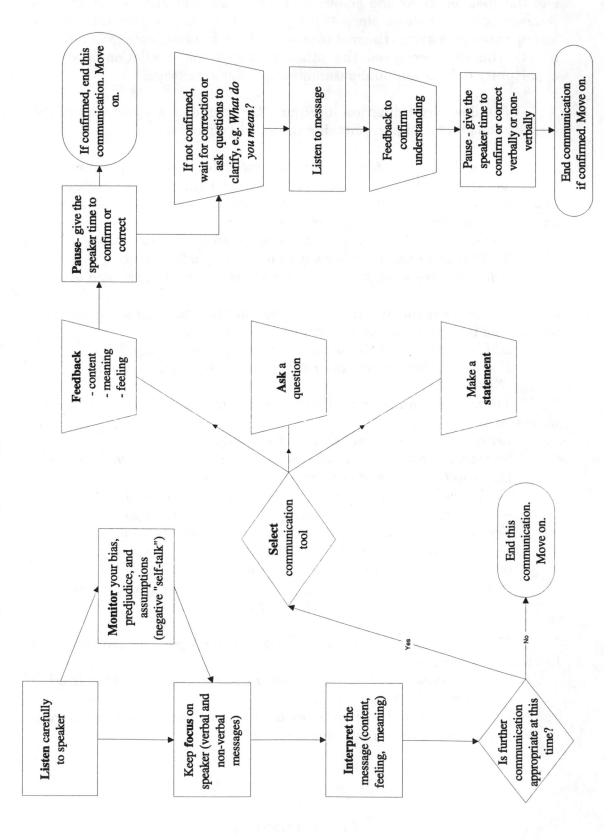

Some tips to avoid common mistakes in paraphrasing:

- Don't use a formula with every paraphrase beginning with the same words.
- Don't paraphrase everything. Emphasize key points and strong statements containing emotional and/or factual data that deserve confirmation, acknowledgment, repetition, or clarification.
- Don't parrot by using the same words. Translate into your own words and make the paraphrase shorter than the original message.
- Don't say, *I understand how you feel*. This can irritate people who resent your assumption that you know how they feel when you may not have been in the same situation.

The diagram in Figure 23 shows how mediators use feedback loops to reduce miscommunication and misunderstanding.

Figure 23. Removing the Barriers
to the Communication Process — Level III

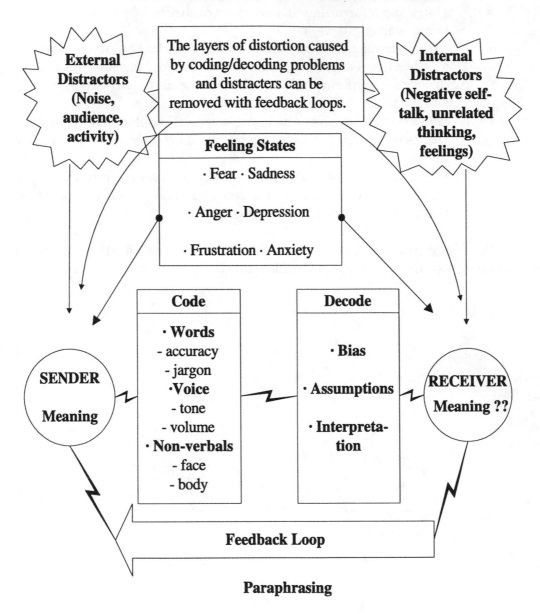

The layers of distortion caused by coding/decoding problems and distracters can be removed with feedback loops.

External Distractors (Noise, audience, activity)

Internal Distractors (Negative self-talk, unrelated thinking, feelings)

Feeling States

· Fear · Sadness

· Anger · Depression

· Frustration · Anxiety

Code

· **Words**
- accuracy
- jargon
· **Voice**
- tone
- volume
· **Non-verbals**
- face
- body

Decode

· **Bias**

· **Assumptions**

· **Interpreta-tion**

SENDER

Meaning

RECEIVER

Meaning ??

Feedback Loop

Paraphrasing

CONTENT   FEELING   MEANING

6. REFRAMING

The ability to reframe is a skill that is essential to the art of mediation. A reframe is a response to a message being sent from one party to another that intends to redirect, limit, or shape the perception of the message so that the message and its response become more constructive. Frames control how people perceive and interpret the situation they are in, the information being communicated, and the decisions they must make. Reframing operates by building on some constructive element or aspect of the message while changing the context or frame that surrounds the constructive element. The purpose is to minimize or eliminate some negative or unproductive dimensions of the original message. The problem part of the message may be a threat, a focus on the past about which nothing can be done, or insulting, offensive language.

Reframing is often called for when one party makes a statement that is likely to be received by another party as domineering, bullying, unconditionally demanding, or otherwise unproductive. Reframing is possible because every message is subject to interpretation. The mediators choose a positive interpretation and ascertain whether the sender and those hearing the message will accept their interpretation.

The following are examples of reframing.

1. Reframing a position focus to an interest focus.
> If a party says:
> *We're not budging. We have financial commitments to our members that we have to keep. We insist on full compensation of $200,000 and there is no way we will take a penny less!*
>
> The mediator could reframe this by saying:
> *So fair monetary compensation is a critical piece of the overall settlement for you because you have people counting on it and on you.*
>
> This reframe deletes the specific position or demand and focuses on the underlying interests: equity and meeting constituents' expectations.

2. Reframing a judgment focus to a problem focus.

    If a party says:
He is a liar. He doesn't deserve our trust. All we have seen is a bunch of broken promises.

    The mediator could reframe this by saying:
So you will need safeguards to be built into the agreement in order to be confident that it will be carried out?

    This reframe deletes the accusatory language and refocuses on the problem to be solved.

3. Reframing a blame focus to a need focus.

    If a party says:
She has let down the kids again and again; drinking, not showing up when she's supposed to . . . what a worthless excuse for a mother!

    The mediator could reframe this by saying:
I'm hearing your anger and your worry about the impact on the children. In the future, you want the assurance of consistent, reliable behavior from her whenever she has a commitment to be with the children. What specific steps would you like to see happen?

    This reframe sidesteps all of the accusations about past conduct and focuses on one interpretation of the underlying need of the speaker. The mediator concludes by suggesting a specific, future focus.

4. Reframing a past focus to a future focus.

    If a party says:
That's the last straw. In the last five years that I have known you I don't think I have ever seen you show up for an appointment on time.

    The mediator could reframe this by saying:
It sounds to me like you're really fed up with waiting and you want to make sure that the rest of our meetings begin promptly. Shall we try to develop a schedule that will work for everyone?

    This reframe changes the focus from past performance to a future issue to be discussed.

5. Reframing an individual problem focus to a shared problem focus.
If a party says:
We're not in the entertainment business in running the public schools. Sometimes kids have to be in classes they don't want to take and it's up to the parents to get them to accept it.

The mediator could reframe this by saying:
Both school officials and parents are concerned about kids' attitudes in school. Are there ways you can be helpful to the parents in working on Jimmy's attitude?

This reframe keeps the responsibility for the problem (the child's attitude in school) from being placed solely on one party (the parents).

Some tips for successful reframing:

- Make sure that your reframe retains a key element of the original message;
- Acknowledge clear expressions of emotion;
- Watch for resistance from the sender. Pause to give them a chance to object to the reframe;
- Don't smooth over conflict when it needs to be sharply expressed to define the issues and get the message across to the other side.

The flow chart diagram in Figure 24 provides a graphic view of the steps in the process of reframing the speaker's message.

Figure 24. Reframing Process

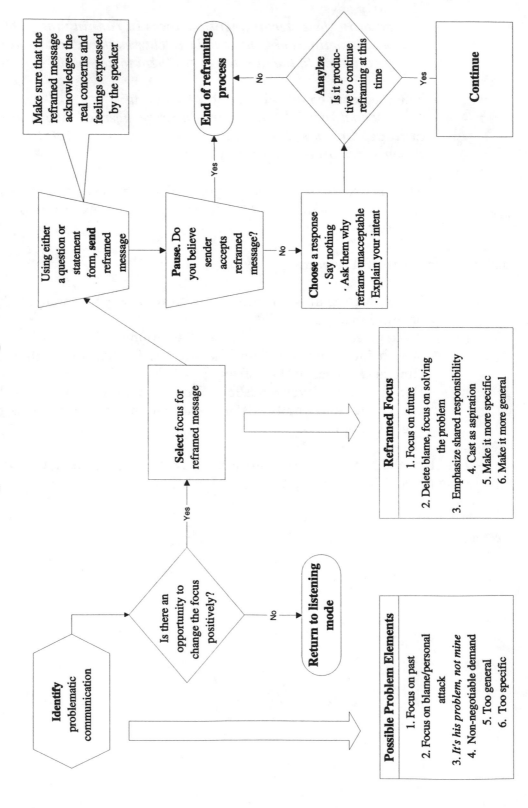

7. SUMMARIZING

Paraphrasing clarifies and ensures understanding at the time a message is delivered. Summarizing establishes more long-term understanding and keeps things on track by listing, synthesizing, and reviewing important information. Summarizing also checks the status of the process. A skillful summary ensures understanding by repeating key information, keeps things on track by reminding people where they are, and makes sure there is clarity before moving on to another point.

There are three issues that we have been discussing: (1).... (2).... (3).... I have a sense that you are ready to move on and come back to these later.

There are several agreements that you have already reached. They include: (1).... (2).... (3).... This leaves two issues that have not been addressed: the sale price of the rental property and the selection of a realtor. Can you think of anything else that needs to be covered?

End a meeting with a summary of what has been done, what will happen next, and what remains to be addressed:

We completed our work on what the new job description would be if you stay with the office. John will check with the City Attorney on the status of the new regulation on leave without pay that you have proposed and report to us at our next meeting at 9 a.m. Tuesday. We will then discuss that regulation and the salary level and benefits package.

Begin a meeting with a summary of what has gone before:

We covered two issues in the last session, (1).... (2).... but did not discuss the pension benefits. Are you ready to move on to this issue?

Ask the parties to sum up where they are:

In what areas do you believe you have made the most progress?
Review for me the two or three areas that most concern you.

8. CLARITY IN SENDING MESSAGES

When the mediators wish to communicate information to the parties, they need to make sure they are understood. They also may need to assist or coach the parties to send messages to the other side that are more likely to be heard and understood.

The following are suggestions for clear messages.

- Replace abstract concepts with concrete descriptions.
  <u>Instead of</u>
  I am concerned about pessimistic statements about the chances for settlement.
  <u>Try</u>
  I am concerned when you say that you want your lawyer to file motions now because I believe it could cause everyone to become more defensive and therefore limit our ability to reach agreement in mediation.
- Send *I* messages by beginning statements about your concerns, feelings, purposes, perceptions, opinions, and judgments with *I* or *We*, not *You*.
  <u>Instead of</u>
  You're rambling and not being very clear.
  <u>Try</u>
  I'm having trouble following you.
  <u>Instead of</u>
  You're jumping to the next thing before we are finished with this issue.
  <u>Try</u>
  I am concerned that we need to finish the discussion of the house before moving on to school placement.
- Accept personal responsibility for interpretation and avoid placing blame, and putting others on the defensive with attacks and criticism.
  <u>Instead of</u>
  You're not telling me the whole truth.
  <u>Try</u>
  I have trouble accepting this information without some supporting documents.
  <u>Instead of</u>
  You are ruining the process by failing to produce the necessary information.
  <u>Try</u>
  I am troubled by the pace of the mediation due to the lack of available information.

Thus, clarity in communications including concrete descriptions, sender orientation, and personal responsibility is the final piece of communication skills work. Underlying these techniques is the intent to improve the quality of mutual understanding which lies at the heart of interest-based problem solving and the entire mediation process.

Figure 25. Communication Skills

II.   VALUES AND FEELINGS

SIGNIFICANCE

The goal of the mediation process is to increase the possibility of a durable agreement by creating an environment in which constructive and creative communication can take place. An agreement requires that people make a decision on a course of action. It is not possible, in most cases, to assist people in making decisions without understanding something about their personal preferences, feelings, and values. The mediators must help the parties to see the problem, and each other, with new eyes. The values they hold and the feelings they have about their current situation and the people on the other side(s) of the dispute create a filter or lens through which all communication and behavior is screened. In order to work with these dynamics, mediators must be comfortable engaging with disputants at an honest level of feeling. The verbal and non-verbal language of emotion and values is an important vocabulary to master.

VALUES

Values are the standards and principles that we use to determine what is right or wrong, fair or unjust. When people feel strongly about something, values are often at work. Examples of values include:

Equity	*Family*
Freedom	*Environment*
Security	*Safety*
Patriotism	*Health*
Growth	*Peace*
Education	*Cooperation*
Harmony	*Competition*
Quality	*Frugality*

For mediators, the identification of disputants' values leads to the ability to understand their decision-making process. However, this understanding is not always easy to achieve. Our values are deeply imbedded in who we are. Sometimes we express them explicitly, but frequently values are not clearly identified. Instead, they lie beneath the surface of communications.

Mediators must be alert to language that implies the presence of values. Here are three clues to listen for:

- The use of extreme language: *worthless, irresponsible, outrageous.* Words that judge or blame the other side, their positions and behavior.
- Reference to a venerable source: *the Constitution says, our therapist says, the child support guidelines say.*
- Prediction of dire consequences: *If I don't get the house, the children will be crushed and their entire sense of security will be destroyed.*

When mediators sense values being communicated, these explicit or implicit statements should be explored. For example, if a party holds several values in relation to the issue in conflict, mediators can test the strength of the values relative to each other to determine if one is more significant to the party. Values cannot be bartered away, but they can be prioritized by the holder. For example, if a party in an employment dispute values freedom and economic security, that person can choose to place more importance on a negotiated settlement that maximizes financial gains but accepts supervision arrangements that limit her ability to do the job exactly the way she chooses. If the conflict involves deep-seated values, the mediators can help the parties look beyond the values in direct conflict to search for a superordinate value that all the parties can agree upon. For example, partners fighting over the dissolution of their business may agree to focus on ways to lawfully avoid taxes as an overriding value. Another approach to values in conflict is to create an option for each party to exercise their competing value in a personal sphere of influence. For example, in a divorce where the parents have conflicting religious values, instead of a winner take all approach to the child's religious training, each parent may agree to introduce the child to that parent's religious beliefs during the child's time with that parent.

PARTY FEELINGS

One of the subjective arts of mediation is the management of the process of ventilation of emotion. Most mediators believe that the opportunity to clearly express strong feelings related to the conflict is an essential part of the process. Failing to foster this opportunity increases the likelihood of deadlock and frustration. It is helpful to keep in mind the following guidelines.

- When one person is ventilating, mediators must pay attention both to the speaker and to the receiver. People have varying tolerances for hearing strong emotions directed towards them. Ventilation is counterproductive when it overwhelms or embitters and polarizes the receiver, making dialogue impossible. Watch body language.
- There is a big difference between ventilation and personal attacks. Encourage those ventilating to use *I* statements, instead of *you* statements.
- If necessary, stop the speaker and ask him or her to reformulate the statement. You may invoke a "no personal attack" ground rule and enforce it as needed.
- When feelings are not being expressed, consider probing, using questions such as:

    How does this feel to you?

    Do you have any emotional reactions you are willing to share with us?

- If feelings are not revealed in joint session, caucus may be a place where you can get more emotional information from the parties.
- Inject feeling issues into the mediation with reality-testing questions:

    If you agree to her proposal to buy you out, how will it feel to you a year or two down the road if she closes the business or sells it to someone else?

    How will you feel if your father tells you that you didn't ask for enough money?

Awareness of the importance of feelings, skill in managing the process of expressing emotion between the parties, and the ability to stay in touch with the emotional states of the parties are essential tools for successful mediation.

As illustrated in Figure 26, feelings and values shape the attitudes and behaviors of the parties.

Figure 26. Relationship of Values and Feelings to Behavior

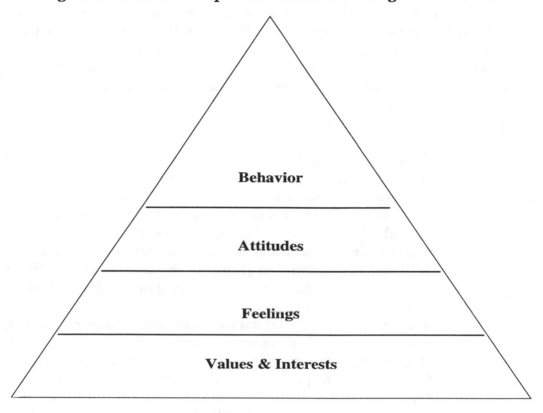

Behavior

Attitudes

Feelings

Values & Interests

MEDIATOR FEELINGS

It is not possible to assist people in confronting their feelings and exploring how their feelings are either assisting or hindering their work in the mediation process if the mediators are not comfortable with their own feelings. It is important that the mediators communicate feelings and discuss feelings openly, without hesitation. It is also important that the mediators understand what kinds of responses and behaviors in others evokes strong feelings in them and pushes their buttons.

The art of mediation is not being neutral in the sense of being free from all values, opinions, and feelings about the parties and the subject matter of the dispute. The mediators' task is to be aware of their own prejudices, opinions, values, and feelings so that they can be privately acknowledged and monitored in order to work effectively with a broad spectrum of individuals.

When the mediators are influenced emotionally by the behavior of someone, they are in a mode of reacting to them instead of responding based upon their best professional judgment. They have been "hooked." The job of the mediators is not to avoid getting hooked by people at all costs, since all of us get hooked sometimes. The important skill is to unhook quickly and get back on track as an impartial helper to the parties in conflict.

Some aids to unhooking include:

- Believe that people are flawed, not evil. When we encounter people in conflict, they are often under the influence of very powerful emotions: fear, anger, anxiety, and depression. We may not see the best side of them. It helps to deal with the difficult side when we believe that evil is rare.
- Pause before responding. If you take time to breathe deeply and briefly reflect on your response, you increase the likelihood that you can short circuit an inappropriate, automatic response.
- Remember mistaken judgments. With reflection we can develop a clear mental picture of a person whom we completely misjudged, by stereotyping them or labeling them as bad, uncouth, mean-spirited, or cruel. If we can remember a significant instance of misjudging someone, this can be a reminder of the dangers of getting hooked.
- Use your co-mediator. The mediators can ask each other for private feedback, outside the mediation session on their reactions. They can also ask one another to take the lead in dealing with a difficult party.

Figure 27 illustrates both common "hooks" that can influence a mediator and some of the tools which can assist a mediator to overcome the hooks.

Figure 27. Getting Unhooked

Recognize Possible Hooks
· Behavior (manner of speaking, emotional expression, negotiating tactics, being difficult) · Personal characteristics (race, ethnicity, gender, disability, sexual orientation, appearance) · Situational factors (values, similarity to the mediator's personal experience)

Aids to Unhook
· Assume that people are flawed, not evil · Breathe deeply and regularly · Remind yourself of a time when you completely misjudged someone · Use your co-mediator as a source of feedback and assistance

III. THE NEGOTIATION PROCESS

OVERVIEW

The techniques of collaborative negotiation are at the heart of the mediation process. It is essential to effective mediation that the mediators have an understanding of the dynamics of negotiation and have the ability to promote constructive negotiation behavior between or among the parties. The best collaborative negotiations are educational processes, with both sides increasing their knowledge and understanding of the other while they work together toward an agreement which encompasses all of their needs.

The goal of the collaborative negotiation process used in mediation is to generate a discussion of issues and needs so the parties can solve their problems by informed, joint, voluntary decisions. This requires that the parties identify the points about which they differ and communicate with each other in order to develop a mutual understanding about their respective concerns and interests. Communication is followed by development of options for settlement. Then, the parties explore the costs and benefits of each option and make selections of those which will work the best for them. An agreement which concludes a successful negotiation may include exchanges of things which are either tangible or intangible, of commitments for the future, and of statements about the past.

Some people approach negotiations from a competitive rather than a collaborative perspective. Their goal is to win — to best the other person in order to achieve a larger share of limited resources. Skillful mediators need to understand the workings of this process of distributive negotiations as well, in order to supervise the dynamics of what is happening and in order to explore whether a shift to collaborative negotiations might be more productive.

ISSUES, INTERESTS, POSITIONS

Issues are the WHAT of negotiations: the subjects, things, and topics that must be addressed in the negotiations. In a labor mediation, issues could include wages, hours, grievance procedures, or safety conditions. In a divorce mediation, issues could include the house, the pension plans, the children's need for parenting, and the MasterCard bill. To identify issues, ask questions such as:

What do we have to discuss?
What tangible things can and must be dealt with?

What are the different aspects of this problem?
What are some different ways to view this situation?

Interests are the WHY of negotiations. They describe the reasons or the underlying needs and concerns that motivate people to ask for certain kinds of outcomes. In a labor mediation, the interests of management could include profitability, job security of top management (based on getting the right deal), and freedom from too much union involvement in management decisions. The interests of the union could include economic security for their members, health and safety of members, and freedom from arbitrary management action. In a divorce mediation, the interests of either or both parties could include financial security, freedom to live their lives without the interference of others, and positive image in the eyes of the children.

To identify interests, ask questions such as:

How will getting (your position) satisfy you?
What are your goals?
Why won't their offer meet your needs?

Positions are the HOW of negotiations. Positions describe possible outcomes or solutions, i.e., how the dispute could be settled. In a divorce mediation, positions could include: *I get the house; we share time with the children absolutely equally; you pay me $1,000/month alimony for five years so I can finish school and support myself.* In a labor mediation, positions could be *$12.00/hour with $1.50/hour overtime, three steps in the grievance procedure with binding arbitration by an independent party, and formation of a ten member safety committee with five representatives appointed by labor and five by management.*

To identify positions, ask questions such as:

What do you want?
What's your bottom line?
What offer will you put on the table?
What's your response to their proposal?

Mediators need to be aware of the distinctions between issues, interests and positions. The mediation should begin by defining what issues there are to resolve, and acknowledging the parties' positions on these issues. The mediation should then proceed to explore the parties' interests. Finally, it should move to identification and evaluation of the options that will meet, to the maximum extent possible, the interests of all parties.

DISTRIBUTIVE BARGAINING

Distributive bargaining is based on competition between the parties. The outcome is seen as dependent on the power and cunning of the negotiator. Distributive bargaining involves the parties arguing over and posturing around the positions which are the preferred results which they seek. In order to maximize their chances at achieving their positions, the parties work to manipulate each other's perceptions. Typically, in a competitive negotiation the parties will determine the best possible outcome they hope to achieve — their target point — and begin their demands significantly above that outcome so as to conceal it and leave themselves room to bargain down to it. However, they know that they are willing to settle for less than their target point, so they also identify the lowest outcome they will accept — their bottom line. This bottom line represents the point at which they will deadlock rather than go lower. In distributive negotiations, the overlap of the parties' bottom lines creates the bargaining range of the negotiation within which settlement can be achieved, unless one or both of the bottom lines are shifted. During the course of the negotiation, a sequence of positions with rationales and justifications is put forward by the negotiators as they move slowly toward their respective bottom lines, coupled with arguments which defend each side's position and seek to persuade the other side to give in. An agreement is reached if the parties' positions meet before a bottom line or non-negotiable limit is reached. This process is portrayed in Figure 28.

Figure 28. Illustrative Bargaining Range

Party A seeks $1,000 from party B, believes the most she can possibly get is $800 [TARGET POINT], and will settle for $500 but not less [BOTTOM LINE].
Party B is willing to pay no more than $700 [BOTTOM LINE], but hopes to settle for $300 [TARGET POINT].

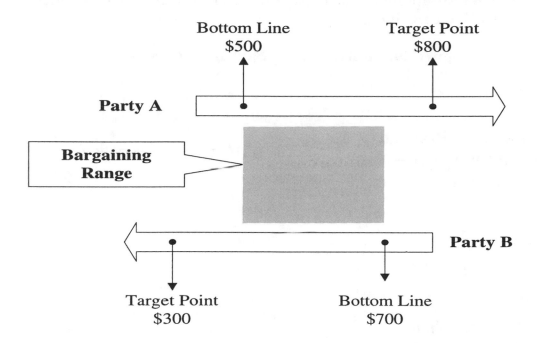

Distributive bargaining can be a useful and efficient way of dealing with a single issue problem in which only finite resources are available for the solution. A classic example of a situation where distributive bargaining is frequently used is the purchase of a car. The price of the car is the issue, and the dollars to fund the purchase are the finite resource. The car salesperson is unwilling to disclose the least for which the car will be sold and the buyer is unwilling to disclose the most she or he is willing to pay. Offers and counteroffers are exchanged, often with much posturing. If buyer and seller agree on an amount before one of them reaches a bottom line, the car will be sold. Distributive bargaining is often used in the settlement of damage cases, where negligence, injury and fault are translated into a negotiated dollar amount.

INTEREST-BASED BARGAINING

Interest-based or problem-solving bargaining emphasizes the attempt to satisfy individual needs or interests, not only for one party, but for all participants in the negotiations. Its emphasis is significantly different than distributive bargaining in that the parties attempt to make their real interests and needs known to each other as an educational process. Then alternatives can be explored which integrate, to the greatest extent possible, need and interest satisfaction for all participants. Figure 29 is an illustration of interest-based bargaining.

Figure 29. Interest-Based Bargaining Model

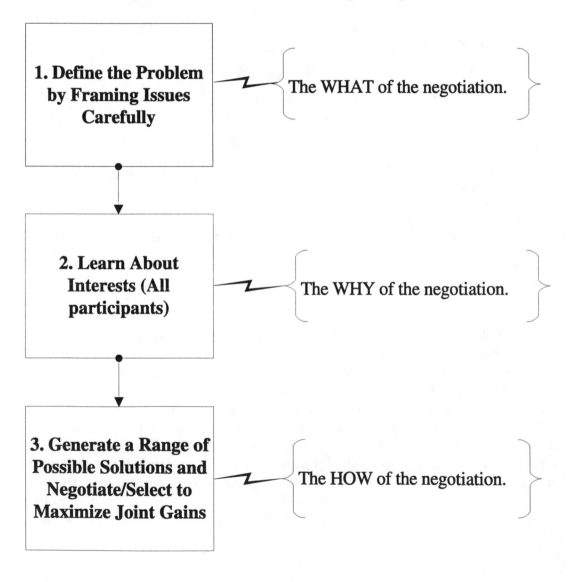

UNDERSTANDING INTERESTS

There are three types of interests that can be involved in negotiations: substantive, procedural, and psychological.

1. Substantive interests are the interests that people usually think of when considering what they want. They include specific levels of money, goods, services, or resources. Substantive interests can often be ascertained by asking, *Would you describe what it is you want and why it is important to you.* A key question to identify substantive interests is *Can you tell us what you want to have at the end of this process?*

2. Procedural interests are the interests that relate to the way that things are done. They include schedules, procedures, and protocols. A key question to identify procedural interests is *How do you want this dispute to be handled and in what way should the outcome be managed?*

3. Psychological interests are associated with the way people are treated or the way relationships are dealt with. Such things as "saving face" or "being treated with respect" are psychological interests. Psychological interests can rarely be accessed with a direct question, although the inquiry *What might help you put this behind you and feel okay?,* may work.

It is only by understanding the parties' interests that the mediators can guide discussions and communications toward an interest-based agreement. An agreement which provides some level of satisfaction for each party's substantive, procedural, and psychological interests is more likely to be a durable settlement.

TRANSITIONS FROM POSITIONS TO INTERESTS

The parties increase the likelihood that they will become involved in a contest of wills which preempts the thoughtful development of creative options when they focus on positions. An important part of the mediators' job is to help the parties make the transition from locking into positions to exploring interests. The following techniques will help the mediators do this.

- Moving on from positions when they are voiced and continuing the parties' dialogue on the issues and underlying interests.
- Using *Why . . . ?* questions, *Why is that what you want?, Why will it meet your needs?, Why isn't their idea acceptable to you?, Why are you motivated to deal with them?,* to determine what interests underlie the position.
- Labeling and describing the interests, then checking this understanding with the parties.
- Asking the parties when they are countering positions with positions, what their concerns are about the position the other party has articulated, as opposed to having them defend their preferred counterpart.
- Suggesting that there might be an alternative to one party getting what they want and the other party not getting what they want. Frame the discussion around possible solutions that will work for all parties.
- Identifying and separating out substantive, psychological, and procedural interests which may be lumped together in a party's statement of their position.
- Asking what general principle underlies a stated position, then going on to see if the parties can agree upon the principle even if they cannot agree upon the position.
- Reminding the parties that the problem has elements of commonality of interests and the possibility of all sides benefiting.
- Separating the problem from the personalities, so that the parties focus on the issues, not on each others' faults.
- Helping the parties to generate multiple options and suggesting that the positions stated, as well as the other options, merits further investigation to determine how the parties' interests might best be satisfied.

See Appendix II, Worksheet 2, Interest Analysis, for a structured approach which allows mediators to analyze the parties' interests in order to develop a strategy that leads toward the best opportunity for a negotiated agreement.

EVALUATING OFFERS

In order for a party to decide whether a negotiated resolution of a dispute is wise or acceptable, that party must address the merits of the offer, as well as the question of what he or she will do if negotiations break down and there is no agreement. In evaluating the offer itself, parties may be aided by examining possible ways of measuring the offer in terms of value and fairness. These can include comparison with other resolutions (precedent), or decisions (court cases), seeking neutral opinions, or researching market values. Parties may look at independent alternatives, i.e., *What can I do on my own to deal with this issue no matter what you do?* They can look at interactive alternatives, i.e., *What can we do together to deal with this issue?* Finally, they can look at third party alternatives, i.e., *Who else can help the two of us resolve this issue?* The acronym, BATNA, is often used by mediators. It stands for Best Alternative To Negotiated Agreement. It refers to what each party plans to do if a negotiated agreement cannot be reached. The purpose of exploring BATNAs is to help the parties to consider their options carefully before rejecting an offer that is as good or better than their best realistic alternative. In considering each alternative to a negotiated agreement the parties need to consider:

- How much will it cost,
- How long will it take,
- What is the best possible realistic result,
- What is the worst possible realistic result,
- What are the potential direct risks,
- What are the potential indirect risks, including:
  — personal costs,
  — emotional costs,
  — physical costs,
  — social costs,
  — time allocation costs,
  — resource allocation costs,
  — lost opportunity costs.

Only in the context of this full exploration of costs and alternatives can parties make an informed decision on whether to accept or reject any option which is before them. It is also important to test offers against the interests of the parties and ask them to consider how well a proposed solution satisfies their substantive, procedural, and psychological interests.

See Appendix II, Worksheets 3, 4, and 5, for examples of decision-making tools which can assist the parties in evaluating offers.

IV.   THE NATURE OF CONFLICT

CONFLICT DEFINED

Conflict is a state of disagreement, opposition, contention, competition, or tension between individuals or groups of people. This state is based on a real or perceived incompatibility among the parties to the conflict. This incompatibility may involve the past, the present, or the future of the parties. Conflict is a universal condition that exists in all types of human relationships and in all cultures.

As mediators, we seek to help participants in conflict explore their real and perceived incompatibility in order to maximize their interest satisfaction while minimizing the costs of the conflict. The constructive and destructive potential of conflict often motivates participants. Parties seek to avoid the very real costs of conflict or to capitalize on the opportunities presented by the resolution of the conflict. Therefore it is important that mediators be aware of the dimensions of conflict.

Conflict is destructive when it:

- takes people away from important priorities,
- builds barriers that inhibit the ability to understand each other and work together,
- decreases productivity,
- lowers morale,
- leads to harmful behavior (fighting, insults),
- injures people physically or psychologically,
- polarizes relationships, increasing an "us against them" feeling, or
- increases distrust and suspicion.

Conflict is constructive when it:

- leads to open dialogue,
- offers an opportunity to solve problems,
- increases understanding, communication, and respect,
- increases productivity,
- results in healed or strengthened relationships,
- improves negotiation, communication, and problem-solving skills,
- relieves tension and anxiety by permitting a release of buried emotions, or

- raises morale.

Proponents and practitioners of mediation have an underlying assumption that conflict need not be destructive. Conflict is natural and can be healthy and useful if it is dealt with openly in a fair process that prevents escalation into violent or exploitative behavior.

BEHAVIOR IN CONFLICT

The mediation process is designed to develop the constructive dimensions of conflict and manage its destructive potential. This design has a structure, logic, and integrity that influences the parties to restrain or modify behavior intended to exploit, harm, or dominate, substituting strong advocacy of personal or group goals. In order for the participants to make the shift from competitive to cooperative participation, mediators must often wrestle with one or more attitudes that underlie destructive behavior in conflict.

- Win/Lose — This is a sense that there are only two possible results for each party. One must win and one must lose. With this perceived limitation of the possibilities, it is easy for competitive dynamics to escalate as each side attempts to win or avoid losing.
- No Hope — This pessimistic mind-set can become a self-fulfilling prophecy as one or more of the parties gives up on any positive outcomes and closes their thinking to new options. If there is no possible way for anything positive to emerge, behaviors that make sure the other side loses as well, or giving in to end the conflict, become acceptable choices.
- Holy War — By "demonizing" the other side, competitive, destructive, and even unethical behavior becomes justified as righteous and necessary to deal with the enemy.

Each of these attitudes has natural behavioral fallout that tends to exacerbate the conflict and drive it toward destructive outcomes. Implementation of the mediation process coupled with the mediators' intervention skills attempt to alter these attitudes. To change win/lose thinking and to develop hope, the mediators encourage the generation of multiple options, so that new possibilities may creatively address both sides' interests. To put a truce in place, and humanize the enemy, mediators interpret each side to the other in an honest, multi-dimensional light, guiding each side to think about the conflict from the other's perspective. At every stage of the process, all sides are given opportunities to engage in dialogue with each other without being dominated. The mediators' stock-in-trade is the management of the escalation factors in conflict. Mediators respond to actual and potential conflict escalation by focusing on variables that often decrease the conflict level.

Figure 30 illustrates common behaviors, attitudes, and beliefs that can escalate and de-escalate conflict.

Figure 30. Managing Conflict

POTENTIAL ESCALATORS

· Multiply issues

· Polarize by stereotyping and generalization

· Threaten and use coercive tactics

· Agitate with others outside the mediation

· Perceive only available outcome as win-lose

· Believe that conflicts are contests

· Feel victimized by others

POTENTIAL DE-ESCALATORS

· Increase direct contact between the participants

· Improve communication

· Build momentum by working on easier issues first or fractionating bigger issues into manageable pieces

· Identify common interests

· Identify superordinate goals and values

· Change what isn't working

· Offer face-saving opportunities that permit modification of behavior and stated positions

· Work on the limited, selective perceptions of participants so their views of each other are more complete

MEDIATOR ATTITUDES

As mediators, we do not come to the conflicts of others free of our own values, attitudes, and emotions. Candid and thorough self-assessment is necessary if we are to be helpful to others. Among the most essential areas of insight is our own personal style or tendencies when we ourselves are in conflict.

It is not uncommon for people to have negative attitudes about conflict. If we were raised to be nice, to avoid the direct expression of anger, or to value harmony above truth, we may tend to avoid conflict. We may smooth over differences rather than surface them openly. If we were raised in an environment in which we needed to fight and compete to get our needs met, we may have a much tougher, "me-first" approach to conflict. All of us have been marked and influenced by our previous experiences with conflict. The possible sources are many: culture, parents and family, peers, church, mass media, and social organizations. Our history may cause us to adopt a one-dimensional stance toward all conflict situations, or we may act one way in conflicts at home with our family and a different way in conflicts at work.

Mediators help disputants choose and implement the approach to the conflict that is wisest in the situation at hand. You must be aware of your own tendencies in order to avoid coloring the situation with your own unconscious preferences. For example, if you tend to value harmony and cooperation, will you influence the parties to reach a premature or inadequate agreement lacking in durability? If you value strength and assertiveness, will you encourage the participants to stand firm, overlooking the real costs of impasse and the value of an agreement that satisfies some, but not all of their interests?

CAUSES OF CONFLICT

To implement the mediation process for a particular dispute, it is helpful to consider the sources of the conflict. There are five major types of conflict from which issues in a dispute emerge:

- Values — These are the deep beliefs that people use to judge good and bad or fair and unfair. They often emerge as "should" and "should not." When people try to impose their values on others, or deny the values of others, conflict results.
- Interests, needs, and preferences — When an activity or desire of one is perceived to be incompatible with another people will

engage in conflict to achieve their needs. *I can't get my needs met without limiting your ability to meet your needs.*

- Relationships — Problems in the relationship that produce conflict include powerful emotions such as anger and frustration, victimization, poor communication, and negative patterns of interaction.
- Control of resources — Time, space, money, power, and property that the parties will not share, or which they believe are inadequate to share satisfactorily, are resources that can generate conflict.
- Information and Meaning — When information is inadequate, or there are disagreements about the relevance or significance of information, conflict can result.

The goal of mediation is to achieve a voluntary agreement that is durable. If the mediators are unable to guide the participants in exploring the real roots of their conflict, it is unlikely that a lasting settlement will result. Thus a complete mediation agreement recognizes the roots of the conflict and contains solutions which will operate to alleviate these root causes. If a partial, interim, or provisional agreement is all that can emerge, the mediators' job is to make sure the parties consciously choose it, appreciating the real nature of the conflict, its long-term consequences, and the ways in which the incomplete agreement fails to alter the root causes of the conflict.

APPROACHES TO CONFLICT

There are five major approaches to dealing with conflict. In any given conflict there may be elements of more than one approach used by each participant.

- Competition — my way — win/lose.
    It's either me or him.
    I'm right, you're wrong.
  A clear use of power and force to achieve goals.
- Collaboration — our way — win/win.
    We can work this out.
    Let's reason together.
  An open, problem-solving approach to meet everyone's interests at the highest possible level.
- Compromise — halfway — half/win.
    Win a little and lose a little.
    Split the difference.
  A pragmatic approach of trading concessions to make a deal.

- Avoidance — no way — no/win.
  Forget it.
  It's not worth fighting over.
  A denial of the existence of conflict or a total unwillingness to deal with the issues.
- Accommodation — your way — lose/win.
  Appeasement.
  Anything to get this over with.
  Giving the other side what they ask or demand.

Figure 31 displays the five basic approaches to conflict along two axes: first, maximizing benefit to one's self, and second, maximizing benefit to the other person.

Figure 31. Conflict Options

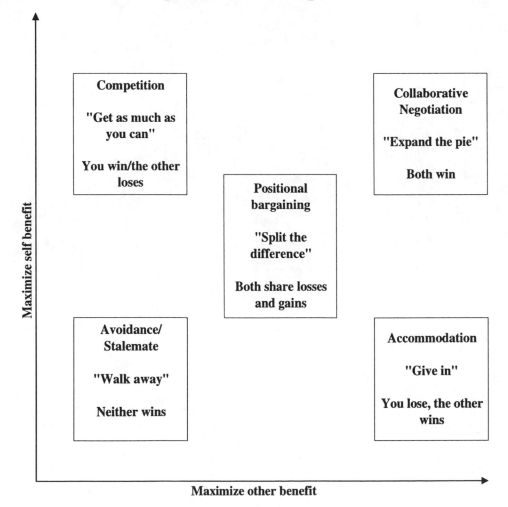

The Art of Mediation

Although the values that underlie the mediation process encourage cooperation and collaboration, any one of the five approaches to the issues in conflict in a mediation may be the wisest and most appropriate for one or both of the participants at some time. As mediators we strive to make sure the collaborative possibilities have been explored. If so, the parties' choice to take another approach, after weighing the costs and benefits, should not be resisted.

V.   MEDIATING ACROSS CULTURES

One of the most serious issues facing the development of mediation is how differences in culture, ethnicity, and gender impact the process. Several scholars have suggested that traditionally disadvantaged groups such as the poor, people of color, women, and gays, will fare worse in mediation. They posit that because mediation is a private, non-reviewable process, bias and prejudice will be more likely to emerge and produce unfair results. The mediation community has tended to dismiss these concerns, saying that competent, well-trained mediators can mediate any dispute between any people. There are several empirical studies, however, that suggest that this may not be true.

The first involves a carefully constructed experiment in which black, white, male, and female investigators were sent to purchase cars. They were of similar ages and educational backgrounds, they were dressed alike, they had undergone intensive training so that they would respond identically to car salespersons' techniques, and they even drove up to the dealerships in identical cars. The results stunningly demonstrated the existence of racial and gender bias. White men bought cars the cheapest, black men paid about $400 more than white men, white women paid almost $800 more than white men, and black women paid over $1,200 more than white men. This carefully controlled study demonstrates that racial and gender prejudice does exist in America, and that women and African Americans do come out worse, at least when buying cars.

A second study, performed by the University of New Mexico Schools of Law and Sociology, demonstrated a similar phenomenon in small claims court mediations in Albuquerque, New Mexico. Hundreds of civil court cases were randomly assigned to adjudication or mediation and then were tracked both objectively and subjectively through court records and interviews. The study found that disputants of color, who in this sample were more than 85 percent Hispanic, had less favorable monetary outcomes in court-adjudicated cases than did white disputants. More significantly, disputants of color fared even worse in mediation than they did in adjudication, and also worse than did white disputants in mediation. Indeed, a claimant of color in mediation was likely to receive fifteen percent less than a white claimant, while a respondent of color was likely to pay eighteen percent more than a white respondent. This disparity in mediated outcomes disappeared, however, when the case was mediated by two co-mediators of color. This strongly suggests that the ethnicity of the mediators, if not their actions, has a powerful impact on the outcome of the mediations.

Women, as a whole, fared as well or better than men in both adjudication and mediation in the small claims court study. This does not mean that we can disregard concerns about women in mediation. It simply means that in the context of civil disputes where the amount in controversy is less than $5,000, gender does not appear to influence outcome. It may well be that in different types of disputes, such as custody, divorce, criminal, or larger civil cases, women do come out worse in mediation than do men.

The UNM study data also demonstrate that gender of mediators impacts on outcome. Two female co-mediators were most likely to have their cases achieve agreements, two male mediators were least likely to have agreements in their cases, and mixed gender co-mediation pairs fell roughly in the middle.

What these two studies suggest is that differences in gender and ethnicity of both mediators and disputants are quite likely to influence the results of mediations. While we don't know what causes this influence, that is, whether mediator actions and attitudes, disputant actions and attitudes, or both, are causing these results, we do know that there is a problem which cannot be dismissed by saying that *a good mediator can mediate anything*. In the short run, it seems that we must pay attention in three significant areas. The first is to increase the training mediators receive in intercultural work in order to increase mediator sensitivity and awareness. The second is to increase the training mediators receive in power balancing, so that they have more tools to use in mediating cases with weaker and stronger disputants. The third is to change intake procedures before mediations begin in order to focus more clearly on these issues of culture, gender, ethnicity and fairness. The result might be to screen more cases out of mediation, or to choose special mediators, or particular mediation locations, or even to put disputants through a special pre-mediation orientation training. Meanwhile, a great deal more empirical work must be undertaken to explore the causes of disparate outcomes in mediation and to learn what interventions might ameliorate or erase this phenomenon. Figure 32 suggests some important dimensions of competence for skilled mediators when working with people whose cultural background is different from theirs.

Figure 32. Suggestions for Cultural Competence

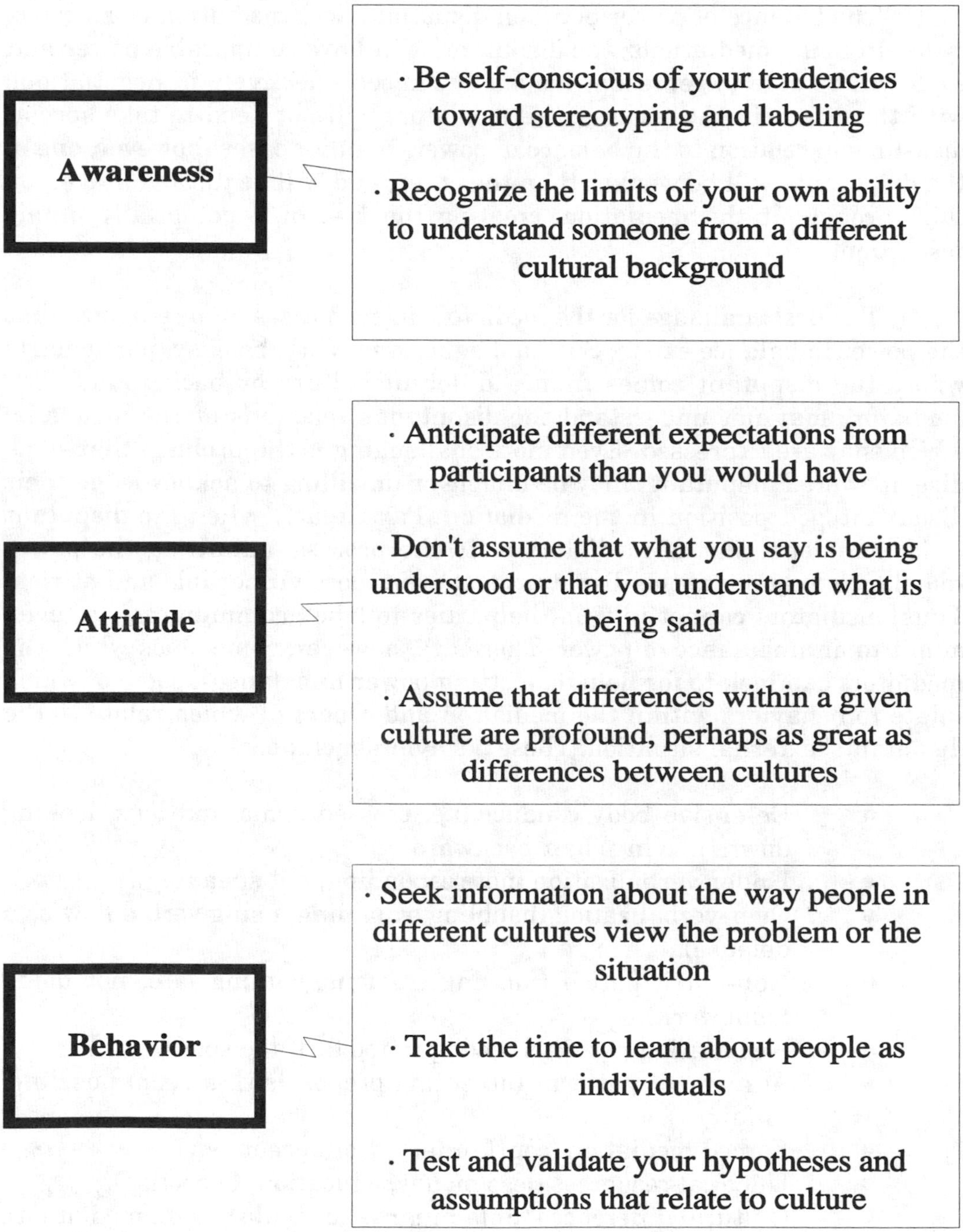

Awareness

- Be self-conscious of your tendencies toward stereotyping and labeling

- Recognize the limits of your own ability to understand someone from a different cultural background

Attitude

- Anticipate different expectations from participants than you would have

- Don't assume that what you say is being understood or that you understand what is being said

- Assume that differences within a given culture are profound, perhaps as great as differences between cultures

Behavior

- Seek information about the way people in different cultures view the problem or the situation

- Take the time to learn about people as individuals

- Test and validate your hypotheses and assumptions that relate to culture

VI. POWER BALANCING

The balance of power between disputants in a mediation is a serious issue. In many mediations, the disputants will have comparable power and each will be able to represent herself or himself effectively in negotiations with the other. In these cases, the mediators will not need to take special measures in relation to the balance of power. In other cases, however, one of the disputants will be weaker than the other, and will be disadvantaged by this throughout the mediation, creating the risk of a potentially unfair resolution.

The first challenge for the mediators in such cases is to recognize that the power imbalance exists. Such a diagnosis may not be easy, particularly where the disputant comes from a different culture or background. The mediators may not understand the disputant's reactions or the means by which they are expressed. Even more challenging is the problem that some disempowered disputants may be unable or unwilling to acknowledge their disadvantaged position in the mediation. Particularly when the disputant lacks confidence in the mediators or in the process, admitting the power imbalance may make the disputant feel even more vulnerable and at risk. Thus, mediators cannot rely on the parties to label, communicate, or even admit to an imbalance of power. There are, however, some clues which the mediators can look to for help in spotting power imbalances, some of which relate to behaviors within the mediation and others of which relate to the disputants' external situation. These behaviors include:

- Defensive body conduct (i.e. crossed arms and legs, looking down, moving chair backwards).
- Under-verbalization (not responding, not speaking).
- Over-verbalization (babbling, rambling, using verbal flow as a defense).
- Non-participation (missing sessions, coming late, not doing homework).
- Negotiation patterns (giving in too fast, too soon).
- Agreement patterns (accepting proposals that seem puzzling, unfair).
- Forced mediation (court order, prior agreement).
- Unequal resources (less money, education, expertise).
- Cultural differences (unfamiliar with legal system, mediation).
- Prior history (physical abuse, emotional abuse).

POWER SOURCES

Since power imbalance is a serious issue, it is important to remember that power relationships in a dispute are fluid, multi-faceted, and subject to change during the mediation process. Mediators must be aware of the different forms of power that may be at play in a given situation. A common error is to limit the definition of power to the ability to hurt or do damage. A more inclusive definition would add the ability to influence the decisions of others. The following ten items are commonly encountered types of power.

1.   Authority
       The power of authority comes from a formal structural position that delivers power and influence to the holder of the position. Examples of these positions include judges, school superintendents, managers, and parents. This authority may include the power to decide and/or the control of the procedures by which decisions are made.

2.   Sanction
       The power of sanction stems from the perceived or actual ability to inflict harm or to interfere with another's ability to achieve goals.

3.   Information
       The power of information comes from expertise, i.e., the possession of knowledge or information about a particular subject or control over access to information.

4.   Nuisance
       The power of nuisance or interference is often available, even to those who seem to be without power. It is based on the ability to slow down, discomfort, or inconvenience others to a greater or lesser degree.

5.   Association
       The power of association is an indirect form of power that derives from proximity to, alliance with, or relationship with others possessing power.

6.   Characteristics
       The power of personal or moral characteristics includes determination, communication ability, confidence, and the ability to invoke moral principles and appeal to values held by others.

7.   Resources
       The power of resource control stems from the ability to deliver or deny desirable resources such as money, land, labor, and materials to others.

8.   Status Quo
       The power of the status quo rests with the party who benefits from or is satisfied with the existing arrangement, because it usually requires more effort to change a situation than to continue it.

9.   Reward
       The power of reward comes from providing incentives and things people desire such as money, recognition, promotion, or social approval.

10.   Procedure
       The power of procedure comes from managing or controlling the processes that must be used to accomplish tasks.

Using Worksheet 1 in Appendix II, mediators can reflect on the sources of power possessed by the parties.

BALANCING POWER

When the mediators suspect a possible power imbalance, there are a number of interventions which might be appropriate.

- Call a caucus to discuss the problem.
- Only mediate in separate sessions so the disadvantaged party is buffered from the higher power party.
- Use speaker phones or other electronic communication devices to keep the parties separate but speaking with each other.
- Increase the structure in mediation sessions, to ensure that the disadvantaged party has an equal opportunity to think and speak.
- Increase mediator power and control, putting pressure on the higher power party.

- Restructure the mediation environment with more formal physical protection such as tables and other barriers.
- Confront the higher power party and discuss whether the exercise of their power to force an agreement is fair and/or in their overall interest.
- Take a long break to give the disadvantaged party time to assess their predicament and develop options.
- Slow the pace of mediation because speed tends to favor dominant parties.
- Use co-mediation so that one mediator can explicitly ally with the disadvantaged party.
- Bring in an advocate for the disadvantaged party.
- Bring in a friend, family member, priest or community representative for the disadvantaged party.
- Bring in an expert to assist the disadvantaged party.
- Bring in attorneys so the disadvantaged party has representation.
- Assign homework to increase the disadvantaged party's information level.
- Provide pre-mediation education and training to increase the disadvantaged party's skill level.
- Change the language in which the mediation is conducted and mediate in the disadvantaged party's primary language.
- Change the location of the mediation to a place which is familiar and comfortable to the disadvantaged party.
- Study the culture of the disadvantaged party to learn if there are other approaches to resolving the dispute which might be more appropriate.
- Brainstorm with the disadvantaged party about what is needed to balance power.
- Recommend individual therapy.
- Recommend group therapy.
- Recommend a support group.

The goal of these interventions is to explore changing time, space, language, information, and interpersonal dynamics to reduce the imbalance of power in a mediation.

Figure 33 describes the sources of mediator power and some major options to influence the ways that power is affecting the mediation process.

Figure 33. Dealing with Power in Mediation

A's real and perceived power relative to B + the willingness to use the forms of power available = **APPLIED POWER**	**Possible Forms** · Formal authority · Reward · Sanction · Resource · Status Quo · Procedure · Nuisance · Information · Associational · Characteristic	B's real and perceived power relative to A + the willingness to use the forms of power available = **APPLIED POWER**

Balance of Power

Mediation Process & Mediator Behavior

Sources of Mediator Power	**Major Mediator Power Interventions**
· Control of the physical setting · Knowledge of the process · Control of the agenda (Stages, Transitions, Timing , Information) · Control of the "frame" or context · Directing communication (control of who speaks and for how long) · Ability to use uncertainty (reality-testing, best-case/worst-case) · Impartiality/Ethical stance	· Caucus and discuss power issues · Change format to provide additional time and space · Change the pace · Introduce/impose ground rules · Arrange for advocacy/support for the disadvantaged party · Arrange for expertise/information for the disadvantaged party · Help the disadvantaged party identify sources of power that can be tapped · Educate the disadvantaged party about negotiation · Confront the high power party (Is the exercise of their power...(a) fair, (b) in their interest?)

VII. THE CAUCUS

A caucus is a separate meeting between the mediators and one of the parties. It is a different setting with different opportunities for the mediators to use their interactive analytical, probing, and persuasive skills. Some mediators use the caucus in every case, while others never use it. We recommend that you experiment with using caucuses in your mediation simulations so that you can learn how this structural variation of the mediation process might work for you.

Things mediators can do in a caucus include the following:

- Ask for information which has not been revealed in joint session, particularly in sensitive areas.
- Restate what has been heard in open session to verify or to bring out what was really meant instead of what was said.
- Ask for specific behavior from the party which might accomplish what that party wants. It is important not only to ask a party what the other party could do, but also whether there is anything that this caucusing party thinks she or he can do to move toward agreement. Also it may be useful to ask what one party might be willing to do in return for something the other party has said he or she is willing to do.
- Reality-test with the party to determine how their proposals and their behaviors are serving or not serving their stated objectives and interests.
- Give honest feedback and communicate in a manner that might not be possible in a joint session, since totally open and honest communication between parties does not always produce a desirable result, and can lead to an escalation of hostility and even to impasse.
- Communicate information which is inappropriate for a joint session because of its impact on the balance of power between the parties.

The caucus can provide some of the following benefits:

- Avoid damaging the relationship between the parties.
- Allow ventilation in a safe and private manner.
- Prevent one party from manipulating the other emotionally.
- Allow the mediators to confront a party without causing a loss of face.
- Avoid deadlock in negotiations.

- Permit more effective power balancing.
- Surface emotions.
- Hear secrets.
- Allow a cooling-off time.
- Allow the mediators to share their perceptions with the party to moderate or modify that party's point of view.
- Allow for reality testing of the accuracy of a party's perception in order to create some doubt.
- Assist a party in formulating an acceptable or positive offer.
- Encourage parties to stop threats and to commit to de-escalating activities.
- Educate an unskilled party about more effective negotiation behaviors.
- Generate new proposals.
- Act as a reality tester for a determined party to help assess the nature of their proposal, the likelihood of its acceptance, and the costs and benefits of continued firmness.

There may be occasions when a caucus is the primary method of working with the parties. In other situations, a caucus may be called early in the process and then the parties will meet together in joint session for the rest of the mediation. Sometimes, the final bargaining stage may require one or more caucuses to define and close the bargaining range in order to reach an agreement.

The mechanics of caucusing include the following practical areas of concern:

- Mediators need to agree that caucus is appropriate at this point in the mediation.
- Mediators need to elicit parties' agreement to participate in caucus.
- Parties and mediators need to decide who will go first (mediators should avoid splitting up and meeting one-on-one with parties simultaneously, because the team approach of co-mediation is lost).
- Mediators need to balance time between the parties so that they do not appear to favor one side.
- Long caucus sessions may work best in separately scheduled meetings, so that the other party is not forced to wait too long.
- Even when caucusing on a specific topic, it is usually best to start in a general format, such as *How are you doing?* or *What do you think?*

- Before the caucus begins, the mediators must be clear with the parties about how information revealed in the caucus will be handled. There are four approaches.

    (1.) <u>Nothing</u> said to the mediators will be shared with the other party.

    (2.) <u>Nothing</u> said to the mediators will be shared <u>unless</u> the party gives permission.

    (3.) <u>Anything</u> said to the mediators may be shared with the other party <u>unless</u> the mediators are specifically directed to keep the information private.

    (4.) <u>Everything</u> said in the caucus may be shared with the other party.

If the second or third approach is followed, it is essential that the caucus end with an agreement as to what information may be shared and what information is private.

Problem areas for caucusing can include:

- Mediators are ordinarily able to be more direct and honest in a caucus, but to the extent that mediators confront someone, they can also alienate that person.
- Ground rules about confidentiality in caucusing and how information will be shared with the other party must be clearly established to avoid perceived betrayals.
- A caucus may create a perception of an alliance between the mediators and a caucusing party.
- A party may attempt to manipulate mediators emotionally in a caucus setting.

Use Figure 34 as a guide to using a caucus.

Figure 34. Caucus

Uses
• Check for participant's understanding without causing embarrassment in front of another.
• Explore bottom lines.
• Confront a participant about difficult behavior.
• Encourage the expression of emotion by one participant without risk of offending another.
• Discuss sensitive topics and hear information that a participant might not share in joint session.
• Help a participant develop an offer or evaluate the consequences of no agreement.

Checklist
• Determine that a caucus is appropriate.
• Decide whether you will ask parties or announce that a caucus will take place.
• Determine whom you will meet with first or let the parties choose.
• Balance time between the parties (consider scheduling separate long caucuses to avoid substantial waiting periods).
• Clarify how caucus information may/may not be shared.
• Usually start with an open-ended question to find out what is going on from the party's point of view.
• End by confirming understandings, actions that will be taken, and any private information the mediators should not share.

VIII. ETHICAL ISSUES

Currently there are no specific governing standards for the practice of mediation, because there are no recognized organizational entities with enforcement powers over mediators. There are, however, several model or proposed mediator codes of ethics which have been promulgated by such groups as the Society for Professionals in Dispute Resolution, the Academy of Family Mediators, and the American Bar Association, which can be looked to for guidance. These are reproduced in the Ethics Section of these materials, Appendix I. Additionally, mediators who come from other professions, such as law, accounting, medicine, or mental health, continue to be subject to the ethical codes of those professions. Of course, all mediators must also follow any applicable laws in the jurisdictions where they practice.

CONFIDENTIALITY

Typically, the most complex ethical problems faced by mediators occur in the area of confidentiality. The first thing the mediators must do in relation to issues of confidentiality is to determine whether there are any laws in the jurisdiction where they practice which create an evidentiary privilege between mediators and their clients. If there is such legislation or court rule, it will determine under what circumstances communications in mediation may be treated as confidential. If no legislation, court rule, or case law recognizing a mediation privilege exists, then it is not correct for mediators to tell their clients that communications in mediation will be treated as confidential, although they are likely to be inadmissible under the rule of evidence which protects settlement discussions. A reference to this evidentiary rule can be included in the mediation agreement to clarify the parties' intent to be protected by its terms.

There are three major areas where mediators may face a court order which requires them to reveal information from a mediation. The clearest case where confidentiality will be breached because courts will require the mediator to reveal information is one in which there is a reporting duty imposed by law, e.g., the duty to report suspected child abuse or neglect. Unless there is a blanket mediation privilege in the jurisdiction, the mediator must follow the legal requirements regarding the information that must be revealed. A second area where the court may require the mediator to testify is when there is a subpoena in an unrelated case, e.g. a criminal prosecution in which the state seeks to compel the mediator to give evidence or turn over documents from a mediation.

The area of largest realistic concern, however, is the one where the mediator is most likely to be allowed to protect information. This occurs when the mediator is subpoenaed in the case in which the mediator actually worked. Most mediators handle protection of this category of communications by contractually binding the parties to agree not to call them as witnesses in the

Agreement to Mediate. Often mediators will ask the parties to agree to be responsible for the time and costs of resisting a subpoena as well. This contractual agreement does not require that a mediation privilege be recognized in the jurisdiction. While there are only a handful of reported cases dealing with this situation, mediators around the country describe their local courts as being willing to enforce contractual barriers to involving the mediators in subsequent litigation in the same case.

Because of the complexity of the area of confidential communications, some mediators eschew the use of this word altogether in the contracting stage of mediation, agreeing instead to keep client communications "private" and not to reveal them unless legally required.

Issues of confidentiality, or privacy, also arise in the mediation itself. One issue occurs when communications are received in individual caucus sessions during a mediation. There are no firm rules about how information from a caucus session should be handled. The mediator may agree to reveal nothing without the client's permission, or may agree that everything except those communications which the client specifically asks be held private may be revealed, or may agree that everything said in the caucus may be revealed. It is important that the mediator discuss the issue of information revealed in caucus with the clients before the caucus begins. This ensures that there is a shared understanding regarding what use may be made of the information they reveal.

The second confidentiality issue within the mediation involves communications between the mediators and attorneys, mental health professionals, experts, and other persons outside the mediation. It is important in these communications that the mediators discuss with the parties what, if any, issues they authorize the mediators to discuss outside the mediation. The parties will also have to waive confidentiality separately with the attorneys or therapists with whom the mediator plans to confer. Often medical and mental health professions will require a signed release from the client. Because such communications may be critical to the success of the mediation, exploring client consent to engage in them can be very important.

LAWYER-LAY CO-MEDIATION

A second constellation of ethical issues in mediation stems from limitations imposed by the legal profession. These include prohibitions against fee-splitting, which may be unwittingly violated by attorneys who co-mediate with non-lawyers. The safest solution is to have the clients pay each mediator separately, or pay a third-party organization, i.e. the mediation office, which can then pay each mediator separately as an independent contractor. Similar pitfalls may exist in relation to how lawyers and non-lawyers are permitted to list their names in cards and materials describing their mediation association. Some of the regulations may seem petty and nonsensical. For instance, in some jurisdictions an attorney may list his or her name as part of a nonlegal association, but may not use the initials "J.D." (Juris Doctor) or the abbreviation "Esq." after the name. Attorneys must check the opinions of their state bar disciplinary committee before structuring the office documents and payment system in their mediation practice to avoid the risk of censure.

PRACTICING LAW

Underlying issues such as fee division and professional listing is the larger question of whether practicing mediation constitutes the practice of law. There are a surprising number of ethical opinions around the country saying that it does. Most of these opinions are ten to fifteen years old, and may be subject to modification in today's climate of acceptance of mediation and ADR. Particularly in those jurisdictions where such opinions exist, however, non-lawyer mediators must be wary of being accused of engaging in the unauthorized practice of law, which often may be treated as a criminal offense.

Non-lawyers will be viewed as practicing law if they give legal advice rather than legal information to the clients. Unfortunately, the distinction between these two activities is fuzzy at best. It is permissible for a non-lawyer to describe what the law is; it is more problematic to discuss its interpretation or application in a particular case. It is not permissible for a non-lawyer to advise clients about what to do in relation to the law. One of the great advantages of lawyer/non-lawyer co-mediation is that it removes the non-lawyer from these confusing strictures because the lawyer can lead discussion of the legal issues in the mediation. The lawyer-mediator can also alleviate the appearance of practicing law problems which may arise when non-lawyer mediators draft mediation agreements for the parties.

REPRESENTATION VERSUS MEDIATION

Even the lawyer in mediation would not choose to be seen as practicing law, however, because to do so would create problems of conflicts of interest. A recent amendment to the American Bar Association Model Rules of Professional Conduct, ethical rule ER 5.7, focuses on mediation and other law-related services. It requires that the lawyer-mediator ensure that the mediation services are distinct from the provision of legal services and that the person receiving the mediation services know that she or he is not receiving legal services and that the protections of the client-lawyer relationship do not exist. If this standard is not met, all of the ethical duties owed to clients by lawyers under the Model Rules may apply.

In traditional adversary representation, the lawyer represents only one person or entity. In limited circumstances, following carefully prescribed rules, the lawyer may represent all the clients in a case. In mediation, however, the lawyer-mediator represents no one. This concept is central to mediation, because it is the source of the mediator's neutrality. The lawyer-mediator would be charged with protecting the interests of the disputants if representing one or all of the disputants. From this would flow a duty to be responsible for the outcome of the mediation, and the lawyer-mediator rather than the disputants would become responsible for both the existence and the content of an agreement.

It is also the difference in roles and responsibilities between mediators and other professionals which gives rise to the intake problem of how a case comes into an office and how communications are handled. The risk stems from the fact that at least a limited lawyer-client relationship may be created by even preliminary telephonic interactions. This would mean that any information learned by the lawyer-mediator would be privileged and protected by the attorney-client relationship. This privileged information, received in a different role, would make it at least theoretically impossible for the lawyer to serve as a neutral third-party mediator in the case. While conflicts of interest may be waived following full disclosure and explanation, it is certainly better practice to avoid this problem altogether by making a clear initial determination regarding whether the client is there to seek adversary legal representation or mediation services. Prohibitions on role switching and potential conflicts of interest also mandate a conflicts check before a case is accepted for mediation. This requires that the mediator ascertain that no one in the office has had a prior personal or professional association with any of the parties in the current dispute.

COMPETENCE

Perhaps the most central area of ethical concern for mediators involves the duty to perform mediation services competently. The many facets to this duty include: possessing the requisite skills, training, and expertise to handle the dispute in question; having sufficient time to prepare and handle the case adequately; performing services like drafting promptly; following through on any other commitments made to the parties in mediation; and not becoming emotionally embroiled in the case, either with the subject matter or the parties themselves. One of the great advantages of co-mediation is that it offers a straightforward solution to many of these problems.

CONCLUSION

All of these areas of ethical concerns are relatively new, and have not yet developed clear and satisfying answers. Over the next decade, substantial change and development in regard to ethical standards for mediators are likely. Practitioners in the field need to stay closely involved in these issues, both in order to keep informed about them and, more important, to help shape the overall development of the profession of mediation.

SECTION FOUR: PRACTICAL ISSUES

THE PROFESSION AND PRACTICE OF MEDIATION

Over the last ten years we have offered mediation trainings to hundreds of lawyers, law students, judges, mental health professionals, accountants, managers, and lay people. We usually end our trainings by asking participants what questions they have about the profession and practice of mediation. The intent of this chapter is to provide brief guidance in response to frequently asked questions. Our answers are not exhaustive and do not discuss all of the questions in depth. They are intended to give a starting point and direction to the beginning mediator.

I. MEDIATION AS A PROFESSION

1. *What options exist for getting mediation experience?*

- Many community mediation centers utilize volunteers to deliver services. Some of these organizations have structured apprenticeship programs. Contact your local center for details.
- Settlement week programs conducted by the courts use lawyers, judges, accountants, psychologists, and other professionals in quasi-mediator roles as settlement facilitators. Contact your court and offer your services.
- Enter into an arrangement to work with an experienced mediator using one of the following options:
  — Develop your own cases and use the experienced mediator as a resource to guide you.
  — Ask the experienced mediator to co-mediate with you.
  — Find an experienced mediator who is willing to let you act as co-mediator in his or her cases or to let you observe actual mediations.
- There are numerous informal opportunities to practice your skills as a mediator, limited only by your own imagination and degree of initiative. The world is filled with conflict and many of the parties cannot afford to hire independent professionals. You can be invaluable as a problem-solving resource.
  — Act in the role of mediator, peacemaker, or problem-solver on a non-profit board or in a church congregation.
  — Offer to lead a brainstorming session for a community group, parent-teacher group, neighborhood association, or church executive board.
  — Mediate disputes between children.
  — Help resolve conflicts on the job where you work.

— If you are a manager, mediate between employees whom you supervise.
— Within your organization, work with disputing departments, divisions, teams, or committees, to bring them together.
— Play a mediator role to help your law or business partners work out a thorny problem.
— In a complex case with multiple attorneys, act in a mediator role to bring all sides into a more constructive negotiation process to search for an agreement that meets everyone's interests, including those of your client.
— When you represent a client comprised of multiple decision-makers (a business partnership, a closely held corporation with several major shareholders, an estate with several heirs, a non-profit corporation with several members on the board) who are in conflict, act as a mediator to help them work toward agreement.
— Think like a mediator in the next dispute in which you are personally involved. Ask questions to uncover interests, reframe hostile, difficult responses, and set aside your own point of view temporarily to listen fully and actively to the other side.

2. *What else can I do to develop my skills as a mediator?*

There is no hard and fast answer to this question. What we suggest as approaches should be tailored to your situation and background. Although experience is an essential element of professional competence, there are other ways to increase your knowledge.

• Consider joining one or more dispute resolution organizations and reading their newsletter and publications. There are many good articles about mediation practice and theory which you can locate at a university library. All of the national mediation organizations have annual conferences that you might attend (see list in question 4). They offer presentations on topics of interest, developments in the field, and insights based on current research. Mediation and dispute resolution are discussed on several sites on the internet as well.

• Reread all of your notes and the mediation manual to refresh the insights that came out of the training.

- Commit to taking a follow-up mediation training in the next twelve months. Another training can provide different perspectives and it will give you more role-playing practice. Many people, anxious to develop a new career path, underestimate the skills and knowledge that quality mediation demands. No 40-hour training can produce instant mediator competence.

- Plan to receive relevant cross-training. If you are a mental health professional and want to mediate divorce cases, attend a family law seminar. If you are an attorney and want to mediate child custody cases, attend a seminar on child development. If you want to mediate in a subject matter area that is new to you, e.g. construction disputes, find out more about the issues in the area. Seek out a subject matter expert. Attend a seminar on current issues in construction law.

- Look at Appendix IV, the Selected Bibliography, pick items that interest you and begin to read in the field. If you are not sure where to start, read *Getting to Yes* by Fisher and Ury and *Getting Past No* by Ury. Mediation is a process of assisted negotiation. The heart of the mediators' job is to encourage constructive negotiation. Anything you can do to deepen your understanding of negotiation will enhance your ability as a mediator.

- Increase your understanding and self-awareness with therapy, meditation, peer counseling, and journal-keeping.

3. *Can I make a living as a mediator? How?*

There are a small but growing number of salaried jobs in the ADR field. Some governmental and private organizations have ADR positions. For example, the legal staff of a city, state, or federal agency may employ an ADR specialist who coordinates cases and advises others on the use of ADR. Large corporations or other business entities may also employ dispute resolution specialists. A few major law firms have designated attorneys who act as ADR specialists. Community mediation centers have salaried executive staff and mediators. A number of organizations are developing internal mediation programs in which employees, as a part of their job, mediate disputes. Most people working in the field do not make their living exclusively as mediators. The most common pattern of private mediation practice is comprised of lawyers or mental health professionals who do some mediation and practice their profession as well. Many of the people who are full time in the mediation and ADR fields combine the practice of mediation and other ADR roles with teaching and training others.

If you are interested in starting a private practice as a mediator, you should be prepared (a) to take some time to build a practice and (b) to spend significant time marketing yourself and your skills. We do see the field growing in the foreseeable future. Mediation is mentioned in newspaper and magazine articles with increasing frequency, and ADR has been singled out as a growth field in the service industries.

Don't think of mediation skills as only being an asset for those who are working professionally as mediators. If you become more skilled as a conflict resolver and a problem solver, you will also have enhanced your effectiveness, skill level, marketability, and value in a variety of other vocational roles including management, administration, counseling, and law practice. People who can communicate skillfully, promote collaboration, and help others solve problems are essential parts of most organizations.

4.   *What mediation networks/organizations exist?*

- Many state bar organizations have committees or sections that focus on ADR. The American Bar Association has a Dispute Resolution section which publishes a newsletter.
- The Society for Professionals in Dispute Resolution (SPIDR) is a national organization. Its base is broad, including mediators and arbitrators in every conceivable subject matter area: family, commercial, environmental, public policy, international, and organizational.
- The Academy of Family Mediators (AFM) focuses on disputes involving family members, primarily divorce and child custody issues. *Mediation Quarterly* is a publication which comes with membership in AFM and it has a strong practice orientation.
- The Association of Family and Conciliation Courts (AFCC) focuses on disputes of families.
- Conflict Net is an on-line computer network for people interested in conflict resolution and mediation. There are also dispute resolution networks on E-Mail.

5. **What standards and licensing requirements are there for mediators?**

Almost none at the present. While a few states have developed limited licensing standards for mediators, most have none in place. The standards that do exist tend to focus on court-annexed mediation services and who is eligible to provide them. There is, however, a trend toward developing professional standards. AFM has established different tiers of membership. To qualify as a "Practitioner" member, you must submit agreements from mediations you have been responsible for and meet extensive training requirements. AFM and SPIDR have ethical guidelines. The American Bar Association has draft ethical guidelines for attorneys acting as family mediators. The American Arbitration Association, the American Bar Association, and the Society of Professionals in Dispute Resolution have collaborated to produce model standards of conduct for mediators. We do foresee increasing use of standards in the profession of mediation. It is likely that some sophisticated consumers may look to these standards in selecting mediators.

6. **How can I decide whether to co-mediate?**

Every mediator must decide whether and when to co-mediate. The following checklist can serve as a guide when you consider this question.

POSITIVES:

- Gives two heads which are better than one (greater insight and skills present in team).
- Permits cultural diversity (by including different cultures on the team, mediators can model cooperative problem solving, respect for differences).
- Facilitates power balancing (by creating a team which neutralizes ethnic/gender/other identity issues by mirroring disputants).
- Allows you to bring in a partner with special expertise or experience (increases efficiency of mediation team).
- Protects against off days (one mediator may be on and cued into the disputants' needs and concerns, even if the other is not).

- Builds learning curve (working together with someone provides a source of immediate feedback and a way to process your experiential learning in mediation).
- Bolsters neutrality (with two mediators it is more difficult for a party to coalesce with and compromise the neutral force in the mediation).
- Allows the weight to be shared (mediation is hard work and in co-mediation, one co-mediator can take the lead, while the other co-mediator watches for opportunities).
- Permits allying (with two mediators, one can link with each disputant when necessary).
- Divides work (if flip chart recording is used, one co-mediator can focus on recording information while the other remains focused on the parties).

NEGATIVES:

- Limits the ability to do your own thing (requires that both mediators be team players).
- Can cause co-mediator confusion (co-mediators need signals and procedures for times when they disagree about the process or direction of the mediation).
- Requires co-mediator relationship work (co-mediators need knowledge of each other's strengths and weaknesses in order to support each other, work together effectively, and learn new skills together).
- Impacts mediator economics and potential cost to the parties (two or more people to pay instead of one).

II. MEDIATION ETHICS

7. *What should I do if one of the parties lies in mediation?*

The availability of sufficient, accurate information is a foundational element of a durable agreement. If one of the parties is intentionally providing false information, this strikes at the heart of the integrity of the mediation process. There are several approaches mediators can take:

- Educate the person about the importance of full disclosure to support a fair, durable agreement;
- Confront the lie in a private caucus, ask for an explanation, and, if appropriate, indicate that you will terminate the mediation unless fair disclosure is made;
- Use a procedural device to shape the negative behavior such as an affidavit requiring the parties to swear that certain information is correct; or
- Ignore the issue or let it be the subject of negotiation and trade-off if both sides can assess its relative accuracy, importance, and value.

8. *If I hold a professional license, for example, as a psychologist, social worker, accountant, or attorney, and also act as a mediator, are there any issues with which I should be concerned?*

Licensed professionals carry the ethical obligations of their profession into the mediation setting, so they must always be aware of both their professional and their mediator requirements. The key word is clarity. Be clear with your mediation clients about how your licensed role relates to the mediation process.

If you are a psychologist or mental health professional, be aware of the questions regarding "switching hats." These questions include:

- When can a therapist mediate with one or more former clients?
- Can a therapist who mediated a case later act as a therapist for one or both parties or their children?

The safest position is that you should not switch hats. If a mediator decides to do so, there are two bases to touch. First, insure a clear understanding between you and your clients leading to informed consent on their part. Second, make an independent assessment that the previous relationship will not impair your ability to function professionally and ethically in the subsequent role.

If you are an attorney, it is relatively easy to explain the difference between the mediation and advocacy/advice-giving roles, but what to do with your legal experience is a more difficult issue. It is important to decide if you will provide anything more than basic legal information such as, *This is a community property state. That means that almost everything you receive or earn after the date of the marriage belongs to the two of you equally. The most common exceptions are* . . . Beyond giving basic legal information, you must answer a series of questions for yourself:

- Will you talk about what the local judge is known to do in cases like theirs?
- Will you talk about how the state appellate court has interpreted the legal standard that applies to the situation in the mediation?
- Will you make predictions about how a court would rule on their disputed issues?
- Will you advise them on the legal and procedural posture of their case?

Each step you take that moves from legal information to legal advice puts your appearance of neutrality at risk, and may be construed as assuming the role of legal representative. Some lawyer-mediators are willing to share both legal information and advice with their clients using techniques like speaking in the voice of each party's lawyer to neutralize the situation. The lawyer-mediator may even move his or her chair next to each participant while saying *If I were your lawyer, I would argue that you should get . . . because . . . . But if I were your lawyer, I would argue that such a result is neither legal nor equitable because* . . . . Other lawyer-mediators are unwilling to assume the burden of staying abreast of law and practice, or are unwilling to open themselves to potential legal malpractice, or feel that there is no way to neutralize the impact of legal evaluation and advice on the outcome of the process.

9. *What should I look for to determine if a case is appropriate for mediation?*

For the past decade, the dispute resolution community has been expanding the list of cases that can be mediated. There are a number of factors to consider. First, the parties must have the capacity to mediate. They must be able to make independent decisions and take personal responsibility for those decisions. Individuals with impairing mental illness or who are active substance abusers are not usually candidates for mediation.

Second, a severe power imbalance could make a case inappropriate for mediation. For example, if there is consistent pattern of physical and/or psychological abuse in a divorce case that has left one party in fear of displeasing the other, the victimized individual may be unable to negotiate effectively to protect their interests.

Third, if the case involves only distributional, win-lose issues such as the amount of money the victim of an auto accident will receive, mediation can be used, but it may not be the most effective ADR process. The distributional focus of the dispute may be outweighed by the presence of a future relationship, arguing for mediation. If not, another process such as settlement facilitation or early neutral evaluation could be a better choice.

Even if the case is appropriate for mediation, the timing may be wrong to begin the mediation. For example, a proposed partnership dissolution mediation may come to you with the information that one partner has just announced that he wants to start a competing business after a twenty-year partnership. The other partner is completely surprised and emotionally devastated. It is likely that the surprised partner will not be prepared to carefully consider all of the decisions to be faced without some time and assistance to come to terms emotionally with the end of the partnership. When the psychological pain of the conflict is new and raw, one or both parties may not be ready for the dialogue and negotiation dimensions of the mediation process.

Figure 35 captures these and other danger signs that demand the mediators' full attention until either the concerns are put to rest or the mediation process is ended.

Figure 35. Danger Signs

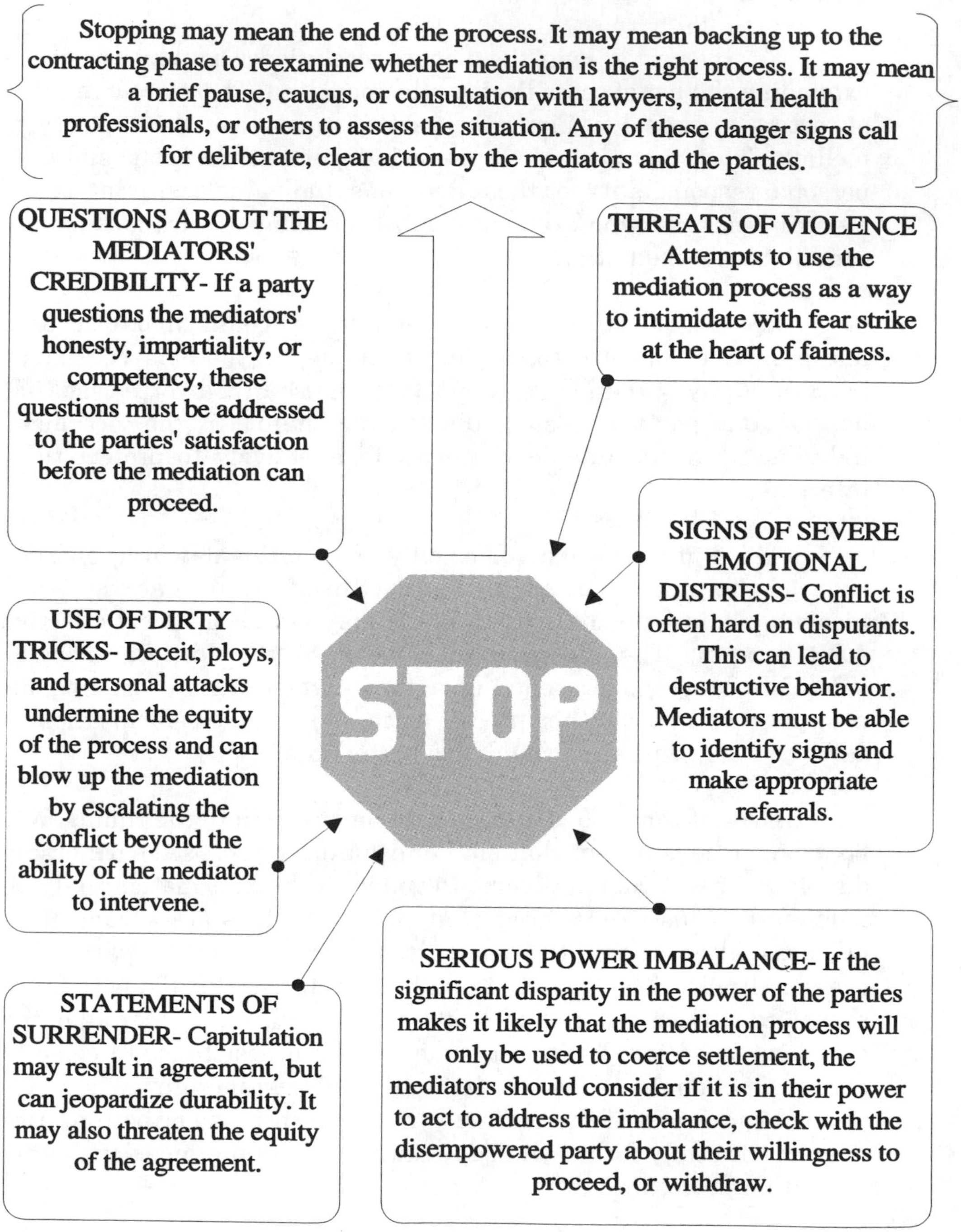

Stopping may mean the end of the process. It may mean backing up to the contracting phase to reexamine whether mediation is the right process. It may mean a brief pause, caucus, or consultation with lawyers, mental health professionals, or others to assess the situation. Any of these danger signs call for deliberate, clear action by the mediators and the parties.

QUESTIONS ABOUT THE MEDIATORS' CREDIBILITY- If a party questions the mediators' honesty, impartiality, or competency, these questions must be addressed to the parties' satisfaction before the mediation can proceed.

THREATS OF VIOLENCE Attempts to use the mediation process as a way to intimidate with fear strike at the heart of fairness.

SIGNS OF SEVERE EMOTIONAL DISTRESS- Conflict is often hard on disputants. This can lead to destructive behavior. Mediators must be able to identify signs and make appropriate referrals.

USE OF DIRTY TRICKS- Deceit, ploys, and personal attacks undermine the equity of the process and can blow up the mediation by escalating the conflict beyond the ability of the mediator to intervene.

STOP

STATEMENTS OF SURRENDER- Capitulation may result in agreement, but can jeopardize durability. It may also threaten the equity of the agreement.

SERIOUS POWER IMBALANCE- If the significant disparity in the power of the parties makes it likely that the mediation process will only be used to coerce settlement, the mediators should consider if it is in their power to act to address the imbalance, check with the disempowered party about their willingness to proceed, or withdraw.

10. **What should I do if I believe the mediation should be terminated, either because it is fruitless or because the case seems inappropriate?**

We believe that mediators have an ethical responsibility to the parties to protect the integrity of the process. If the mediators believe that there is no possibility of agreement, they should inform the parties and discuss whether the parties have perspectives or information that could change the mediators' opinion. If not, the mediators should terminate the mediation. One sample mediation agreement in Appendix III has a provision that gives the mediator this authority.

A case that initially seems appropriate for mediation may become inappropriate during the process, for example, when one of the parties who is a recovering alcoholic starts drinking again and comes to a session inebriated. The mediators' duty to protect the process requires that the mediators stop it unless the parties provide additional information or assurances that permit the mediators to change their assessment about appropriateness. In the example, the alcoholic may agree that the mediation should be temporarily suspended while he or she seeks professional help. Once he or she is in treatment, with the knowledge and approval of the treating professional, the mediation might resume.

III.   MEDIATION AS A BUSINESS

11.   *What suggestions do you have about starting a mediation practice?*

- Make a commitment to professional development so that you are deserving of the trust and confidence of people in need.
- Network actively. Tell likely referral sources about your intentions so they become possible sources of business. Be willing to invest significant time in developing a caseload.

12.   *How do mediators get cases and referrals?*

The general sources of new case referrals are:

- Satisfied former clients who tell people about you;
- Professionals who regularly deal with people in crisis and conflict (lawyers, psychologists, counselors, ministers, accountants);
- Publicity and advertising (yellow pages ad, your name in an article about mediation in the newspaper, a speech to the Rotary, Lions, or Kiwanis Clubs, an appearance on talk radio discussing mediation);
- Other mediators who know of your work and send you their friends and family or cases they don't want or can't handle.

The critical element is a reputation for competence and skill. If you are perceived as someone who can deliver quality services, you are more likely to be referred cases.

13.   *How do mediators charge for their services? What are the going rates?*

Most for-fee mediation is paid for on an hourly basis. Rates vary depending on the use of co-mediation and the background and experience of the mediators. For co-mediation, most rates fall in the range of $80-250/hour to be divided by the team. For solo mediation, the range is about $40-150/hour. Many licensed professionals in private practice, such as attorneys and psychologists, charge their standard hourly rate. This means that rates in large, urban areas may be higher than the ranges we have suggested.

Some mediators charge retainers or deposits at the beginning of the mediation. Most collect from their clients at the end of each session. Some charge for telephone conferences, preparation time outside of sessions, and time spent drafting agreements. Others do not charge for this time. It is absolutely essential to reach a clear fee agreement that deals with all of these issues with your clients before the mediation begins.

14.   *Is there significant risk of professional liability as a mediator?*

We are not aware of any reported cases of mediators being sued for professional malpractice. The low rates charged by insurance companies for malpractice coverage also indicate that people whose job it is to monitor risk consider the exposure to be low. Many mediators adopt the risk reducing practice of requiring that all parties in mediation have independent legal counsel.

15.   *What kind of liability insurance is available for professional mediators?*

Professional liability (malpractice) insurance is available for less than $500/year through membership in the Society for Professionals in Dispute Resolution (SPIDR), the Association of Family and Conciliation Courts (AFCC), or the Academy of Family Mediators (AFM). If you perform fewer than ten mediations per year, the cost may be even less. Licensed professionals, for example, lawyers or mental health professionals who already carry malpractice insurance, may be able to have a rider issued by their existing carrier at no additional premium or for a modest fee. There is no requirement that a mediator carry professional liability insurance in order to mediate. There is no custom in the field regarding malpractice insurance coverage. Many mediators choose not to carry this insurance.

16.   *What should I do if I am sued or subpoenaed?*

Consult an attorney. If you have malpractice insurance coverage and the suit claims professional negligence, inform your insurance carrier. They may provide an attorney. Take copies of any court papers and your mediation file containing your contract, notes, and documents for the case. You will note that one of the sample mediation contracts in Appendix III contains a clause requiring the party who attempts to subpoena information to pay your attorney's fees to fight the subpoena. If you belong to one of the professional organizations (SPIDR, AFM, or AFCC) you may want to contact them for assistance or information that may help in your defense.

17. *What case file documentation is appropriate and necessary to maintain?*

Practices on documentation vary among mediators. We recommend that you have a written contract with your clients if you are in private practice. The contract should spell out fees and other aspects of the mediator-client relationship. We have included samples of different agreements in Appendix III. Clarity about the rules and the boundaries of your role as a mediator are essential to inform your clients about what they can and should expect of you. We believe that this will also decrease the possibility that someone would file a claim against you because she or he believes that you acted unprofessionally or carelessly.

There is no standard practice regarding notes and documents generated during the mediation. Some community mediation centers destroy notes made at the end of the mediation. Most mediators in private practice retain notes and documents for some period of time. Retention of notes and documents enables private mediators to review the mediation in the event the parties return for follow-up work. It also could assist the mediators in defending themselves against a future complaint by a client. Original documents (tax returns, deeds, or legal papers.) should be returned to the client as soon as they have been copied for the file.

IV. MEDIATION AS A PROCESS

18. *What kind of visual aids, if any, do mediators use to assist the parties?*

The most commonly used tool is the easel with flip chart pad. By writing key points (issues, interests, options) on the pad in front of all parties, mediators provide a clear focus to keep everyone on track. Flip charts also help mediators to keep their notes accurate because they are in plain view. Misunderstandings can surface as the mediator's summary interpretation is reviewed. With little drawing talent, mediators can also use the flip chart to illustrate and educate with diagrams and charts. The worksheets in Appendix II are examples of the kind of visual aids that mediators use. Handouts can also be used as aids to assist parties in negotiating effectively and making wise decisions. In cases with multiple parties, flip chart pages taped to a wall can act as minutes of the session. With continuing enhancement of existing technology, we anticipate growing use of portable computers and LCD panels that permit overhead projection of settlement language on a screen.

19. *How do mediators usually set up their working areas to enhance effective communication?*

Room setup is not always within the mediators' control, especially if a courthouse or other public facilities are being used. If the mediators have a choice, they should arrange for a location with the following attributes:

- Quiet with minimal noise and external distraction.
- Soundproof, so that discussions or raised voices will not be heard by people outside the room.
- Comfortable, so that the participants can relax.
- Convenient, with a nearby caucus space or waiting area.
- Equipped, so that drinks (water, sodas, coffee) and bathrooms are available.

Some mediators prefer to work around tables, others do not like to use them unless absolutely necessary because they form a barrier between people. If the mediation requires reference to objects or documents, it may be inconvenient to work without a table. For more relational mediations, tables can be physical and psychological components that keep people apart or make people feel more protected.

Chairs should be positioned so that everyone can see and hear other participants easily. We prefer to keep a distance between the chairs of the disputants that prevents them from leaning and touching or gesturing at the other in threatening or offensive ways. We also want the chairs of the disputants to be at an angle to each other so they can easily make eye contact but are not in a confrontational face-to-face physical position.

In large group sessions, semi-circular seating arrangements facing a wall on which flip chart pages are posted are often helpful. When observers are present but are not participating at the table, a "fish bowl" offers a logical and effective format, putting the participants in the center and the observers around them.

Figure 36 depicts four common room setup options.

Figure 36. Room Setup Options

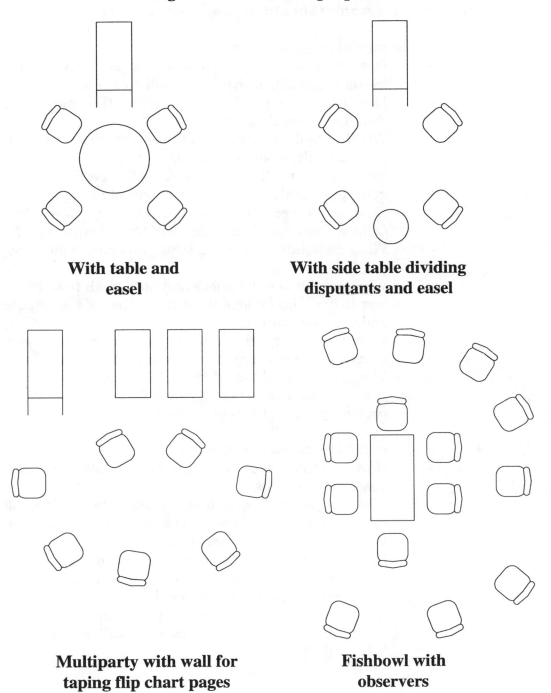

With table and easel

With side table dividing disputants and easel

Multiparty with wall for taping flip chart pages

Fishbowl with observers

20. *Can you give us a checklist of the common issues that practicing mediators should be prepared to address?*

- Issues related to getting clients:
    — How to describe your services in advertising (i.e. mediation, ADR, arbitration, conflict resolution, etc.)?
    — How to generate public appearances (i.e. radio, TV, churches, local clubs, schools, etc.)?
    — Whether to do mailings (i.e. to lawyers, mental health professionals, businesses, etc.)?
    — How to perform effective networking (i.e. getting known, getting referrals, getting connections, etc.)?
    — How to answer the phone (i.e. *Law and Mediation Offices, Center for Counseling and Conciliation*, etc.)?
    — What materials to send (i.e. letter, brochure, videotape, etc.)?
    — Who to talk to on the phone and how much to talk (i.e. how to limit discussions about the subject of the dispute and the other party)?
    — Whether to charge for first session (i.e. should you give a free sample or charge from the start)?
    — Whether to do individual or joint first sessions (i.e. can you learn more from meeting each disputant separately first or by seeing them together)?

- Issues related to structuring a practice:
    — How to handle your ad in the phone book (i.e. costs, deadlines, contents)?
    — Whether you will agree to be responsible for bringing other party(s) into mediation (i.e. will you contact them and try and persuade them to participate)?
    — How to perform intake of new cases, including:
        — your role and its clarity (i.e. attorney/mediator/ mental health professional, etc.)?
        — your initial discussions with the parties (i.e. how much of the dispute specifics will you learn in advance)?
    — Whether to co-mediate:
        — if so, who is the right co-mediator for this case (i.e. level of experience, special expertise, gender, ethnicity, etc.)?

- Whether you are competent:
  - is this case appropriate for your level of experience (i.e. are you getting in over your head)?
  - does this case require special expertise (i.e. is it technical in subject matter)?
  - does this case involve issues which are highly charged for you, so that your neutrality may be compromised (i.e. is it a volatile parent-child conflict which brings up memories of your own childhood)?
- How to respond to emergencies:
  - are you being asked to do too much (i.e. to mediate a complex case in one weekend because there is a court hearing Monday)?
  - are you being asked to work too fast (i.e. to mediate a divorce in one session because that's all the parties can afford)?
  - are you being asked to disregard your prior experience with what works in this kind of case (i.e. to agree that the roots of the conflict will never be explored)?
- How to set up your office:
  - furniture (i.e. couches or chairs, tables or open space)?
  - reception/waiting area (i.e. comfort, size)?
  - phone (i.e. who will answer it)?
  - acoustics (i.e. privacy concerns)?
- How to handle fees:
  - how much? (i.e. your per/hour rate)?
  - how to divide? (i.e. if you co-mediate)?
  - whether to charge for first session (i.e. should you give a free sample or introduction)?
  - retainer (i.e. will you require one, if so, how much)?
  - work outside of actual mediation sessions (i.e. will you charge, if so, how and how much)?
  - ethical issues (i.e. are you violating fee-splitting prohibitions)?

- Issues related to the mediation process:
  - What to do about ground rules:
    - should you have them at all (i.e. will you wait and respond when and if problems arise)?
    - interruptions (i.e. will you restrain the parties from interrupting each other)?
    - future focus (i.e. will you exhort the parties to focus on the future)?
    - voice level (i.e. will you forbid yelling)?
    - personal attacks (i.e. will you ban name calling)?
  - How to deal with and explain confidentiality/privacy issues:
    - court proceedings (i.e. will parties agree not to call you as a witness in this case)?
    - child abuse (i.e. what are your reporting duties)?
    - criminal behavior (i.e. what are your reporting duties)?
    - caucus (i.e. what will you do with information heard from one side)?
    - attorneys and mental health professionals (i.e. may you communicate with them)?
  - How to fulfill the role of mediator:
    - judgment (i.e. how do you suspend this and remain neutral for the parties)?
    - muscle (i.e. how much pressure will you exert)?
    - legal advice (i.e. will you give it)?
    - switch to other process such as arbitration (i.e. are you willing to do this)?
    - decision making (i.e. will you ever undertake this)?
  - How to manage homework:
    - clear assignments (i.e. do parties understand what is expected of them)?
    - enforcement/follow through (i.e. what will you do if the parties don't do their homework)?
    - documentation (i.e. will you put assignments in writing)?

The Art of Mediation

- How to use experts:
  - what fields are necessary (i.e. law, medicine, child development, valuation, accounting, etc.)?
  - how to choose (i.e. parties' choice, their lawyers' choice, mediator's choice, etc.)?
  - how to pay (i.e. in advance, split 50-50 by parties, out of trust account, etc.)?
  - confidentiality (i.e. you need permission to discuss case with them)?
- How to draft agreements:
  - form (i.e. informal, legal, etc.)?
  - initial drafting (i.e. mediators or attorneys)?
  - review by attorneys (i.e. will you suggest/require this)?
  - will you draft and file court documents (i.e. switch to representative lawyer role)?

SECTION FIVE: APPENDICES

SECTION FIVE: APPENDICES
TABLE OF CONTENTS

APPENDIX I: ETHICAL MATERIALS

ETHICAL MATERIALS

TABLE OF CONTENTS

ACADEMY OF FAMILY MEDIATORS
STANDARDS OF PRACTICE
FOR FAMILY AND DIVORCE MEDIATION*
Adopted 1985

I.   Preamble

Mediation is a family-centered conflict resolution process in which an impartial third party assists the participants to negotiate a consensual and informed settlement. In mediation, whether private or public, decision-making authority rests with the parties. The role of the mediator includes reducing the obstacles to communication, maximizing the exploration of alternatives, and addressing the needs of those it is agreed are involved or affected.

Mediation is based on principles of problem solving that focus on the needs and interests of the participants; fairness; privacy; self determination; and the best interest of all family members.

These standards are intended to assist and guide public, private, voluntary, and mandatory mediation. It is understood that the manner of implementation and mediator adherence to these standards may be influenced by local law or court rule.

II.   Initiating the Process

A.   Definition and Description of Mediation. The mediator shall define mediation and describe the differences and similarities between mediation and other procedures for dispute resolution. In defining the process, the mediator shall delineate it from therapy, counseling, custody evaluation, arbitration, and advocacy.

B.   Identification of Issues. The mediation shall elicit sufficient information from the participants so that they can mutually define and agree on the issues to be resolved in mediation.

C.   Appropriateness of Mediation. The mediators shall help the participants evaluate the benefits, risks, and costs of mediation and the alternatives available to them.

D.   Mediator's Duty of Disclosure

      1.   <u>Biases</u> The mediator shall disclose to the participants any biases or strong views relating to the issues to be mediated.

Reprinted with permission of the Academy of Family Mediators

2. <u>Training and Experience</u> The mediators' education, training, and experience to mediate the issues should be accurately described to the participants.

III. Procedures

The mediators shall reach an understanding with the participants regarding the procedures to be followed in mediation. This includes but is not limited to the practice as to separate meetings between a participant and the mediator, confidentiality, use of legal services, the involvement of additional parties, and conditions under which mediation may be terminated.

A. Mutual Duties and Responsibilities. The mediator and the participants shall agree upon the duties and responsibilities that each is accepting in the mediation process. This may be a written or verbal agreement.

IV. Impartiality and Neutrality

A. Impartiality. The mediator is obligated to maintain impartiality toward all participants. Impartiality means freedom from favoritism or bias, either in word or action. Impartiality implies a commitment to aid all participants, as opposed to a single individual, in reaching a mutually satisfactory agreement. Impartiality means that a mediator will not play an adversarial role.

The mediator has a responsibility to maintain impartiality while raising questions for the parties to consider as to the fairness, equity, and feasibility of proposed options for settlement.

B. Neutrality. Neutrality refers to the relationship that the mediator has with the disputing parties. If the mediator feels, or any one of the participants states, that the mediator's background or personal experiences would prejudice the mediator's performance, the mediator should withdraw from mediation unless all agree to proceed.

C. Prior Relationships. A mediator's actual or perceived impartiality may be compromised by social or professional relationships with one of the participants at any point in time. The mediator shall not proceed if previous legal or counseling services have been provided to one of the participants. If such services have been provided to both participants, mediation shall not proceed unless the prior relationship has been discussed, the role of the mediator made distinct from the earlier relationship, and the participants given the opportunity to freely choose to proceed.

D. Relationship to Participants. The mediator should be aware that post-mediation professional or social relationships may compromise the mediator's continued availability as a neutral third party.

E. Conflict of Interest. A mediator should disclose any circumstance to the participants that might cause a conflict of interest.

V. Costs and Fees

A. Explanation of Fees. The mediator shall explain the fees to be charged for mediation and any related costs and shall agree with the participants on how the fees will be shared and the manner of payment.

B. Reasonable Fees. When setting fees, the mediator shall ensure that they are explicit, fair, reasonable, and commensurate with the service to be performed. Unearned fees should be promptly returned to the clients.

C. Contingent Fees. It is inappropriate for a mediator to charge contingent fees or to base fees on the outcome of mediation.

D. Referrals and Commissions. No commissions, rebates, or similar forms of remuneration shall be given or received for referral of clients for mediation services.

VI. Confidentiality and Exchange of Information

A. Confidentiality. Confidentiality relates to the full and open disclosure necessary for the mediation process. A mediator shall foster the confidentiality of the process.

B. Limits of Confidentiality. The mediator shall inform the parties at the initial meeting of limitations on confidentiality, such as statutorily or judicially mandated reporting.

C. Appearing in Court. The mediator shall inform the parties of circumstances under which mediators may be compelled to testify in court.

D. Consequences of Disclosure of Facts Between Parties. The mediator shall discuss with the participants the potential consequences of their disclosure of facts to each other during the mediation process.

E. Release of Information. The mediator shall obtain the consent of the participants prior to releasing information to others. The mediator shall maintain confidentiality and render anonymous all identifying information when materials are used for research or training purposes.

F. Caucus. The mediator shall discuss policy regarding confidentiality for individual caucuses. In the event that a mediator, on consent of the participants, speaks privately with any person not represented in mediation, including children, the mediator shall define how information received will be used.

G. Storage and Disposal of Records. The mediator shall maintain confidentiality in the storage and disposal of records.

H.   Full Disclosure. The mediator shall require disclosure of all relevant information in the mediation process, as would reasonably occur in the judicial discovery process.

VII.   Self-Determination

A.   Responsibilities of the Participants and the Mediator. The primary responsibility for the resolution of a dispute rests with the participants. The mediator's obligation is to assist the disputants in reaching an informed and voluntary settlement. At no time shall a mediator coerce a participant into agreement or make a substantive decision for any participant.

B.   Responsibility to Third Parties. The mediator has a responsibility to promote the participants' consideration of the interests of children and other persons affected by the agreement. The mediator also has a duty to assist parents to examine, apart from their own desires, the separate and individual needs of such people. The participants shall be encouraged to seek outside professional consultation when appropriate or when they are otherwise unable to agree on the needs of any individual affected by the agreement.

VIII.   Professional Advice

A.   Independent Advice and Information. The mediator shall encourage and assist the participants to obtain independent expert information and advice when such information is needed to reach an informed agreement or to protect the rights of a participant.

B.   Providing Information. A mediator shall give information only in those areas where qualified by training or experience.

C.   Independent Legal Counsel. When the mediation may affect legal rights or obligations, the mediator shall advise the participants to seek independent legal counsel prior to resolving the issues and in conjunction with formalizing an agreement.

IX.   Parties' Ability to Negotiate

The mediator shall ensure that each participant has had an opportunity to understand the implications and ramifications of available options. In the event a participant needs either additional information or assistance in order for the negotiations to proceed in a fair and orderly manner or for an agreement to be reached, the mediator shall refer the individuals to appropriate resources.

A.	Procedural Factors. The mediator has a duty to ensure balanced negotiations and should not permit manipulative or intimidating negotiation techniques.

B.	Psychological Factors. The mediator shall explore whether the participants are capable of participating in informed negotiations. The mediator may postpone mediation and refer the parties to appropriate resources if necessary.

X.	Concluding Mediation

A.	Full Agreement. The mediator shall discuss with the participants the process for formalization and implementation of the agreement.

B.	Partial Agreement. When the participants reach a partial agreement, the mediator shall discuss with them procedures available to resolve the remaining issues. Without Agreement Termination by Participants. *[sic]* The mediator shall inform the participants of their right to withdraw from mediation at any time and for any reason.*[sic]*

C.	Termination by Participants. The mediator shall inform the participants of their right to withdraw from mediation at any time and for any reason.

D.	Termination by Mediator. If the mediator believes that participants are unable or unwilling to participate meaningfully in the process or that a reasonable agreement is unlikely, the mediator may suspend or terminate mediation and should encourage the parties to seek appropriate professional help.

E.	Impasse. If the participants reach a final impasse, the mediator should not prolong unproductive discussion that would result in emotional and monetary costs to the participants.

XI.	Training and Education

A.	Training. A mediator shall acquire substantive knowledge and procedural skill in the specialized area of practice. This may include but is not limited to family and human development, family law, divorce procedures, family finances, community resources, the mediation process, and professional ethics.

B.	Continuing Education. A mediator shall participate in continuing education and be personally responsible for ongoing professional growth. A mediator is encouraged to join with other mediators and members of related professions to promote mutual professional development.

XII.   Advertising. A mediator shall make only accurate statements about the mediation process, its costs and benefits, and the mediator's qualifications.

XIII.   Relationship with Other Professionals

A.   The Responsibility of the Mediator Toward Other Mediators/ Relationship with Other Mediators. A mediator should not mediate any dispute that is being mediated by another mediator without first endeavoring to consult with the person or persons conducting the mediation.

B.   Co-mediation. In those situations where more than one mediator is participating in a particular case, each mediator has a responsibility to keep the other informed of developments essential to a cooperative effort.

C.   Relationships with Other Professionals. A mediator should respect the complementary relationship between mediation and legal, mental health, and other social services and should promote cooperation with other professionals.

XIV.   Advancement of Mediation

A.   Mediation Service. A mediator is encouraged to provide some mediation service in the community for nominal or no fee.

B.   Promotion of Mediation. A mediator shall promote the advancement of mediation by encouraging and participating in research, publishing, or other forms of professional and public education.

SOCIETY OF PROFESSIONALS IN DISPUTE RESOLUTION

ETHICAL STANDARDS OF PROFESSIONAL RESPONSIBILITY*

Adopted June 1986

Introduction

The Society of Professionals in Dispute Resolution (SPIDR) was established in 1973 to promote the peaceful resolution of disputes. Members of the Society believe that resolving disputes through negotiation, mediation, arbitration and other neutral interventions can be of great benefit to disputing parties and to society. In 1983, the SPIDR Board of Directors charged the SPIDR Ethics Committee with the task of developing ethical standards of professional responsibility. The Committee membership represented all the various sectors and disciplines within SPIDR. This document, adopted by the Board on June 2, 1986, is the result of that charge.

The purpose of this document is to promote among SPIDR Members and Associates ethical conduct and a high level of competency among SPIDR Members, including honesty, integrity, impartiality and the exercise of good judgment in their dispute resolution efforts. It is hoped that this document also will help to (1) define the profession of dispute resolution, (2) educate the public, and (3) inform users of dispute resolution services.

Application of Standards

Adherence to these ethical standards by SPIDR Members and Associates is basic to professional responsibility. SPIDR Members and Associates commit themselves to be guided in their professional conduct by these standards. The SPIDR Board of Directors or its designee is available to advise Members and Associates about the interpretation of these standards. Other neutral practitioners and organizations are welcome to follow these standards.

Scope

It is recognized that SPIDR Members and Associates resolve disputes in various sectors within the disciplines of dispute resolution and have their own codes of professional conduct. These standards have been developed as

---

Reprinted with permission of the Society of Professionals in Dispute Resolution

general guidelines of practice for neutral disciplines represented in the SPIDR membership. Ethical considerations relevant to some, but not to all, of these disciplines are not covered by these standards.

General Responsibilities

Neutrals have a duty to the parties, to the profession, and to themselves. They should be honest and unbiased, act in good faith, be diligent, and not seek to advance their own interests at the expense of their parties.

Neutrals must act fairly in dealing with the parties, have no personal interest in the terms of the settlement, show no bias toward individuals and institutions involved in the dispute, be reasonably available as requested by the parties, and be certain that the parties are informed of the process in which they are involved.

Responsibility to the Parties

1. Impartiality. The neutral must maintain impartiality toward all parties. Impartiality means freedom from favoritism or bias either by word or by action, and a commitment to serve all parties as opposed to a single party.

2. Informed Consent. The neutral has an obligation to assure that all parties understand the nature of the process, the procedures, the particular role of the neutral, and the parties' relationship to the neutral.

3. Confidentiality. Maintaining confidentiality is critical to the dispute resolution process. Confidentiality encourages candor, a full exploration of the issues, and a neutral's acceptability. There may be some types of cases, however, in which confidentiality is not protected. In such cases, the neutral must advise the parties, when appropriate in the dispute resolution process, that the confidentiality of the proceedings cannot necessarily be maintained. Except in such instances, the neutral must resist all attempts to cause him or her to reveal any information outside the process. A commitment by the neutral to hold information in confidence within the process also must be honored.

4. Conflict of Interest. The neutral must refrain from entering or continuing in any dispute if he or she believes or perceives that participation as a neutral would be a clear conflict of interest. The neutral also must disclose any circumstance that may create or give the appearance of a conflict of interest and any circumstance that may reasonably raise a question as to the neutral's impartiality.

5. Promptness. The neutral shall exert every reasonable effort to expedite the process.

6. The Settlement and Its Consequences. The dispute resolution process belongs to the parties. The neutral has no vested interest in the terms of a settlement, but must be satisfied that agreements in which she or he has participated will not impugn the integrity of the process. The neutral has a responsibility to see that the parties consider the terms of a settlement. If the neutral is concerned about the possible consequences of a proposed agreement, and the needs of the parties dictate, the neutral must inform the parties of that concern. In adhering to this standard, the neutral may find it advisable to educate the parties, to refer one or more parties for specialized advice, or to withdraw from the case. In no case, however, shall the neutral violate Section 3, Confidentiality, of these standards.

Unrepresented Interests

The neutral must consider circumstances where interests are not represented in the process. The neutral has an obligation, where in his or her judgment the needs of parties dictate, to assure that such interests have been considered by the principal parties.

Use of Multiple Procedures

The use of more than one dispute resolution procedure by the same neutral involves additional responsibilities. Where the use of more than one procedure is initially contemplated, the neutral must take care at the outset to advise the parties of the nature of the procedures and the consequences of revealing information during any one procedure which the neutral may later use for decision making or may share with another decision maker. Where the use of more than one procedure is contemplated after the initiation of the dispute resolution process, the neutral must explain the consequences and afford the parties an opportunity to select another neutral for the subsequent procedures. It is also incumbent upon the neutral to advise the parties of the transition from one dispute resolution process to another.

Background and Qualifications

A neutral should accept responsibility only in cases where the neutral has sufficient knowledge regarding the appropriate process and subject matter to be effective. A neutral has a responsibility to maintain and improve his or her professional skills.

Disclosure of Fees

It is the duty of the neutral to explain to the parties at the outset of the process the bases of compensation, fees, and charges, if any.

Support of the Profession

The experienced neutral should participate in the development of new practitioners in the field and engage in efforts to educate the public about the value and use of neutral dispute resolution procedures. The neutral should provide *pro bono* services, where appropriate.

Responsibilities of Neutrals Working on the Same Case

In the event that more than one neutral is involved in the resolution of a dispute, each has an obligation to inform the others regarding his or her entry in the case. Neutrals working with the same parties should maintain an open and professional relationship with each other.

Advertising and Solicitation

A neutral must be aware that some forms of advertising and solicitations are inappropriate and in some conflict resolution disciplines, such as labor arbitration, are impermissible. All advertising must honestly represent the services to be rendered. No claims of specific results or promises which imply favor of one side over another for the purpose of obtaining business should be made. No commissions, rebates, or other similar forms of remuneration should be given or received by a neutral for the referral of clients.

For further information, please contact the International SPIDR Office:

SPIDR
815 15th Street, NW, Suite 530
Washington, DC 20005
202-783-7277

**FAMILY LAW SECTION OF THE
AMERICAN BAR ASSOCIATION**
750 N. Lake Shore Drive
Chicago, Illinois 60611

<u>STANDARD OF PRACTICE
FOR LAWYER MEDIATORS
IN FAMILY DISPUTES</u>*
Adopted August, 1984

PREAMBLE
FOR THE PURPOSES OF THESE STANDARDS, FAMILY MEDIATION IS
DEFINED AS A PROCESS IN WHICH A LAWYER HELPS FAMILY
MEMBERS RESOLVE THEIR DISPUTES IN AN INFORMATIVE AND
CONSENSUAL MANNER. THIS PROCESS REQUIRES THAT THE
MEDIATOR BE QUALIFIED BY TRAINING, EXPERIENCE AND
TEMPERAMENT; THAT THE MEDIATOR BE IMPARTIAL; THAT THE
PARTICIPANTS REACH DECISIONS VOLUNTARILY; THAT THEIR
DECISIONS BE BASED ON SUFFICIENT FACTUAL DATA; AND, THAT
EACH PARTICIPANT UNDERSTANDS THE INFORMATION UPON
WHICH DECISIONS ARE REACHED. WHILE FAMILY MEDIATION MAY
BE VIEWED AS AN ALTERNATIVE MEANS OF CONFLICT
RESOLUTION, IT IS NOT A SUBSTITUTE FOR THE BENEFIT OF
INDEPENDENT LEGAL ADVICE.

I.   THE MEDIATOR HAS A DUTY TO DEFINE AND DESCRIBE
        THE PROCESS OF MEDIATION AND ITS COST BEFORE
        THE PARTIES REACH AN AGREEMENT TO MEDIATE.

SPECIFIC CONSIDERATIONS:

Before the actual mediation session begins, the mediator shall conduct
an orientation session to give an overview of the process and to assess the
appropriateness of mediation for the participants. Among the topics covered,
the mediator shall discuss the following:

A.   The mediator shall define the process in context so that the
participants understand the differences between mediation and other
means of conflict resolution available to them. In defining the process,

---

Reprinted with permission of the American Bar Association

the mediator shall also distinguish it from therapy or marriage counseling.

B.　　The mediator shall obtain sufficient information from the participants so they can mutually define the issues to be resolved in mediation.

C.　　It should be emphasized that the mediator may make suggestions for the participants to consider, such as alternative ways of resolving problems and may draft proposals for the participants' consideration but that all decisions are to be made voluntarily by the participants themselves, and the mediator's views are to be given no independent weight or credence.

D.　　The duties and responsibilities that the mediator and the participants accept in the mediation process shall be agreed upon. The mediator shall instruct the participants that either of them or the mediator has the right to suspend or terminate the process at any time.

E.　　The mediator shall assess the ability and willingness of the participants to mediate. The mediator has a continuing duty to assess his or her own ability and willingness to undertake mediation with the particular participants and the issues to be mediated. The mediator shall not continue and shall terminate the process, if in his or her judgment, one of the parties is not able or willing to participate in good faith.

F.　　The mediator shall explain the fees for mediation. It is inappropriate for a mediator to charge a contingency fee or to base the fee on the outcome of the mediation process.

G.　　The mediator shall inform the participants of the need to employ independent legal counsel for advice throughout the mediation process. The mediator shall inform the participants that the mediator cannot represent either or both of them in a marital dissolution or in any legal action.

H.　　The mediator shall discuss the issue of separate sessions. The mediator shall reach an understanding with the participants as to whether and under what circumstances the mediator may meet alone with either of them or with any third party. Commentary:　The mediator cannot act as lawyer for either party or for them jointly and should make that clear to both parties.

I.   It should be brought to the participants' attention that emotions play a part in the decision-making process. The mediator shall attempt to elicit from each of the participants a confirmation that each understands the connection between one's own emotions and the bargaining process.

II.   THE MEDIATOR SHALL NOT VOLUNTARILY DISCLOSE INFORMATION OBTAINED THROUGH THE MEDIATION PROCESS WITHOUT THE PRIOR CONSENT OF BOTH PARTICIPANTS.

SPECIFIC CONSIDERATIONS:

A.   At the outset of mediation, the parties should agree in writing not to require the mediator to disclose to any third party any statements made in the course of mediation. The mediator shall inform the participants that the mediator will not voluntarily disclose to any third party any of the information obtained through the mediation process, unless such disclosure is required by law, without the prior consent of the participants. The mediator also shall inform the parties of the limitations of confidentiality such as statutory or judicially mandated reporting.

B.   If subpoenaed or otherwise noticed to testify, the mediator shall inform the participants immediately so as to afford them an opportunity to quash the process.

C.   The mediator shall inform the participants of the mediator's inability to bind third parties to an agreement not to disclose information furnished during the mediation in the absence of any absolute privilege.

III.   THE MEDIATOR HAS A DUTY TO BE IMPARTIAL.

SPECIFIC CONSIDERATIONS:

A.   The mediator shall not represent either party during or after the mediation process in any legal matters. In the event the mediator has represented one of the parties beforehand the mediator shall not undertake the mediation.

B.   The mediator shall disclose to the participants any biases or strong views relating to the issues to be mediated, both in the orientation session, and also before these issues are discussed in mediation.

C.   The mediator must be impartial as between the mediation participants. The mediator's task is to facilitate the ability of the participants to negotiate their own agreement, while raising questions as to the fairness, equity and feasibility of proposed options for settlement.

D.   The mediator has a duty to ensure that the participants consider fully the best interests of the children, that they understand the consequences of any decision they reach concerning the children. The mediator also has a duty to assist parents to examine the separate, and individual needs of their children and to consider those needs apart from their own desires for any particular parenting formula. If the mediator believes that any proposed agreement of the parents does not protect the best interests of the children, the mediator has a duty to inform them of this belief and its basis.

E.   The mediator shall not communicate with either party alone or with any third party to discuss mediation issues without the prior consent of the mediation participants. The mediator shall obtain an agreement from the participants during the orientation session as to whether and under what circumstances the mediator may speak directly and separately with each of their lawyers during the mediation process.

IV.   THE MEDIATOR HAS A DUTY TO ASSURE THAT THE MEDIATION PARTICIPANTS MAKE DECISIONS BASED UPON SUFFICIENT INFORMATION AND KNOWLEDGE.

SPECIFIC CONSIDERATIONS:

A.   The mediator shall assure that there is full financial disclosure, evaluation and development of relevant factual information in the mediation process, such as each would reasonably receive in the discovery process, or that the parties have sufficient information to intelligently waive the right to such disclosure.

B.   In addition to requiring this disclosure, evaluation and development of information, the mediator shall promote the equal understanding of such information before any agreement is reached. This consideration may require the mediator to recommend that either or both obtain expert consultation in the event that it appears that additional knowledge or understanding is necessary for balanced negotiations.

C.   The mediator may define the legal issues, but shall not direct the decision of the mediation participants based upon the mediator's interpretation of the law as applied to the facts of the situation. The mediator shall endeavor to assure that the participants have a sufficient understanding of appropriate statutory and case law as well as local judicial tradition, before reaching an agreement by recommending to the participants that they obtain independent legal representation during the process.

V.   THE MEDIATOR HAS A DUTY TO SUSPEND OR TERMINATE MEDIATION WHENEVER CONTINUATION OF THE PROCESS WOULD HARM ONE OR MORE OF THE PARTICIPANTS.

SPECIFIC CONSIDERATIONS:

A.   If the mediator believes that the participants are unable or unwilling to meaningfully participate in the process or that reasonable agreement is unlikely, the mediator may suspend or terminate mediation and should encourage the parties to seek appropriate professional help. The mediator shall recognize that the decisions are to be made by the parties on the basis of adequate information. The mediator shall not, however, participate in a process that the mediator believes will result in harm to a participant.

B.   The mediator shall assure that each person has had the opportunity to understand fully the implications and ramifications of all options available.

C.   The mediator has a duty to assure a balanced dialogue and must attempt to diffuse any manipulative or intimidating negotiation techniques utilized by either of the participants.

D.   If the mediator has suspended or terminated the process, the mediator should suggest that the participants obtain additional professional services as may be appropriate.

VI. THE MEDIATOR HAS A CONTINUING DUTY TO ADVISE EACH OF THE MEDIATION PARTICIPANTS TO OBTAIN LEGAL REVIEW PRIOR TO REACHING ANY AGREEMENT.

SPECIFIC CONSIDERATIONS:

A.   Each of the mediation participants should have independent legal counsel before reaching final agreement. At the beginning of the mediation process, the mediator should inform the participants that each should employ independent legal counsel for advice at the beginning of the process and that the independent legal counsel should be utilized throughout the process and before the participants have reached any accord to which they have made an emotional commitment. In order to promote the integrity of the process, the mediator shall not refer either of the participants to any particular lawyers. When an attorney referral is requested, the parties should be referred to a Bar Association list if available. In the absence of such a list, the mediator may only provide a list of qualified family law attorneys in the community.

B.   The mediator shall inform the participants that the mediator cannot represent either or both of them in a marital dissolution.

C.   The mediator shall obtain an agreement from the husband and the wife that each lawyer, upon request, shall be entitled to review all the factual documentation provided by the participants in the mediation process.

D.   Any memo of understanding or proposed agreement which is prepared in the mediation process should be separately reviewed by independent counsel for each participant before it is signed. While a mediator cannot insist that each participant have separate counsel, they should be discouraged from signing any agreement which has not been so reviewed. If the participants, or either of them, choose to proceed without independent counsel, the mediator shall warn them of any risk involved in not being represented, including where appropriate, the possibility that the agreement they submit to a court may be rejected as unreasonable in light of both parties' legal rights or may not be binding on them.

MODEL STANDARDS OF CONDUCT FOR MEDIATORS*
Final Draft
Adopted April 8, 1994

Introductory Note

The initiative for these standards came from three professional groups: the American Arbitration Association, the American Bar Association, and the Society of Professionals in Dispute Resolution.

The purpose of this initiative was to develop a set of standards to serve as a general framework for the practice of mediation. The effort is a step in the development of the field and a tool to assist practitioners in it — a beginning, not an end. The standards are intended to apply to all types of mediation. It is recognized, however, that in some cases the application of these standards may be affected by laws or contractual agreements.

Preface

The standards of conduct for mediators are intended to perform three major functions: to serve as a guide for the conduct of mediators; to inform the mediating parties; and to promote public confidence in mediation as a process for resolving disputes. The standards draw on existing codes of conduct for mediators and take into account issues and problems that have surfaced in mediation practice. They are offered in the hope that they will serve an educational function and provide assistance to individuals, organizations, and institutions involved in mediation.

Mediation is a process in which an impartial third party — a mediator — facilitates the resolution of a dispute by promoting voluntary agreement (or "self-determination") by the parties to the dispute. A mediator facilitates communications, promotes understanding, focuses the parties on their interests, and seeks creative problem solving to enable the parties to reach their own agreement. These standards give meaning to this definition of mediation.

I.   Self-Determination: A Mediator Shall Recognize that Mediation is Based on the Principle of Self-Determination by the Parties.

Self-determination is the fundamental principle of mediation. It requires that the mediation process rely upon the ability of the parties to

_____

Reprinted with permission of the American Bar Association

reach a voluntary, uncoerced agreement. Any party may withdraw from mediation at any time.

COMMENTS: * The mediator may provide information about the process, raise issues, and help parties explore options. The primary role of the mediator is to facilitate a voluntary resolution of a dispute. Parties shall be given the opportunity to consider all proposed options.
* A mediator cannot personally ensure that each party has made a fully informed choice to reach a particular agreement, but it is a good practice for the mediator to make the parties aware of the importance of consulting other professionals, where appropriate, to help them make informed decisions.

II.   Impartiality: A Mediator Shall Conduct the Mediation in an Impartial Manner.

The concept of mediator impartiality is central to the mediation process. A mediator shall mediate only those matters in which she or he can remain impartial and evenhanded. If at any time the mediator is unable to conduct the process in an impartial manner, the mediator is obligated to withdraw.

COMMENTS: * A mediator shall avoid conduct that gives the appearance of partiality toward one of the parties. The quality of the mediation process is enhanced when the parties have confidence in the impartiality of the mediator.
* When mediators are appointed by a court or institution, the appointing agency shall make reasonable efforts to ensure that mediators serve impartially.
* A mediator should guard against partiality or prejudice based on the parties' personal characteristics, background or performance at the mediation.

III.   Conflicts of Interest: A Mediator Shall Disclose All Actual and Potential Conflicts of Interest Reasonably Known to the Mediator. After Disclosure, the Mediator Shall Decline to Mediate Unless All Parties Choose to Retain the Mediator. The Need to Protect Against Conflicts of Interest Also Governs Conduct that Occurs During and After the Mediation.

A conflict of interest is a dealing or relationship that might create an impression of possible bias. The basic approach to questions of conflict of interest is consistent with the concept of self-determination. The mediator has a responsibility to disclose all actual and potential conflicts that are reasonably known to the mediator and could reasonably be seen as raising a question about impartiality. If all parties agree to mediate after being informed of conflicts, the mediator may proceed with the mediation. If, however, the conflict of interest casts serious doubt on the integrity of the process, the mediator shall decline to proceed.

A mediator must avoid the appearance of conflict of interest both during and after the mediation. Without the consent of all parties, a mediator shall not subsequently establish a professional relationship with one of the parties in a related matter, or in an unrelated matter under circumstances which would raise legitimate questions about the integrity of the mediation process.

<u>COMMENTS:</u>   * A mediator shall avoid conflicts of interest in recommending the services of other professionals. A mediator may make reference to professional referral services or associations which maintain rosters of qualified professionals.

* Potential conflicts of interest may arise between administrators of mediation programs and mediators and there may be strong pressures on the mediator to settle a particular case or cases. The mediator's commitment must be to the parties and the process. Pressures from outside of the mediation process should never influence the mediator to coerce parties to settle.

IV.   Competence: A Mediator Shall Mediate Only When the Mediator Has the Necessary Qualifications to Satisfy the Reasonable Expectations of the Parties.

Any person may be selected as a mediator, provided that the parties are satisfied with the mediator's qualifications. Training and experience in mediation, however, are often necessary for effective mediation. A person who offers herself or himself as available to serve as a mediator gives parties and the public the expectation that she or he has the competency to mediate effectively. In court-connected or other forms of mandated mediation, it is essential that mediators assigned to the parties have the requisite training and experience.

COMMENTS: * Mediators should have available for the parties information regarding their relevant training, education and experience.
* The requirements for appearing on a list of mediators must be made public and available to interested persons.
* When mediators are appointed by a court or institution, the appointing agency shall make reasonable efforts to ensure that each mediator is qualified for the particular mediation.

V.   Confidentiality: A Mediator Shall Maintain the Reasonable Expectations of the Parties with Regard to Confidentiality.

The reasonable expectations of the parties with regard to confidentiality shall be met by the mediator. The parties' expectations of confidentiality depend on the circumstances of the mediation and any agreements they may make. A mediator shall not disclose any matter that a party expects to be confidential unless given permission by all parties or unless required by law or other public policy.

COMMENTS: * The parties may make their own rules with respect to confidentiality, or the accepted practice of an individual mediator or institution may dictate a particular set of expectations. Since the parties' expectations regarding confidentiality are important, the mediator should discuss these expectations with the parties.
* If the mediator holds private sessions with a party, the nature of these sessions with regard to confidentiality should be discussed prior to undertaking such sessions.
* In order to protect the integrity of the mediation, a mediator should avoid communicating information about how the parties acted in the mediation process, the merits of the case, or settlement offers. The mediator may report, if required, whether parties appeared at a scheduled mediation.
* Where the parties have agreed that all or a portion of the information disclosed during a mediation is confidential, the parties' agreement should be reported by the mediator.

* Confidentiality should not be construed to limit or prohibit the effective monitoring, research, or evaluation of mediation programs by responsible persons. Under appropriate circumstances, researchers may be permitted to obtain access to statistical data and, with the permission of the parties, to individual case files, observations of live mediations, and interviews with participants.

VI. Quality of the Process: A Mediator Shall Conduct the Mediation Fairly, Diligently, and in a Manner Consistent with the Principle of Self-Determination by the Parties.

A mediator shall work to ensure a quality process and to encourage mutual respect among the parties. A quality process requires a commitment by the mediator to diligence and procedural fairness. There should be adequate opportunity for each party in the mediation to participate in the discussions. The parties decide when and under what conditions they will reach an agreement or terminate a mediation.

COMMENTS:

* A mediator may agree to mediate only when he or she is prepared to commit the attention essential to an effective mediation.

* Mediators should only accept cases when they can satisfy the reasonable expectations of the parties concerning the timing of the process. A mediator should not allow a mediation to be unduly delayed by the parties or their representatives.

* The presence or absence of persons at a mediation depends on the agreement of the parties and mediator. The parties and mediator may agree that others may be excluded from particular sessions or from the entire mediation process.

* The primary purpose of a mediator is to facilitate the parties' voluntary agreement. This role differs substantially from other professional-client relationships. Mixing the role of a mediator and the role of a professional advising a client is problematic, and mediators must strive to distinguish between the roles. A mediator should therefore refrain from providing professional advice. Where appropriate, a mediator should recommend that parties seek outside professional advice, or consider resolving their dispute

through arbitration, counseling, neutral evaluation, or other processes. A mediator who undertakes, at the request of the parties, an additional dispute resolution role in the same matter assumes increased responsibilities and obligations that may be governed by the standards of other professions.

* A mediator shall withdraw from a mediation when incapable of serving or when unable to remain impartial.

* A mediator shall withdraw from the mediation or postpone a session if the mediation is being used to further illegal conduct, or if a party is unable to participate due to drugs, alcohol, or other physical or mental incapacity.

* Mediators should not permit their behavior in the mediation process to be guided by a desire for a high settlement rate.

VII.   Advertising and Solicitation: A Mediator Shall Be Truthful in Advertising and Solicitation for Mediation.

Advertising or any other communication with the public concerning services offered or regarding the education, training, and expertise of the mediator shall be truthful. Mediators shall refrain from promises and guarantees of results.

COMMENTS:
* It is imperative that communication with the public educate and instill confidence in the process.
* In an advertisement or other communication to the public, a mediator may make reference to meeting state, national, or private organization qualifications only if the entity referred to has a procedure for qualifying mediators and the mediator has been duly granted the requisite status.

VIII. Fees: A Mediator Shall Fully Disclose and Explain the Basis of Compensation, Fees, and Charges to the Parties.

The parties should be provided sufficient information about fees at the outset of a mediation to determine if they wish to retain the services of a mediator. If a mediator charges fees, the fees shall be reasonable considering, among other things, the mediation service, the type and complexity of the matter, the expertise of the mediator, the time required, and the rates customary in the community. The better practice in reaching an understanding about fees is to set down the arrangements in a written agreement.

COMMENTS: * A mediator who withdraws from a mediation should return any unearned fee to the parties.
* A mediator should not enter into a fee agreement which is contingent upon the result of the mediation or amount of the settlement.
* Co-mediators who share a fee should hold to standards of reasonableness in determining the allocation of fees.
* A mediator should not accept a fee for referral of a matter to another mediator or to any other person.

IX.   Obligations to the Mediation Process.

Mediators have a duty to improve the practice of mediation.

COMMENTS: * Mediators are regarded as knowledgeable in the process of mediation. They have an obligation to use their knowledge to help educate the public about mediation; to make mediation accessible to those who would like to use it; to correct abuses; and to improve their professional skills and abilities.

APPENDIX II: CHECKLISTS AND WORKSHEETS

CHECKLISTS AND WORKSHEETS

Table of Contents

Worksheet 1. Power Analysis[*]

Name of Party	1.	2.	3.	4.
Sources of Power (for each party assess type of power possessed by that party) (consider the relative strength of the power source)				
Authority- derives from position within a structure that carries certain decision-making options				
Reward- the perceived or actual ability to grant rewards (money, recognition, promotion, etc.)				
Sanction- the perceived or actual ability to inflict harm or seriously interfere with another's ability to satisfy her/his interests				
Resource- control over things people value ($$$, materials, labor, etc.) Also can be negative...the ability to deny others access to resources or force them to expend them				
Status Quo- Who benefits from the way things are now? It is usually easier to keep things the same than it is to change them				
Procedure- control over the procedures by which decisions are made and actions occur				
Information- comes from knowledge and skill in a particular area or possession of/ access to information about a certain matter				
Nuisance- the ability to cause discomfort, impose costs, or delay others as they attempt to satisfy their interests				
Association- derives from association with other people with power or the creation of power through group action				
Characteristic- comes from individual attributes, e.g. self-assurance, persuasiveness, determination, endurance, & charisma or the ability to invoke moral principles and appeal to values held by others				

[*]For mediators to use as a diagnostic aid to consider the forms of power available to disputants.

The Art of Mediation

Worksheet 2. Interest Analysis[*]

1. Identify Type of Interest to Be Satisfied ☞	Substantive- needs or desires that refer to goods, space, money, resources, security, authority, or quality (the content of the agreement)	Procedural- needs or desires that refer to specific types of behavior, the way things are done, time frames, and methods to be used for input & decision-making	Psychological - the needs or desires that refer to how one feels, how one is treated, "face", image, or conditions for ongoing relationships
2. List Parties ▼	**List interests for each party by type ▼**		
A.			
B.			
C.			
D.			
3. Analyze how parties' interests relate to each other. List interests for all parties by category. ▼			
Shared- satisfying this interest benefits more than one party to the dispute ☞			
Complementary- satisfying this interest for one party does not hurt other parties ☞			
Conflicting- more for one party means less for another (zero-sum) ☞			

----

[*]For mediators to use as a diagnostic aid to identify and compare the interests of the disputants that may need to be satisfied to reach an agreement.

Worksheet 3. Evaluating Offers[*]

✎ What's my last offer to you?	✎ What's your last offer to me?	✎ What are the ± impacts of impasse? *What will happen to me if we don't agree?*
✎ **What's my alternative?** *What will I do if we don't agree?*	✎ **What's your alternative?** *What do I think you will do if we don't agree?*	✓ **Economic-** *What will it cost me in attorney's fees, court costs, other expenses, & the value of my time, if we don't agree?* ✓ **Psychological-** *How will impasse affect me in terms of stress & emotions?* ✓ **Social-** *How will impasse affect my relationships, reputation, & ability to deal with others?*
✎ **What kinds of satisfaction do I want?** ❑ Substantive ❑ Procedural ❑ Psychological	✎ **What kinds of satisfaction do I think you want?** ❑ Substantive ❑ Procedural ❑ Psychological	✓ **Ethical-** *Are there any impacts on my sense of morality, fairness, & doing the right thing?*
✎ **What standards, objective criteria, or principles is my offer based upon?** *What makes my offer fair & reasonable?*	✎ **What standards, objective criteria, or principles is your offer based upon?** *What makes your offer fair & reasonable?*	✓ **Time/Opportunity-** *What effect will impasse have on my ability (time and energy) to pursue other useful activities & keep existing commitments?* ✓ **Other risks/impacts**

---

[*]For mediators to use as a guide to lead disputants through careful consideration of offers BEFORE they accept or reject an offer. If there is a break between sessions, use as a handout to have disputants work through as homework for the next session.

Worksheet 4. Decision Worksheet A[*]

- NO -	Decision Factors- criteria, values, standards, interests, or needs	+ YES +
5 4 3 2 1		1 2 3 4 5
	❶	
	❷	
	❸	
	❹	
	❺	
TOTAL=____		TOTAL=____

[*]For mediators to use by drawing on a flip chart or as a handout to give disputants a structured way to make a YES/NO decision about a specific proposed solution or to be used to evaluate each proposed solution on individual sheets. Take a score for each disputant on each decision factor, e.g. a +5 if one person's response to that factor is strongly affirmative and a -2 for a second person is mildly negative. Then total the positive and negative numeric scores, compare, and use as a basis for more discussion of the disputant's assessment, or compare score sheets on each proposed solution.

Worksheet 5. Decision Worksheet B*

Step 1. List the options to consider. Spend time developing options and possibilities. When you have no option to a proposal by the other party in negotiation, you have very little power. If there are more than 3 options use another sheet. ▶

1.

2.

3.

Step 2. List criteria (decision factors) to weigh in making the decision. Consider all of your interests and needs, e.g. cost, time, reputation, stress level, future economic security, moral principle, attitude toward risk, impact on future relationship, impact on relationship with others, intuition, career potential, environmental impact, etc. ▶

Step 3. Weight the criteria on a 1-5 scale, 5 = most, 1 = least important. Make sure the weights are accurate in relationship to each other. Consider ranking the most important criterion first. ▶

Step 4. Use the criteria to rank the option on a 1-5 scale, based on the level it satisfies that criteria, 1=low, 3= medium, 5=very high. Place this ranking in the box on the left side of this column for each option. ▶

Step 5. Multiply the number obtained in Step 3 by the ranking number in the next column [Step 4] to obtain a weighted score. Place this ▶ score in the box immediately to the right of the ranking. Repeat the process for each option.

		Option 1. Ranking	Option 1. Score	Option 2. Ranking	Option 2. Score	Option 3. Ranking	Option 3. Score
A.							
B.							
C.							
D.							
Total scores for each option- add all #s from Step 5 & compare ☞							

---

*For mediators to use by creating a simplified version on a flip chart and leading one or more disputants through the assessment of options. It can also be used as a handout to give a disputant for work outside of a mediation session to develop and assess their options.

APPENDIX III: FORMS

MEDIATION FORMS

TABLE OF CONTENTS

PART ONE: AGREEMENTS TO MEDIATE

1. **CLIENT INFORMATION**[*]

NITA MEDIATORS, INC.
CLIENT INFORMATION

Q: What is mediation?

Mediation is a voluntary process. An independent, impartial person or persons helps individuals, groups, or organizations who are having conflicts and disagreements to discuss and negotiate resolutions. All parties must agree on the final solution which resolves a dispute through mediation. Therefore, mediation is different from arbitration in which a third party acts as a private judge and makes a decision. It is also different from litigation where lawyers for the parties argue in front of a judge or jury who makes a decision.

Q: Why should I consider mediation?

1.   To increase the odds of an agreement.

The people involved in a dispute (difficult personalities and strong feelings) or the problem underlying a dispute (complex issues and intractable positions) can make it difficult to reach a resolution. Mediators can improve the parties' communications and help them to focus on the real issues with a productive, creative approach. When there is disagreement and conflict, people get locked into positions and fight with each other in ways that are destructive, time-consuming, and costly. All the energy spent on fighting leaves little strength for negotiating effectively and solving the problem. By meeting with the parties, together and separately, mediators can encourage them to explore their interests carefully and search for all possible options. Using mediators increases the likelihood of a negotiated settlement by bringing the skills, creativity, and influence of trained, impartial third parties to bear on the problem.

2.   To save time and money.

When you can't reach a negotiated settlement without assistance, you may feel that filing a lawsuit is your only alternative. The litigation process can be expensive and time-consuming. There are no guarantees of positive

---

[*]This form can be mailed to prospective clients before the contracting stage to provide answers to common questions.

outcomes when you go to court. By pursuing litigation, you risk allowing someone else (a judge or jury) to impose a decision on you. Even after you file a lawsuit, statistics show that 80 to 90 percent of court cases settle before trial. Unfortunately, many of these settlements occur only after the parties have expended significant amounts of money and time in the process. Many of these risks of losing time and money can be avoided if you negotiate a solution directly and retain control over the outcome. Furthermore, a lawsuit can take a year or more just to come to trial, then either side can appeal, so a final resolution may be years away. Also, when a case is being litigated, you must spend time meeting with your lawyer to discuss the status of the case, to prepare for hearings or depositions, and to answer written questions from the other side. The time you spend preoccupied with the details of litigation is time that is unavailable for you to further your personal and organizational goals. Trying mediation before filing a lawsuit is like trying medication to treat a health problem before you have surgery. Litigation, like surgery, is a more extreme choice involving additional cost, time, and risks. We often conclude agreements in mediation within three to six weeks by meeting once a week in one or two hour sessions.

3.   To keep your options open.

If mediation doesn't work, you can still sue and go to court. You can also decide to simply walk away from the problem. Mediation is totally voluntary, and if it's not working, any party can end the process and move promptly into litigation or exercise another option.

4.   To reduce emotional costs.

Not only is litigation expensive and time consuming, but it can be very stressful. You may feel that an important part of your life is on hold while you are waiting for a trial date, wondering and worrying about the outcome. If the parties to the conflict are likely to have to deal with each other in the future, using an adversary process like litigation risks polarizing and embittering their relationship. The emotional wounds from fighting may never heal, and these wounds can complicate the parties' future dealings and make it impossible for them to have a satisfactory relationship.

5.   To develop satisfying, lasting agreements.

When the parties, who know their needs better than anyone else, work together, they can customize a negotiated resolution for their unique situation. Judges and juries don't have any special wisdom or insight that lets them understand the practical and psychological needs you have in your family, school, and business affairs. Also, they may be restricted by legal rules that prevent them from addressing all aspects of your conflict in order to develop a real solution. In mediation, there are no rules that limit your ability to deal with the whole picture. Your agreement can cover both legal and non-legal issues and can be more creative, comprehensive, and on-target than an outcome reached through litigation.

6.   To increase compliance.

It is natural to resent decisions imposed on us by others with power. The goal of mediation is to reach an agreement that everyone can live with after all parties have a direct role in negotiating the terms along with a chance to clear the air. When the parties participate in this way they tend to have not only a sense of legal obligation towards the agreement they reached, but also a psychological sense of commitment as well, because it is their very own agreement. This sense encourages feelings of personal, moral obligation and acceptance of the costs as well as the benefits of the agreement. It is often necessary for one or more of the parties to follow through in some significant way to fulfill the terms of an agreement or a court order. When people voluntarily agree to undertake an obligation, they are more likely to follow through in good faith.

7.   To protect your privacy.

Mediation is a private process. There is no lawsuit filed at the courthouse and listed in the newspaper for friends, employers, employees, bankers, reporters, creditors, or others to notice, wonder about, and discuss. There are no hearings and trials open to spectators. In some disputes no public record of any kind may be necessary.

Q: How does mediation work?

The mediators schedule an initial session with all the parties to answer any questions about the process, to help everyone decide whether to mediate, and if so, to sign a mediation agreement covering the ground rules and the payment of fees and costs. Until this agreement is signed, we cannot discuss the conflict in detail. If everyone decides to sign the mediation agreement, we begin to explore the issues at the initial session. Additional sessions are one to two hours each and are usually scheduled one to two weeks apart. Many conflicts can be resolved in three to six full sessions. Cases involving complex issues and cases with angry, polarized parties often take longer.

Generally, the mediators will meet with all parties together in sessions. But sometimes it can be helpful to meet separately with each party. It may be difficult for the mediators to get an open, honest assessment from one or more parties in front of the others. Also, where the feelings and communications of the parties are particularly difficult and bitter, separate meetings allow the mediators to act as a buffer and keep the parties from escalating the conflict.

The role of the mediators is to move the parties beyond personality clashes and historic grievances. Then the mediators can help the parties to improve communication so any future dealings can take place without repeating the difficulties of the past. By reducing the fighting and petty quarreling, the mediators set the stage for each person to look realistically at their interests and their negotiating positions. Taking some tension out of the parties' communications allows everyone to look at the areas of disagreement in more creative ways to seek previously unconsidered options.

Mediation works because it adds a new dimension to the negotiations. Skilled, experienced mediators can:

- increase communication and direct dialogue without jeopardizing the parties' basic bargaining positions or strategies;
- translate positions and proposals into understandable and straightforward language;
- move discussions into areas that have not been fully explored;
- simplify positions, by helping to identify what is important and what is expendable;
- contribute to each party's understanding of the other's view of the issues;
- set the pace of the negotiations, slowing it down or speeding it up as appropriate;
- encourage constructive movement and conciliatory gestures;
- assist all parties to look realistically at the merits of their positions and assess the likely consequences of the alternatives to a negotiated agreement;
- work to ensure that no one becomes defensive or aggressive due to a misinterpretation or emotional reaction;
- make suggestions to encourage reasonableness, rationality, and constructive, creative proposals.

Q: What are the ground rules for mediation?

We incorporate the rules into the mediation agreement that the parties sign. They cover such basic areas as entering the process with an open attitude, maintaining privacy, refraining from subpoenaing the mediators or their records, and making full disclosure of relevant information. In addition, specific rules can be added by the parties depending on the nature of the dispute.

Q: How can I find qualified mediators?

At this time, our state has no licensing or certification process for mediators although many mediators come from a recognized professional background, such as law, psychology, social work, or accounting. You should ask mediators about their background and what specific training and experience they have that qualifies them to help you. As with most other professions, satisfied clients are the best evidence of competence, so you may wish to ask for client references.

The background of competent, professional mediators should show:

- ▸   thorough knowledge of mediation, negotiation, and conflict resolution theory and practice;
- ▸   a solid understanding of psychology and human relations;
- ▸   excellent communications ability;
- ▸   flexibility, patience and a sense of humor;
- ▸   a demonstrated track record of experience;
- ▸   familiarity with the issues involved in the dispute (or the ability to get up to speed on the issues quickly) because of relevant professional background and knowledge.

Q: What does it cost?

Mediators' fees vary a great deal per case. We charge by the hour for our time. Our rate is $____/hour plus gross receipts tax of about six percent. If the dispute involves a non-profit or community service organization, we will consider donating part of our fee. Our time includes the work we do in mediation sessions, phone conferences, preparation between mediation sessions, and preparation of documents. If the case involves out-of-town travel, we will discuss the additional charges for time spent on a case-by-case basis.

Q: How expensive is mediation compared to other dispute resolution options?

For most disputes there are at least six dispute resolution options for most people to consider. For each option, costs to consider include money, time, and stress. These dispute resolution options include:

1. Negotiating a resolution directly with the other side(s). This is the fastest and least expensive approach. It can be difficult and stressful if the relationship and the communications between the parties are poor.

2. Hiring mediators to help the parties directly negotiate a resolution. This is usually the next least expensive approach. If you spend six hours in mediation (say $900 ÷ 2 = $450/each) and each spend three hours to consult with a lawyer about the mediation ($150/hr x 3 = $450/each), the cost could be about $900 each. If the case is complicated or involves the preparation of court documents and filings, the mediators' fees and the legal fees could be substantially more. It is usually clear after two to three mediation sessions if we are making progress on the issues. The stress level of direct negotiation is decreased by the assistance of skilled mediators, but you must be able to take responsibility for speaking up on your own behalf and making decisions.

3. Hiring lawyers and asking your lawyers to negotiate with each other to attempt to resolve the issue. This approach can be more costly. If you estimate eight hours of time for each lawyer to research the issues, advise the client, and negotiate with the other side ($150/hour x 8) you may spend $1,200 per party. As in mediation, this process can move quickly. The stress level may be lessened because you don't have to deal directly with the other side. It may also be increased, however, because you give up some control over the situation to the lawyers. This option compares favorably to mediation in time and money when both lawyers take a pragmatic, problem-solving approach to the dispute. There is, however, a risk of escalation, if bringing advocates for each party to the negotiating table increases the level of tension and conflict. Some lawyers are excellent problem-solvers ("deal-makers") who know how to defuse situations and negotiate skillfully for constructive, workable, and fair agreements. Other lawyers are aggressive

fighters ("deal-breakers") who posture, maneuver, and argue, eliciting defensive or hostile responses from their counterparts resulting in escalation of the conflict with increased time and expense.

4.   Arbitration. Submission of the dispute to binding arbitration can be a relatively inexpensive route to resolution when one or both sides aren't willing to negotiate. Fees for the arbitration service (if any), the arbitrator(s), and the parties' lawyers can still add up to thousands of dollars. Uncomplicated cases could be resolved in a matter of a few months.

5.   Beginning (or continuing) litigation. It is easy for the cost of this option to reach $10,000 or more per party. In disputes with any kind of complexity, the fees can skyrocket. There is also a real possibility that it can take one to two years to reach a resolution. The stress level can be very high as the issues drag on, the costs mount, and you realize how little control you have over the outcome.

6.   Lumping-it by walking away from the situation with whatever you can salvage. Although this takes little time, the money costs and the stress of this decision may be significant.

Q: How can I keep down the cost of mediation?

To take advantage of the mediation process while minimizing the cost, you must be willing to treat mediation as a priority in your life. Prepare carefully for each session. Promptly gather all of the information we request and keep your agreements to check with other people or produce documents. If you need to consult with your lawyer or tax advisor, do this promptly so you are ready to deal with the issue and make a decision. The more legwork and homework you are willing to do between sessions, the faster the process can move along.

Q: Isn't mediation primarily a labor-management procedure for unions and big corporations that are stuck in negotiations?

In the United States, much of our historic knowledge about mediation comes from the labor-management experience. Beginning 25 to 30 years ago, people in business, community services, and the mental health and legal professions began to use mediation in many different settings. These developments accelerated tremendously in the eighties. Some of these uses of mediation include: divorce and child custody cases; environmental and development disputes; car dealer-customer complaints; construction claims; employee grievances; special education-public schools problems; neighborhood controversies; and complex business litigation. Two major international corporations, IBM and Fujitsu, recently used mediation to resolve a trademark/trade secret dispute involving hundreds of millions of dollars in claims!

A few examples of the kinds of mediation that we have personally conducted include:

- ▶ community problems such as growth/development conflicts, and location of unpopular facilities;
- ▶ a dispute between a producer and director involving property rights to a film;
- ▶ problems among home owners in a planned subdivision regarding restrictive covenants and controversial improvements;
- ▶ divorce and post-divorce issues of custody, property division, tax liability, debts, alimony and child support;
- ▶ corporate problems involving boards of directors fighting over policy and control of organizations;
- ▶ organizational, workplace, and commercial problems including employer-employee disagreements, business owner-manager conflicts, staff problems, and partnership disputes;
- ▶ civil rights and discrimination complaints;
- ▶ a dispute between an architect and a property owner regarding cost overruns and construction quality;
- ▶ family business issues including valuation, succession and inheritance;
- ▶ multi-party and complex disputes before and after litigation has begun.

Q: Are there any cases that shouldn't go into mediation?

Mediation does work, even in difficult and unlikely situations, but it isn't a magic bullet. The parties must have a commitment to work on the dispute and negotiate with each other in order to get through the tough spots. When one or more of the parties is intent on causing physical, financial, or emotional harm to the other, mediation is probably not appropriate. This is particularly true if there is recent history of physical violence and intimidation. If any of the parties has serious, ongoing dysfunctions such as alcoholism or drug addiction, they may not have the level of responsibility required by the mediation process. If one party has significantly more power than the other, it may be difficult to build a fair negotiating process. Yet, generally, any time the parties will be dealing with each other in the future, whether by choice or out of necessity, mediation should be considered as a way to increase the possibility of cooperative future dealings. The importance of the future relationship may justify some risk, even when one or more of the factors just listed are present.

Q: If I participate in mediation do I need to hire a lawyer?

We encourage all our mediation clients to have lawyers with whom they can consult as needed, both before they decide to try mediation and throughout the process. This consultation is particularly critical before signing any legally binding agreement resulting from the mediation. As mediators, we cannot ethically represent any of the parties, and we cannot offer legal advice. When the parties negotiate successfully, we prepare a written summary of the understandings reached in mediation, subject to all parties taking it to their lawyers for review and advice.

The role of the lawyer as advisor and counselor is very important to success in mediation. We think of advice from a knowledgeable lawyer as a form of insurance. This makes sure that all bases have been touched, that you understand the implications of the agreement, and that you are not agreeing to something that is fundamentally unfair to you given your legal rights and responsibilities.

Some cases require court papers that only your lawyer can prepare for you. For example, in a divorce, orders must be prepared for the judge to sign. In pending lawsuits, you may need orders approving the settlement agreement and dismissing the lawsuit. We do not prepare any court papers in connection with mediated agreements.

Q: Should I consider mediation if my lawyer advises against it?

If your lawyer discourages you from trying mediation, make sure you understand his or her concerns and ask common-sense questions. Ask about the lawyer's direct knowledge of the mediation process and how it has worked for clients in the past. Ask whether there are some safeguards that can be built in to the mediation process to address the lawyer's concerns. Carefully consider the alternatives to negotiated settlement. Particularly weigh the advantages and disadvantages of litigation. Ask for an estimate of the odds of success if you litigate, including the possibility of an appeal by the losing party. Assess the length of time it will take to get the matter to trial and the estimated cost of litigating the matter through trial and appeals. Also, remember that trying mediation does not prevent you from going to court if the mediation does not result in a satisfactory agreement. For this reason mediation can be a good place to start. Adversarial representation and the commencement of litigation may increase the level of polarization and bad feeling between the parties. This often leads to the use of aggressive and defensive tactics that make clear communication and constructive negotiation difficult or impossible. When the parties forego the opportunity for direct communication assisted by mediators, they often must rely on a communication chain for current information on the dispute. "I'll tell my lawyer, who will tell your lawyer, who will tell you, and then you will respond by telling your lawyer, who tells my lawyer, who will then tell me." It is easy for communication to be misunderstood or fouled up in this process, handicapping the ability of the parties to search for a resolution.

Finally, after listening to the lawyer's concerns, use your common sense. It's your life. It's your dispute. You, not your lawyer, will live with the consequences of your choice.

2. AGREEMENT TO MEDIATE A[*]

NITA MEDIATORS, INC.

AGREEMENT TO MEDIATE

The parties to this agreement are _____
called "Clients" and _____ and _____
called "Mediators."

Clients want the Mediators to assist them in resolving a dispute
relating to _____. The Mediators have agreed to
work with Clients subject to the following terms and conditions:

ROLE OF THE MEDIATORS

1.   Mediation is a voluntary process. It is an alternative to a decision by
a judge or arbitrator. It is also an alternative to the use of lawyers as
intermediaries to negotiate on behalf of their clients. The role of mediators
is to help their clients engage in constructive and creative communication
about and exploration of the issues to reach a mutually acceptable resolution.
The Mediators will not make decisions about "right" and "wrong" or tell the
Clients what to do.

2.   The Clients have the ultimate responsibility for the content of the
agreement. The Mediators will not advise the Clients to accept or reject an
agreement.

COST OF MEDIATION

3.   The Mediators shall be compensated based upon the amount of time
spent on the case. The rate of compensation is $ _____ per hour plus
applicable tax. The Mediators' time includes all time in mediation sessions
and all time spent outside mediation sessions on research, preparation,
document drafting, and phone conferences.

---

*This form should be sent to the prospective clients before the initial contracting session to give them
the opportunity for careful review and consultation with their attorneys.

4.   In some cases an initial deposit is required. In this case:
□ There shall be an initial deposit. The Clients shall pay a deposit of $_____ at the beginning of the mediation. The Mediators shall use the deposit to pay their fees and reimburse themselves for all out-of-pocket expenses. The Mediators shall promptly refund any amount of the deposit that is unearned at the conclusion of the mediation.
□ There shall not be an initial deposit.

5.   Reimbursable out-of-pocket expenses include long-distance telephone charges, copying costs, mileage at 27.5 cents/mile, special mailing and delivery fees (express mail and messenger). The Clients must approve all travel costs and any other expense item over $15.00 in advance.

6.   The total cost of the mediation shall be shared by the Clients as follows:
□ Divided equally between the Clients.
□ Paid in full by _____.
□ Other: _____.

7.   All sums due under this contract shall be paid to _____. If the Clients request a detailed billing including time records, it will be provided within ten business days. Any sums due that are not covered by an initial deposit shall be paid as follows:
□ At the end of each mediation session
□ Within ten business days of receipt of a statement

FULL DISCLOSURE

8.   Adequate, timely information is essential for the Clients to make informed decisions about the wisdom and fairness of an agreement. Therefore, each Client shall produce all information necessary for the Mediators to understand the issues and for the Clients to negotiate knowledgeably. This includes providing each other and the Mediators with all information and documentation that usually would be available through the discovery process in a lawsuit. The Mediators may require either Client to supplement such information. If necessary information is not available, the Mediators may suspend the mediation until the information is available. The Clients recognize that the failure to make full disclosure may jeopardize the durability of the agreement and permit a court to set it aside.

MEDIATORS' AUTHORITY

9.   The Mediators do not have authority to impose a settlement upon the Clients but will attempt to help them reach a satisfactory resolution of their dispute.

10.   The Mediators may hold joint and separate meetings with the Clients as they deem necessary. The Mediators may discuss any statements made to the Mediators by one Client in a separate session with the other Clients unless the Client making the statement specifically requests that the information remain private.

PRIVACY

11.   Mediation sessions are private. Representatives of the Clients and other persons may attend only with the permission of the Clients and with the consent of Mediators.

12.   In order for mediation to work, open and honest communications are essential. Therefore, all written and oral communications of the Clients will be treated as privileged settlement discussions. As such, they shall not be admissible as evidence in court. Specifically, but without limiting the scope of this paragraph, the Clients agree that they will not rely on or introduce as evidence in any arbitral, judicial or other proceeding:

    a.   views expressed or suggestions made by another Client with respect to a possible settlement of the dispute;

    b.   admissions made by another Client in the course of the mediation proceedings;

    c.   proposals made or views expressed by the Mediators; or

    d.   the fact that another Client had or had not indicated willingness to accept a proposal for settlement made or presented by the Mediators.

13.   The Mediators will not reveal anything discussed in mediation to anyone except the Clients without the permission of all Clients unless they are required to do so by law. The Mediators may be required by law to reveal information if they believe that a child is in need of protection or a person is a danger to self or to others.

14.   At no time shall the Clients call the Mediators or anyone employed by the Mediators as a witness or deponent in any legal or administrative proceeding concerning this dispute. To the extent that they may have a right to call the Mediators or their employees as witnesses, the Clients hereby waive this right.

15.   The Clients shall not subpoena or demand the production of any records, notes, documents, or work product of the Mediators in any legal or administrative proceeding concerning this dispute. To the extent that they may have a right to demand the production of this information, the Clients hereby waive this right.

16.   If any Client causes a subpoena to be issued violating the terms of paragraphs 14 or 15, the responsible Client shall pay the Mediators' reasonable attorneys' fees and costs incurred to resist the subpoena and enforce the privacy terms of this agreement.

17.   There are two exceptions to these privacy provisions. First, this agreement to mediate, and any written agreement made and signed by the Clients, as a result of mediation, may be used in any relevant proceeding, unless the Clients agree in writing not to do so. Second, the Mediators may testify and offer records, notes, or work product from the mediation in any legal or administrative proceeding between the Mediators and a Client regarding the Mediators' fees and services.

MEDIATION, LAWYERS, AND COURT

18.   The Mediators are licensed attorneys in the State of Nita. In helping the Clients in the resolution of their dispute, the Mediators will not act as attorneys for either or both parties. The Mediators may provide legal information that is related to the issues in dispute. If requested by the Clients, the Mediators may prepare a settlement agreement necessary for the resolution of the dispute. If the settlement agreement requires any court documents or legal filings to carry out its terms, the Clients must arrange for preparation of the documents by their attorneys.

19.   The Clients acknowledge that they have been advised by the Mediators that:

    a.   They should each have separate legal representation and should consult privately with their respective attorneys for independent, legal advice. This advice may be necessary prior to signing this mediation agreement, during the mediation process, and prior to signing any agreement for the resolution of the dispute;

    b.   Without review and advice by their own independent, legal counsel they may be giving up legal rights to which they are entitled, or running risks of which they are not aware; and

    c.   They should seek independent tax advice from their attorneys or other qualified tax advisors to assess any possible tax consequences related to the issues involved in the mediation.

20.   The Clients recognize that there may be alternative objective and subjective standards to measure the fairness and effectiveness of a resolution to the issues in dispute. The goal of mediation is a lasting agreement that is acceptable to all participants. The outcome of mediation may be different from the result that could be obtained from a court resolution of the dispute.

TERMINATION

21.   All Clients intend to continue with mediation until reaching a settlement agreement. However, because mediation is a voluntary process any Client may withdraw from mediation at any time. All Clients reserve the option, if a satisfactory settlement is not reached, to pursue other available legal options.

22.   The Mediators may end the mediation if any Client fails to make full disclosure of necessary information.

23.   The Mediators may end the mediation if, in their judgment, further efforts will not contribute to a resolution of the dispute.

STAFFING

24. _____ and _____
shall be the Mediators handling this case.

Signed on the _____ day of _____, 19____.

NITA MEDIATORS, INC.

By: _____   _____

CLIENTS

_____   _____

_____   _____

3. AGREEMENT TO MEDIATE B[*]

NITA MEDIATION CENTER

AGREEMENT TO MEDIATE

This is an agreement between _____,
and _____, the Parties, and Nita Mediation Center
as represented by _____, _____.
The Parties have entered into mediation with Nita Mediation Center with the
intention of reaching a consensual settlement of their dispute regarding

_____

_____.

ROLE OF THE MEDIATORS

1.   The Mediators are neutral facilitators who will assist the Parties to
reach their own settlement. They will not make decisions about "right" or
"wrong" or tell the Parties what to do.

RESPONSIBILITY FOR AGREEMENT

2.   The Parties have the ultimate responsibility for the content of the
agreement. The mediators will not advise the Parties to accept or reject an
agreement.

COST OF MEDIATION

3.   The Parties agree to share the cost of mediation according to the terms
of the attached Fee Agreement.

FULL DISCLOSURE

4.   Full disclosure of all information is essential to the mediation process.
Accordingly, there will be a complete and honest disclosure by each of the
Parties to the other and to the Mediators of all information and documents.
This includes providing each other and the Mediators with all information
and documentation that usually would be available through the discovery
process in a legal proceeding. The Parties recognize that if either of them fails

---

*This form should be used in the same way as Agreement to Mediate A. It provides a simpler
alternative style and separates privacy and fees for the clients' attention.

to make full disclosure, the agreement they reach in mediation may be set aside by a court of law.

ENDING MEDIATION

5.   While both Parties intend to continue with mediation until a settlement agreement is reached, it is understood that either or both Parties may withdraw from mediation at any time. If one or both Parties decide to withdraw from mediation, best efforts will be made to discuss this decision in the presence of both Parties and the Mediators. If the Mediators determine that the issues cannot be resolved through mediation they can terminate the mediation.

AGREEMENT

6.   When an agreement is reached, the Mediators will prepare a Memorandum of Understanding. Each party is advised to review this memorandum with his or her own attorney before the agreement is placed in final form and signed.

MEDIATORS ARE NOT LEGAL ADVISORS

7.   The Mediators DO NOT offer legal advice nor do they provide legal counsel. Each party is advised to retain his or her own attorney in order to be properly counseled about his or her legal interests, rights, and obligations.

The Parties acknowledge that without review and advice by their own independent legal counsel they may be giving up legal rights to which they are entitled, or running risks of which they are not aware.

MEDIATION AND COURT

8.   The Parties understand that the outcome of mediation may be different from the result obtained if the dispute had been resolved in court. The goal of mediation is to obtain an agreement with which both Parties are reasonably satisfied.

The Parties understand, however, that while the mediation process can lead to the settlement of issues, it is not a substitute for the legal process and it will still be necessary for both Parties to go to court, if they wish their agreement to be adopted as an order of the court.

I have read, understand, and agree to each of the provisions of this agreement.

_____   _____
Signature   Signature

_____   _____
Date   Date

Nita Mediation Center

_____   _____
Signature   Signature

_____   _____
Date   Date

NITA MEDIATION CENTER

ADDENDUM TO AGREEMENT TO MEDIATE

PRIVACY AGREEMENT AMONG THE PARTIES AND MEDIATORS

In order for mediation to work, open and honest communications are essential. Accordingly, all written and oral communications, negotiations, and statements made in the course of mediation will be treated as privileged settlement discussions. Therefore, they are not admissible as evidence in court.

The Mediators will <u>not</u> reveal anything discussed in mediation without the permission of both Parties. It is understood that the Mediators, by state law, are required to breach this privacy agreement if they have reason to believe that a child is in need of protection.

The Parties agree that they will not at any time, before, during, or after mediation, call the Mediators or anyone associated with Nita Mediation Center as witnesses or deponents in any legal or administrative proceeding concerning this dispute. To the extent that they may have a right to call the Mediators or anyone associated with Nita Mediation Center as witnesses, that right is hereby waived.

The Parties agree not to subpoena or demand the production of any records, notes, work product, or the like of the Mediators in any legal or administrative proceeding concerning this dispute. To the extent that they may have a right to demand these documents, that right is hereby waived.

There are two exceptions to these privacy provisions. First, this agreement to mediate, and any written agreement made and signed by the Clients as a result of mediation may be used in any relevant proceeding, unless the Clients agree in writing not to do so. Second, the mediators may testify and offer records, notes, or work product from the mediation in any legal or administrative proceeding between the mediators and a client regarding the mediators' fees and services.

I have read, understand, and agree to each of the provisions of this agreement.

_____   _____
Signature   Signature

_____   _____
Date   Date

Nita Mediation Center

_____   _____
Signature   Signature

_____   _____
Date   Date

NITA MEDIATION CENTER

FEE AGREEMENT

FOR MEDIATION

_____ and _____ agree
to pay the fee of _____ per hour plus gross receipts
tax for the services of _____ and _____
who are mediating this dispute for Nita Mediation Center. This fee, which is
due and payable at the end of each session, shall be shared by the Parties as
follows:

_____

_____

_____

_____   _____
Signature   Signature

_____   _____
Date   Date

For Nita Mediation Center

_____   _____
Signature   Signature

_____   _____
Date   Date

PART TWO: FINAL AGREEMENTS

1. WORKPLACE AGREEMENT*

MEDIATED AGREEMENT

between
Janice Jay and Elvis Paul

for and with the participation of
John Long, President

Engineering Manufacturing & Development, Inc. (EMD, Inc.)

I.   Purpose

Dr. Jay is an Engineer III in the Chemical-Nuclear Department of EMD. Dr. Paul is in charge of that department. Dr. Jay has filed a complaint charging Dr. Paul with harassment and discrimination. Dr. Paul has filed a complaint charging Dr. Jay with libel and slander. The purpose of this agreement is to resolve the disputes between the Parties, Dr. Jay and Dr. Paul, to specify the responsibilities of each, and to state the expectations of each regarding these matters.

II.   Goal

The goal of this agreement is to achieve a stable relationship between Dr. Jay and Dr. Paul which maximizes their abilities to be productive members of EMD, Inc. and which minimizes the conflict and poor communication between them.

III.   Two-Year Plan

To effectuate the Purpose and Goal of this agreement, the Parties will follow a plan over the next two years (from July 1, 1991 to June 30, 1993) as described in detail below:

       A.   Communications and Problem Solving

             1.   The Parties agree to emphasize true and positive statements about each other and decrease personal opinion and negative statements about each other in their discussions with peers and staff within EMD, Inc.

             2.   The Parties agree that there shall be no private E-Mail, private memos, private questions, or private discussions between them.

---

*This form is an example of an agreement drafted by the mediators and the parties.

3.   The Parties agree that all communications between them shall be in writing, shall first be screened by Director of Personnel, Bob Dean, and shall be passed on only with Dr. Dean's approval of content, subject, rhetoric and style.

4.   In the event that there is an impasse in communications or a dispute between the Parties that requires resolution, the Parties agree to return to mediation using Nita Mediation Center as Mediators.

5.   The Parties agree that any costs incurred for communication, facilitation, and mediation shall be paid equally by Dr. Paul and Dr. Jay.

B.   Commitments from Dr. Paul and EMD, Inc. to Dr. Jay
1.   Assign two lab assistants, paid for from Department funds for up to two years, to assist in research program development.

2.   Protect lab space from reassignment for two years.

3.   Pay $10,000 per year to her discretionary account for two years to assist in research program development.

4.   Prevent this account from being frozen during the two years.

5.   Forgive $5,000 debt owed by Dr. Jay to EMD, Inc.

6.   Provide Dr. Jay with a full explanation of her current salary level and its justification.

7.   Use mediation to resolve disputes with Dr. Jay.

C.   What is expected of Dr. Jay by the end of the two-year period.
1.   Generate at least $150,000 per year in research funds, which will be used to pay for:
        a.   support of at least two master's level lab assistants,
        b.   support of at least one Ph.D. level lab assistant,
        c.   one-fourth of Dr. Jay's salary, and
        d.   operating expenses.

2.   Publish four articles (or have them accepted for publication) in refereed journals.

3.   Complete two technical presentations per year for each of the two years.

4.   Use mediation to resolve disputes with Dr. Paul.

D.   What is expected of Dr. Paul by the end of the two-year period.
1.   Complete the Gender Equality Institute's seminar, Today's Workplace, or its equivalent.
2.   Commit adequate staff clerical support to Dr. Jay for grant and research activities, to be at least ten hours per week of staff time.
3.   Protect Dr. Jay's overhead account for her control and use (i.e. the account will not be frozen) for the two-year period.
4.   Allocate decisions on Dr. Jay's salary to President Long.
5.   Retain Dr. Jay's present office space.
6.   Retain Dr. Jay's present laboratory space.
7.   Engage in reading, seminars or consultation leading to raised consciousness on the issues faced by professional women and ethnic minorities.
8.   Use mediation to resolve disputes with Dr. Jay.

E.   Evaluation of the Two-Year Plan.
1.   President Long shall evaluate compliance with Section A.
2.   Dr. Dean shall evaluate compliance with Section B.
3.   President Long shall evaluate compliance with Sections C and D.
4.   Compliance will be evaluated at the end of the two year period, that is, no later than June 30, 1993, with written evaluations to be produced no later than July 31, 1993.

IV.   Grievances and Causes of Action.

This Agreement settles all grievances and legal actions which exist or might be raised regarding all interactions between the Parties on or before July 1, 1991, and the Parties hereby release each other, EMD, Inc., and its officers and employees from any claims or legal actions arising from such interactions.

The Parties agree to distribute a public letter of disengagement, conforming with the letter and spirit of the provisions of this Agreement. The public letter of disengagement shall be produced under the process specified in Section III-A-3 above.

V. Violations of this Agreement

If either or both of the Parties or President Long believes that any provision of this agreement has been violated, the following procedures shall be utilized:

1. A written complaint will be distributed to the other two participants in this agreement. The complaint will first be reviewed and edited by the screening person designated in section III-A-3 above.
2. Mediation by the designated Mediators will be scheduled.

_____   _____   _____
Dr. Janice Jay   Dr. Elvis Paul   Dr. John Long

_____   _____   _____
Date   Date   Date

2. TERMINATION AGREEMENT*

Memorandum of Agreement

A.   PURPOSE: Health Care Services, Inc. and Jeff Smith want to provide an orderly end to Jeff Smith's employment as an emergency medical technician.

B.   GOALS:
  1.   Protect the privacy and reputation of all parties.
  2.   Settle all claims and obligations related to Jeff Smith's employment with Health Care Services, Inc.
  3.   Enable Health Care Services, Inc. to carry on its business without interference.

C.   Health Care Services, Inc. (HCSI) and Jeff Smith (JS) agree as follows:
  1.   HCSI shall pay JS $5,000 within ten days of executing a formal settlement agreement and the related documents referred to in this memorandum.
  2.   HCSI shall pay an additional $5,004 in nine equal payments of $556/month beginning on September 1, 1993.
  3.   HCSI shall provide security for the payment of the additional $5,004 by a pledge of the following assets of HCSI: (1) 1983 Dodge Truck valued at $2,500; (2) Johnson Controls brand heart monitor valued at $1,500; (3) CompuAdd 486 SX computer with monitor valued at $1,000.
  4.   JS shall release his security in these assets as the value of the payments made equals the value of the pledged asset. HCSI shall specify the item that they wish to have released.
  5.   JS shall provide a full release of all claims against HCSI for medical expenses, legal expenses, punitive damages, disability, wrongful termination, or any other cause of action arising from his employment at HCSI.
  6.   HCSI agrees that it will not disclose any information to potential future employers about the conditions of JS's employment or discharge.
  7.   JS agrees that he will in no way affiliate with or identify himself as associated with HCSI.

---

*This form is an example of a mediation settlement memorandum drafted by the mediators and the parties that will be used by the parties' attorneys to prepare additional documents.

8.   JS agrees that he will not initiate any contact with HCSI, its business premises, or its on-duty, uniformed employees. Any communication between the Parties shall be through their attorneys, their representatives, or by mail. HCSI agrees that it will not direct any of its employees to initiate any contact with JS.

9.   JS shall provide an address for payments to HCSI within ten days of the date of this agreement.

10.   The Parties shall direct their respective attorneys to cooperate in preparing and reviewing all of the documents necessary to implement the intent of this Memorandum of Agreement. HCSI's attorney shall prepare the release and settlement agreement. JS's attorney shall prepare the security pledge agreement.

Signed the _____ day of _____, 199__.

_____   _____

Jeff Smith   Health Care Services, Inc.
                                          By: Sarah Ball, Its President

3. **BUSINESS DISSOLUTION***

AGREEMENT

The Parties to this agreement are Stephen Aims (Steve) and Kathy White (Kathy).

A. PURPOSE — Kathy and Steve want to resolve the last remaining issue from their business partnership that dissolved on December 15, 1988.

B. GOALS —
   1. Sell the parcel of real estate in Nita County (the Nita property). The legal description of this property is attached hereto as Exhibit A, incorporated herein by reference.
   2. Make specific arrangements for division of the proceeds of the sale and disposition of some debts that relate to the property.

C. TERMS OF AGREEMENT —
   1. The Parties will promptly place the Nita property on the market for sale subject to the following terms and conditions:
       a. For forty (40) days from the date of this agreement, the Parties will list the Nita property for sale by owner. Within ten (10) days from the date of this agreement, Steve will notify the present tenant of the property and offer to sell the property to him for the sale price of eighty-eight thousand dollars ($88,000). Steve and Kathy will also arrange for a "For Sale" sign to be placed on the property and an ad to be placed in the newspaper of general circulation in Nita County, within ten (10) days of the date of this agreement.

---

*This form is an example of a final agreement drafted by the mediators with the parties' involvement.

b.   If the Nita property is not under contract within forty (40) days from the date of this agreement, Steve and Kathy agree to sign a listing agreement with a licensed Realtor in the Nita area. Steve and Kathy will contact potential Realtors and confer on the Realtor to handle the property for the Parties. The initial listing price for the property shall be ninety-three thousand dollars ($93,000) unless the Parties mutually agree on a different listing price.

c.   If the property is not under contract to sell within ninety (90) days from the date of this agreement, the Parties agree that the initial listing price may be reduced from $93,000 to $90,000. Any further reduction in the listing price must be mutually agreed upon.

d.   Any offers to buy that involve owner financing must be agreed to by both Parties. Any other terms that do not involve normal and usual terms of sale in Nita County area must be mutually agreed upon.

e.   Any out-of-pocket expenses incurred by either party in order to repair the property prior to sale shall be reimbursed to that party out of the sale proceeds if the Parties agree in advance in writing that the expense is necessary and the party incurring the expense produces receipts to document the expense.

2.   The proceeds from the sale of the house shall be used as follows:

a.   All reasonable and necessary costs of sale shall be paid including:

1.   Closing and escrow fees
2.   Realtor's commission
3.   Title insurance and binder fees
4.   Survey cost (if required by contract of sale)
5.   Tax prorations
6.   Recording fees

b.   Debts to be paid include:

1.   Mortgages owed in the amount of $42,000 (estimated figure).

2. Eighteen thousand dollars ($18,000) owed to Kathy's father, J.R. White. This sum represents $15,000 in principal and $3,000 in interest (reduced from approximately $9,000 in interest) owing on a promissory note signed by both Parties.

c. Any amounts due to the Parties for repair expenses under the terms of paragraph 1.e.

d. The remaining amount shall be divided equally between the Parties.

3. Kathy shall deliver a check in the amount of $5,000.00 to Steve paying in full a debt she owes under the partnership dissolution agreement. This shall take place at the same time as the funds from the closing are paid to the Parties.

4. Steve and Kathy agree to fully cooperate with each other, real estate agents, title company employees, and any other Parties necessary to market, sell, and close on the Nita property. This agreement includes promptly signing and returning documents necessary to the selling process.

5. This agreement has been executed in the State of Nita and shall be governed by its laws. The agreement represents the complete agreement of the Parties. The payment of the money provided for herein and the fulfillment of the other terms of this agreement constitutes a full and final settlement of all of the claims that the Parties have against each other. All Parties have read this agreement carefully, have had the opportunity to consult with independent legal counsel, and have signed the same voluntarily. No amendment of this agreement shall be effective unless in writing and signed by both Parties. The agreement shall be binding on the heirs, successors, and assigns of the Parties.

6. If any disagreements arise that Steve and Kathy are unable to resolve, they will contact Nita Mediation Service and meet for at least one two-hour session to attempt to resolve the issue(s) before pursuing other action.

Signed November _____, 1991.

_____
Kathy White

_____
Steve Aims

STATE OF NITA

COUNTY OF NITA

The foregoing instrument was acknowledged before me this _____ day of November, 1991, by Stephen Aims.

_____
Notary Public

My commission expires:

_____

STATE OF NITA

COUNTY OF NITA

The foregoing instrument was acknowledged before me this _____ day of November, 1991, by Kathy White.

_____
Notary Public

My commission expires:

_____

4.   PARTNERSHIP DISSOLUTION[*]

Agreement

This agreement is between Sean (Sean) Wilson and Toby (Toby) Washington.

A.   Purpose

Sean and Toby want to end their business partnership with an agreement that is fair and mutually acceptable.

B.   Goals

1.   We want to minimize disruption and inconvenience to our existing customers.
2.   We want to protect the privacy of our financial affairs.
3.   We want to preserve our respective professional reputations in the community.
4.   We want to treat each other with respect and acknowledge the mutual work and effort that has led to our success.

C.   Steps We Will Take to Dissolve the Business

1.   We formed the partnership, Blue Sky Builders, on August 26, 1991 in the State of Nita. As of April 30 of this year, we will stop doing business as Blue Sky Builders, a partnership organized and doing business in River City, Nita. Neither of us shall use the name after that date.
2.   We shall pay all current liabilities as of April 30 out of our operating bank account at First Bank. This shall include all payroll taxes. Other than current bills and payroll taxes we do not have any other liabilities.
3.   On April 30, we shall divide the assets of the business as follows:
Sean shall receive as his sole property:
    a.   Ford F250 4x4 pickup
    b.   IBM Pentium computer system and all system and business software
    c.   Lots 5-12 in the Sierra del Sur subdivision
    d.   Bobcat loader

---

[*]This form is an example of a final agreement drafted by the mediators and the parties.

     e.   One-half the cash balance in the operating account at First Bank after payment of the current liabilities

Toby shall receive as her sole property:

     a.   Chevrolet Blazer 4x4 utility vehicle
     b.   Hewlett Packard 4 printer
     c.   Lots 4, 14, 16-19 in the Sierra del Sur subdivision
     d.   All of the power and personal tools owned by the business (saws, hammers, shovels, measures, levels, joiners, power cords, etc.)
     e.   All remaining building materials stored in the storage shed on Lot 4 of the Sierra del Sur subdivision
     f.   One-half the cash balance in the operating account at First Bank after payment of the current liabilities

4.   On May 1, of this year, each of us will arrange to have Pat Baca, vice president of First Bank, issue a new loan for one-half the current balance of our development loan that is secured by the unsold lots of the Sierra del Sur subdivision. This loan number is 5675643. Pat has agreed verbally and in writing to do this. The principal balance on April 30, will be $67,540.00 so each one of us will be personally responsible for the payment of $33,770.00. The note that First Bank will write in each of our names will be secured only by the Lots in the subdivision that belong to that individual under the terms of this agreement. Neither of us will have any responsibility or liability for the debt of the other.

5.   Our business attorney, Fran Joseph, shall file all required notices to dissolve the business with regulatory and governmental authorities. We will also request that she prepare any additional documents necessary to carry out the letter and spirit of this agreement. We anticipate that this bill will not be available when we divide the business cash on April 30. The bill for this work shall be divided equally and each of us shall pay his or her one-half of the bill.

6.   Our business accountant, Gene Kozloski, shall prepare any tax filings necessary for dissolving the business. We anticipate that this bill will not be available when we divide the business cash on April 30. The bill for this work shall be divided equally and each of us shall pay his or her one-half of the bill.

7.   Each of us shall be responsible for paying one half of any tax liability for this or previous years for the business.

8.   Each of us shall be responsible for paying one half of any liability for any business debt, negligence, or mistake that may arise related to our operation of Blue Sky Builders. If either of us receives any notice of a claim that may result in liability, s/he will notify the other in writing within five business days.

9.   Toby shall retain all of the building plans for past projects in her possession. Sean may have access to them at any time during business hours for the next six months. He may take any plans that he wishes to copy at his expense, returning the original to Toby within ten business days.

10.   Sean shall retain all photographs, negatives, and original advertising layouts for the business' construction projects in his possession. Toby may have access to them at any time during business hours for the next six months. She may take any plans that she wishes to copy at her expense, returning the originals to Sean within ten business days.

11.   The business shall pay for an ad to be placed in *The Daily Star* on April 23, to run for one week. This ad shall announce the friendly dissolution of the business and the new address and phone number of each of the new respective businesses.

12.   On April 15, we will send out a letter to former customers, announcing the dissolution and providing our new addresses and phone numbers. Toby will prepare this letter and Sean will approve and sign it before it is sent out.

D.   Comments to Former Customers

1.   Each of us is entitled to maintain a good professional image in the community.

2.   In spite of the our personal disagreements about working styles, we acknowledge the professionalism and skill that each of us has contributed to our business.

3.   We agree that we will refrain from making any negative or critical remarks about the other to customers, suppliers, employees, subcontractors, real estate agents, or lenders.

4.   If anyone asks either of us why the partnership is dissolving, we agree to respond by stating, "We want to pursue individual opportunities and made a mutual decision to part ways. I respect Toby/Sean and wish him/her well."

E.   Dealing With Future Disputes

1.   If we have any disagreements that we cannot resolve ourselves, we agree to return to mediation with Cina Cervantes and Tom Radmiller, and to try, for at least four hours of mediation, to reach an agreement.

2.	If we still cannot resolve the disagreement, we agree to submit any remaining issues to binding arbitration within thirty days from the last mediation session. We will use Jean Chen, an attorney who specializes in business organizations, as the sole arbitrator. If we cannot agree on the rules of the arbitration, we shall use the Commercial Rules of the National Arbitration Forum. If Jean Chen is unavailable or unwilling to act as our arbitrator, we will ask the National Arbitration Forum to appoint an arbitrator.

_____

Sean Wilson

_____

Date

_____

Toby Washington

_____

Date

5. NEIGHBORHOOD DEVELOPMENT AGREEMENT[*]

Agreement Between
Global Development, Inc. And
Westside United Neighborhood Association

The parties to this agreement are Global Development, Inc. (GDI), a Delaware corporation registered to do business in the State of Nita and Westside United Neighborhood Association (Westside), a chartered neighborhood association certified by River City to intervene in zoning and development matters before the Urban Policy Board.

A. Purpose

Westside and GDI want to clarify GDI's plans for a business office park development named WestPark Center (WPC) and the position Westside will take on these plans at an upcoming meeting of the Urban Policy Board of River City. In response to concerns raised by Westside, GDI has revised its original plan submission. GDI will present its revised development plan at the next Urban Policy Board meeting, and wants Westside to support this revised plan.

B. Goals

1.   Westside and GDI want to ensure that the residents of the Westside neighborhood continue to enjoy their homes without any decrease in property values.
2.   GDI and Westside wish to establish a good working relationship so that future concerns can be addressed promptly and effectively.
3.   Westside and GDI want to establish clear procedures to be used by GDI during the construction period of WPC to minimize any disruption of the peace and quiet enjoyment of the Westside residents.
4.   Westside, its residents, and GDI want to acknowledge that each side has dealt with each other in good faith during the negotiation of this agreement with the mediation assistance of Sandora Volcanzik.

C. Submission of the Revised Development Plan for WPC

1.   GDI currently has a development plan for WPC pending before the Urban Policy Board of River City.

---

[*]This form is an example of a final agreement drafted by the mediators and the parties.

2. GDI shall revise the original plan by making the following specific changes:

   a. The total square feet of building space (the "footprint") of the buildings in WPC shall be reduced by 25% from 100,000 to 75,000 square feet.

   b. The main vehicle entrance for WPC shall be changed from 2nd Street to Elm Street.

   c. There shall not be any vehicular ingress or egress from or to 2nd Street.

   d. GDI shall remove any exterior lighting poles and fixtures in excess of ten feet in height that are located within fifty yards of 2nd Street. Any exterior lighting within fifty yards of 2nd Street that GDI believes is necessary for basic building security shall be directed or shielded so Westside residents' property is not significantly impacted.

   e. GDI shall donate a 5,000 square foot parcel of land in the northwest corner of the project to River City for use as a playscape by the general public. GDI shall donate $50,000 to the Recreation Development Fund of River City as an earmarked donation for the purchase of equipment. Prior to donation of the land, GDI, at its expense, shall grade and prepare the site to the specifications of the Recreation Department of River City. After the playscape equipment is installed, GDI shall, at its expense, landscape the site with grass, sand, and trees.

3. GDI shall specify in its development plan that there will be no construction activity after 6 p.m. or before 7 a.m.

4. The Board of Directors of GDI has authorized its Senior Vice President for Development to enter into this agreement.

D. Westside's Position Before the Urban Policy Board

1. Westside shall support the revised development plan with formal testimony provided by an authorized spokesperson.

2. Westside shall specifically request that the WPC development plan, as revised, be approved by the Urban Policy board, and that the issuing of a final permit be expedited so construction can be completed within 18 months in the interest of Westside residents.

3. Westside has reviewed the terms of this agreement with its Board and its membership at a special meeting called in accordance with its bylaws. Its president has been specifically authorized to accept the terms of this agreement.

4. Westside contacted the Recreation Department of River City and received preliminary assurance that the donation of land, equipment, and landscaping for the playscape will be accepted by River City as a charitable donation.

E. Maintaining a Good Working Relationship

1. Westside agrees to accept GDI as a new neighbor with goodwill and to cooperate with GDI as it phases in its operations.
2. Westside shall send a mailing to all resident members announcing this agreement, asking for cooperation, and listing a Westside contact person for any concerns or complaints by residents relating to WPC.
3. Westside shall notify GDC, through its Community Relations Liaison, Jan Topadoria, of any concerns that it receives from residents and will relay information on GDC's response or solution to the Westside member(s) who expressed the concerns.
4. Westside shall designate a primary contact and an alternate, with day and evening phone numbers, so GDC can communicate regularly about project issues that arise.
5. Westside shall include a WPC project update in its regular monthly mailing to members. GDC shall prepare this update and provide 600 copies to Westside at GDC's expense. Westside must receive the update on or before the 25th day of the month in order to include it in the mailing that goes out on the 1st of the next month.

F. Dealing with Future Disputes

1. Westside and GDC agree that any concerns or problems that either has with the other will be brought to the other's attention prior to the concerned party seeking any legal or administrative relief.
2. Westside and GDC believe that they can cooperate in good faith to ensure the successful completion of WPC with minimal disruption to Westside's members. If any problems arise that cannot be informally resolved with contact between GDC's Community Relations Liaison and the officers of Westside, the parties agree to schedule a mediation session within five business days with Sandora Volcanzik, or a substitute mediator agreeable to both parties.
3. If there is no satisfactory resolution in mediation, the parties retain all their options to proceed to seek legal redress.

Global Development, Inc.

By: _____   _____
 Pat Johancourt, Sr. Vice President   Date

Westside United Neighborhood Association

By: _____   _____
 Gene Watkins, President   Date

6. SMALL CLAIMS CONSUMER AGREEMENT[*]

**NITA CITY
METROPOLITAN COURT
MEDIATION CENTER**

Mediation Between: Roy Jones of Roofers, Inc. and Mary Smith

Was Held: This Twenty-First Day of March

With Mediator(s):   Elizabeth Charles and Alfonso Trujillo

The Parties have agreed to the following to settle their dispute about the new roof and front and rear porches which Roofers, Inc. installed for Mary Smith.

—   Mr. Jones and Ms. Smith will inspect the roof together and agree on what needs to be done.

—   Roofers, Inc. will not use Steve or Luis for any repairs to or continuation of the job.

—   The blisters and delaminations will be repaired as agreed after the inspection.

—   Additional gravel will be added to the roof as required/agreed (minimum of 1½ inches on house/none on garage).

—   Mr. Jones will inspect the roof at six-month intervals throughout the warranty period and will call in advance to make appointments for the inspections.

—   The walls will be recoated and stucco applied to achieve a 30-mil brown color.

---

[*]This form is an example of a simple final agreement drafted by the mediators and the parties in a court-annexed program.

— The front and rear porches will have 4-inch strips of trim adhered to the parapets and perforated L-shape gravel stops will be added.

— The inspections will be scheduled by April 1.

— This agreement applies to both the house and the garage.

— Mr. Jones will extend the original warranty for one year from the time that the agreed upon repairs are completed.

— Mr. Jones will pay Ms. Smith $354.57 for the costs she incurred in this matter.

— Upon completion of the terms of this agreement, Ms. Smith will dismiss the lawsuit she filed against Roofers, Inc.

Signed this 25th day of March, 1996.

Parties:

_____   _____

Mediators:

_____   _____

we help people resolve conflicts

7. SMALL CLAIMS NEIGHBORHOOD AGREEMENT*

NITA CITY
METROPOLITAN COURT
MEDIATION CENTER

Mediation Between: Joe and Susie Talbot and Frank and Gail Gordon

Was Held: This Fifteenth Day of October

With Mediator(s):   Dennis Watson and Nancy Larson.

The Parties have agreed to the following to settle their dispute about neighborhood noise:

— Joe and Susie will let out their dog, Snipe, no earlier than 7 a.m.

— Joe and Susie will bring Snipe in by 10 p.m. They will call Frank and Gail before 10 p.m. if there is a problem with bringing Snipe in on time.

— Frank and Gail will call Joe and Susie if Snipe is still barking after 10 p.m. Frank and Gail will not call animal control without talking to Joe and Susie first.

— Joe and Susie authorize Frank and Gail to continue to spray water from their hose to control Snipe's barking during the day.

— Frank and Gail will not let their children make noise in the yard outside their house on weekdays after 10 p.m.

---

*This form is an example of a simple final agreement drafted by the mediators and the parties in a court-annexed mediation program.

—   Joe and Susie will complain to Frank and Gail about their children making noise only if they are making noise after 10 p.m. weekdays or if they damage Joe and Susie's yard.

—   Both families will get back together in one month to determine if Snipe is barking less and if the schedule is working. If there still is a problem, Joe and Gail will take Snipe to the vet and get an anti-bark-collar. At this meeting, they will also determine if noise from Frank and Gail's children has continued to be a problem. If so, Frank and Gail will institute a 9:00 p.m. curfew for their children.

Signed this 18th day of March, 1996.

Parties:

_____   _____

Mediators:

_____   _____

we help people resolve conflicts

APPENDIX IV: SELECTED BIBLIOGRAPHY

Selected Bibliography

The body of mediation literature is expanding rapidly. It is easy for a beginner to be overwhelmed with the choices for reading. Therefore, we have only included a few of the many possible references for the student of the mediation process. After each entry, we provide a brief description of the book's features. The entries are in alphabetical order by title. In specialized areas of mediation practice such as divorce and multiparty cases, we have selected only one entry to help you to begin your investigation.

Dispute Resolution: Negotiation, Mediation, and Other Processes, Second Edition Stephen Goldberg, Frank Sander, and Nancy Rogers, Little Brown and Company, 1992.

This is a comprehensive resource. It is the most widely used law school text. Mediation is placed in the context of the other dispute resolution mechanisms. There are special sections on mediation in the family, public policy, and international contexts. The chapter on negotiation is a good introduction to this area.

Divorce Mediation: Theory and Practice Jay Folberg and Ann Milne, Guilford Press: New York, 1988.

This compilation of articles by leading American practitioners is a good introduction to the specialized area of family mediation practice. Philosophy, theory, techniques, research and applications are covered. The organization of the book makes it easy to find particular topics of interest. Chapter Eleven on Lawyer and Therapist Team Mediation raises important issues for anyone interested in family mediation.

Facing Racial and Cultural Conflict: Tools for Rebuilding Community (Second Edition) Lester P. Schoene and Marcelle E. DuPraw, Program for Community Problem-Solving: Washington, D.C., 1994.

Mediators are beginning to grapple seriously with the issues of power, culture, and diversity. This book looks at conflict in communities and institutions and discusses the cultural assumptions that underlie the predominant model of mediation in the United States. Case situations for different process models are examined, including a New York Latino community, a San Francisco gay community, communities in Hawaii, Native American communities in urban settings, and communities in China.

Getting Disputes Resolved: Designing Systems to Cut the Costs of Conflict William Ury, Jeanne Brett, and Stephen Goldberg, Jossey-Bass: San Francisco, 1988.

   This is the first comprehensive resource offering ways to look at organizational systems to improve the way conflicts are processed, managed, and resolved. The role of mediator as designer of dispute systems is growing. There is an active exchange between the fields of mediation and organization development about creating and implementing systems for institutions to deal productively with interpersonal and group conflict.

Getting Past No: Negotiating with Difficult People William Ury, Bantam: New York, 1991.

   This may be the best book out on negotiation. It is clear, well-written and behaviorally specific. Ury provides many examples from personal, business, organizational, and international settings.

Getting to Yes: Negotiating Agreements Without Giving In, Second Edition Roger Fisher and William Ury, Penguin: New York, 1991.

   This is the classic text on principled or collaborative negotiation. It is an excellent introduction to the principles of cooperation in negotiation. The original edition was criticized by some as being a bit too simplistic, avoiding the hard questions about dealing with power and dirty tricks. This edition includes a section called *Ten Questions People Ask About Getting to Yes* that addresses some of these concerns.

Managing Public Disputes: A Practical Guide to Handling Conflict and Reaching Agreements Susan Carpenter and W.J.D. Kennedy, Jossey-Bass: San Francisco, 1988.

   The authors are veteran practitioners in the field of environmental and public policy conflicts. These issues usually involve complex situations with many participants. After providing a brief theoretical construct and a set of guiding principles, the book describes a step-by-step approach for addressing public, multiparty disputes.

Mediation: A Comprehensive Guide to Resolving Conflicts Without Litigation Jay Folberg and Alison Taylor, Jossey-Bass: San Francisco, 1984.

This book provides a good overview of mediation history and the modern process as practiced in the United States. The authors describe seven stages that are functionally equivalent to the stages in our materials. Chapter six, "Diverse Styles and Approaches to Mediating Conflict" is a good overview of the diverse behavior that practitioners call mediation. The information on ethnic and sociocultural perspectives in chapter thirteen was an early attempt to raise issues of diversity and difference.

Mediation: Law, Policy, Practice, Second Edition Nancy Rogers and Craig McEwen, Clark Boardman Callaghan: Deerfield, Illinois, 1994.

This is a legal desk reference for lawyers and mediators. In addition to some general information about mediation practice and approaches to mediation, it provides an extensive appendix on legislation. Its strengths are the sections on ethics, legal policy, and advising clients about mediation.

The Mediation Process: Practical Strategies for Resolving Conflict Christopher Moore, Jossey-Bass: San Francisco, 1986.

This book was one of the first detailed examinations of mediation in the United States in the modern era (after 1980). The author goes into great detail on the stages of mediation. His twelve stages surpass the number of stages we teach, although the functional pieces are similar to ours. Chapter seven, "Building Trust and Cooperation" is a very good section on an intangible and essential part of the mediators' work.

Negotiating at an Uneven Table: Developing Moral Courage in Resolving Our Conflicts Phyllis Beck Kritek, Jossey-Bass: 1994.

The author is a nurse, health care administrator, and educator. Her book offers a conceptual framework to deal with disputes within hierarchical systems where present and historical inequity (real and perceived) is a factor in the situation. In addition to discussing the moral and ethical dimensions of power imbalances, Kritek offers possible answers to these dilemmas. Mediators who work in organizational settings must be sensitive to the dynamics of power and how these dynamics can play out during the mediation.

The Promise of Mediation Robert Baruch Bush and Joseph Folger, Jossey-Bass: San Francisco, 1994.

This is a controversial addition to the literature that has catalyzed a great deal of discussion. The authors describe in detail the competing mediation philosophies of outcome (or settlement) and process (or transformation/ relationship). They clearly advocate for the transformative role for the mediator. This role emphasizes the mediators' responsibility to empower the parties to act in their own interests and recognize each other as individuals with legitimate needs and interests. The authors' advocacy serves us by prompting mediators to ask some basic questions of themselves: "What is our philosophy?", "Does my style and approach to mediation empower participants?", "Do participants understand and consent to my agenda for the mediation process?"

When Talk Works: Profiles of Mediators Deborah M. Kolb et al., Jossey-Bass: San Francisco, 1994.

This book provides a behind the scenes look at experienced mediators in family, community, international, commercial and public disputes to show us how they really work. Contributors observed the mediators, interviewed them about their work, and reviewed transcripts and tapes of their subjects' mediation sessions to develop a basis for understanding each mediator's philosophy and style. The editor offers a critical view of the gap between the myths and the realities of mediation practice. The book also demonstrates the diversity of styles and philosophies in the field.

SECTION SIX: ROLE PLAYS

ROLE PLAYS

TABLE OF CONTENTS

Role Play Observer Checklist
(use this to make notes about the co-mediators as you watch)

What to Look for by Stage:	Name of Mediator 1:	Name of Mediator 2:
	_____	_____

Contracting

Get parties seated & comfortable

Give clear & complete explanation

Answer any questions

Establish rapport & confidence

Check suitability (stress & conflict levels, ripeness, commitment to the process)

Note possible mutualities

Get agreement signed

Information Gathering and Issue Identification

Emphasize open-ended questions

Elicit facts & feelings

Use active listening (paraphrasing, summarizing, reframing, open responses)

Take the time to establish clarity and understanding

Keep balance between the parties (time, taking turns)

Cut off disputants if needed (personal attacks, dominance, running on, interrupting)

Manage the interaction between disputants (defuse hostility, reframe destructive comments)

Begin to uncover underlying needs & interests (substantive, procedural, psychological)

Permit/encourage expression of feelings

Frame issues neutrally

Ensure issues are clear, complete & confirmed

Discover & acknowledge mutualities

Agenda Setting

List issues clearly using flip chart or alternative

Select method to set agenda

Elicit principles for decision making

Resolving Each Issue

Discover additional information if necessary

Generate options (brainstorming [quantity], other methods)

Explore needs/interests to be met by options

Evaluate options (use principles developed earlier, check alternatives to negotiated agreement, look at consequences of impasse)

Negotiation process (build on mutualities, dovetail differences, manage concessions/compromises, develop packages/trade-offs)

Intervene to balance power. How?

Use of caucus (timing, length, strategies)

Acknowledge agreements & effort of parties

Reviewing Agreements

Combine agreements on issues

Reality-test overall agreement and parts for durability and satisfaction

Confirm terms & check commitments

Overall Things to Watch for

Demeanor and behaviors

Non-verbal signals (neutral, appropriate language, absence of jargon, humor, attentiveness, active listening)

Interaction & cooperation of co-mediators

What did you learn from your observation of the role play?

What mediator behaviors were most helpful in moving the parties along?

JONES AND SMITH

I. JONES AND SMITH

MEDIATOR INFORMATION

This is a private mediation. The case was referred to you by the parties' attorneys. It involves a threat of litigation between neighbors.

The disputants' names are John and Joan Smith (husband and wife) and Willa Jones and Tommie Jones (grandmother and grandchild). Either John or Joan Smith will represent the Smiths and Tommie Jones will represent the Jones at the mediation.

The disputants came to mediation because their lawyers have advised them to do so.

The disputants have received your extensive mediation information (Client Information Form) and mediation agreement (Agreement to Mediate B).

Keep your actual professional identity.

Your fee is $120/hour, payable at the end of each session.

BACKGROUND INFORMATION

The Jones family has lived in the same home on an eight acre farm in the South Valley for the past 30 years. Mrs. Willa Jones is a widow. She lives with her 23 year old grandchild Tommie. Due to a medical emergency last year, Mrs. Jones was forced to sell part of her property to pay her hospital bills. The purchasers were Dr. John Smith and his wife Joan, who bought five acres of the Jones property including an old abandoned adobe house. They purchased the property on a real estate contract ($110,000 total, to be paid in monthly installments over ten years at eight percent interest). They moved in a trailer and began to restore the old adobe.

There has been repeated friction between the Jones and the Smiths ever since the Smiths moved in. First, the Smiths tore down the old fence between the two properties and replaced it with a six foot chain link fence. The Jones complained that this was a zoning violation, and the Smiths countered that the Jones' old storage shed was a hazardous eyesore. Then, the Jones had a big Fourth of July party and several firecrackers exploded in the Smith's chicken coop. Next, the Smiths called animal control and reported that Tommie Jones was abusing his/her dog. Meanwhile, the Jones repeatedly complained to the Smiths that their dogs were running loose, trespassing throughout the neighborhood, and terrorizing the Jones' family and animals.

One night, two months ago, Tommie left his/her grandmother's property and instead of going out the driveway to the street, s/he took his/her truck the back way on an old dirt irrigation road that crosses the back of the property purchased by the Smiths. As s/he neared the Smiths' house, s/he was gunning the engine and had the radio up full blast. The access road was muddy from recent rains and s/he lost control of the vehicle when the Smiths' prize winning potbellied pig, Veronica, dashed out in front of the truck. Tommie hit the pig, slid off the road, and ran over $500 worth of trees that the Smiths had planted the week before. Veronica suffered a broken leg, and the vet bills were $600. Tommie hit the steering wheel and suffered some facial lacerations and bruises. After the accident, s/he ran to the house, woke his/her grandmother, and called the Smiths. They came right over; Dr. Smith cleaned Tommie's minor cuts while Joan tended to Veronica. Dr. Smith noticed that Tommie's eyes were bloodshot and that s/he smelled strongly of alcohol.

One week after the accident, the Smiths presented the Jones with a bill for $1,100 covering the cost of the trees and the vet bills. When the Jones refused to pay, the Smiths withheld $1,100 from their regular monthly real estate payment. They also put up a fence cutting off the Jones' access to the old dirt road.

The Jones' attorney has sent a demand letter to the Smiths advising them that they are delinquent on the real estate contract, summarizing the interest and penalties that are due ($1,200 monthly payment, $250 interest and penalty), and threatening to take legal action to have the barrier on the access road removed. The Smiths' lawyer wrote back enumerating their damages, demanding $1,500 and an apology, and threatening to sue for the full value of Veronica ($7,000) unless the Smiths are reimbursed immediately. After the two attorneys talked on the phone, each recommended that their respective clients try mediation first, before filing suit. The parties agreed to attempt mediation and were referred to you.

CONTRACTING INSTRUCTIONS

Dr. John or Mrs. Joan Smith

You are here by yourself because your husband/wife has an extremely busy work schedule and does not have time to come. You feel perfectly capable of handling this matter alone. Your lawyer has encouraged you to negotiate for "whatever you can get" because the legal wrangling over these issues will cost far more than the amounts at stake. You have authority to handle this mediation in whatever way seems best. You would like to stay out of court and find a way to resolve all these problems in the neighborhood.

INFORMATION GATHERING AND ISSUE IDENTIFICATION

Dr. John or Mrs. Joan Smith

Emotional Facts:

This situation is the last straw! Your neighbor was drunk and driving recklessly. S/he destroyed your property, injured your exotic pig Veronica, and now you are being threatened with lawsuits. Those Jones have been out to get you since the day you moved in. What kind of people are they anyway? They sell you the property, take your money, and then they use explosive fireworks in an effort to murder your chickens, they try to stop the beautification of your farm by calling the county zoning board, and now this person is trying to weasel out of responsibility and ruin your enjoyment of your property. To top it off, you have never heard one word of thanks for your/your spouse's skill and generosity in treating Tommie after the accident, saving him/her the hassle and expense of a trip to the emergency room.

Other Facts:

1. You and your spouse are in your early fifties. You are both well educated. Joan is an advertising executive and John has a successful practice in internal medicine.

2. Your dogs Rambo and Terminator are show-quality German Shepherds. They are high-spirited, but well-trained dogs. Although you try hard to keep them in, and indeed have re-fenced your entire property, they do sometimes squeeze through the front gate. This is probably because you live in the country where everyone's dogs run loose around the neighborhood, excite your dogs, and tempt them to escape.

3. You are sorry Tommie got hurt in the accident, but what about Veronica? The doctor thinks that she will be okay, but she may always walk with a slight limp and her breeding functions may be impaired by the trauma. In fact your vet has recommended that you spay Veronica, which certainly would put an end to your hopes of breeding potbellied pigs on the farm as a revenue producing activity. The least Tommie could do is apologize.

4. In addition to restoring the old adobe into a showcase home, you and your spouse have spent over $50,000 putting in a well and septic system, new barns and fences, and lots of landscaping. Now you have the most beautiful farm in the neighborhood.

5. You are finding life in this rural neighborhood quite difficult. It was your spouse's idea to be a country farmer. You feel isolated from your family, friends, work, and stores, and feel that everyone in this neighborhood is cold and stand-offish. No one ever talks, visits, or says hello. You think that it is likely that the Jones have turned everyone against you.

6. You reviewed all of the purchase papers and the survey plat and could find no indication of a reservation of an easement across your property for the dirt irrigation road. You know that no one told you about this during the property sales negotiations.

ISSUES AND AGENDA

Dr. John or Mrs. Joan Smith

1. You want to get at least a modest amount of money to cover some of your costs, as well as an apology.

2. You want to find a way to get along with the Jones so that you can stop feeling like you are living in an enemy war zone.

3. You want to find a way to get to know the neighbors so you don't feel so isolated and unwelcome.

4. You want to resolve the issue of the use of the old access road.

5. You want to get the Jones to come to you when they have problems, instead of running to the authorities to complain.

6. You want to be sure that no more firecrackers are thrown in the chicken coop.

POINTS OF RESOLUTION

Dr. John or Mrs. Joan Smith

1. Even though you doubt that Veronica was at fault, you can't say for sure what happened so you will forget about the $600. If Tommie would pick up new trees at the nursery and plant them, it would cut the cost to a total of $300 and you will agree to split this cost 50-50 with him/her.

2. You would like to do whatever you can and whatever is reasonable to get along with the Jones. You hate having neighbors who act like enemies.

3. You feel like you must either establish friendly relations with these neighbors, or you might just give up, sell the farm, and move back to town.

4. You withheld the real estate payment based on principle and can write a check to bring the account current as soon as you are satisfied that Tommie is taking responsibility for his/her actions. Obviously, you are not going to jeopardize an investment of more than $100,000 over $1,200.

5. You don't want Tommie gunning his/her truck up and down the access road. You're not sure where it stands legally, you just want your privacy and your animals' safety respected. As long as you can have quiet, privacy, and safety, you will consider proposals from Tommie on the access road issue.

CONTRACTING INSTRUCTIONS

Tommie Jones

Your attorney has told you to show up for this mediation session. You are not sure what is going on. You understand that mediators are knowledgeable about the law, and will tell each of you who is right. You hope this isn't a big waste of time. When you learn that only one of the Smiths is coming to the mediation, you consider leaving since you take this as a lack of personal respect for you. If the mediators explain that mediation is a process which lets the parties define the issues and create solutions, however, you will be interested in continuing. You recognize that this feud has upset the whole neighborhood, and really bothered your Granny. She has been so worried since the accident that her health has taken a turn for the worse and she can't be here today. As much for her sake as anything, you want to get this taken care of. Really, you have nothing to lose by giving this process a try.

INFORMATION GATHERING AND IDENTIFYING ISSUES

Tommie Jones

Emotional Facts:

You can't believe how these jerks have tried to push you around! They think they can walk into a neighborhood and call the shots just because they have a lot of money. They want to make this neighborhood into the city, putting up fences, always complaining . . . bitch, bitch, bitch! Called the sheriff about your Fourth of July party . . . some b.s. about chickens. Called zoning about your shed, claimed it was hazardous and an eyesore. Called animal control about your dog, Spike, (a great big, beautiful Rottweiller-Pitbull cross). Can you believe it — they call animal control when their vicious pack of so-called show dogs is terrorizing the neighborhood! Their dogs are out all the time barking at you and Spike, and even your poor old Granny — coming on your property all the time. And then they have this ridiculous squinchy little black pig who is too weird looking and not big enough to make a decent sized hot dog, and the stupid pig runs right in front of your truck and now your truck is all dented up. And they want you to pay them! You just wish they would move out so things could be peaceful in the neighborhood like they used to be.

Other Facts:

1. You are 23, finished the 11th grade, work odd jobs when you can. You live with your Granny because you hate your step-father.

2. The night you had the wreck, you were doing some serious partying. You were pretty high. When the runty pig ran in front of the truck, you gunned the motor to scare the hell out of the pig, then you hit a muddy spot and lost control of the truck.

3. The damage to your truck is not serious. Since you're pretty handy with tools, you figure that you can fix it for about $100 in parts.

ISSUES AND AGENDA

1. Get the Smiths to keep their dogs in their yard.

2. Get the Smiths to tell you if there is some problem, instead of calling sheriffs, zoning, or animal control.

3. Find out what the Smiths are planning to do with all of their building projects.

4. Have the Smiths talk to you before they do stuff like tearing down fences.

5. Pay as little money as possible since you are between jobs.

6. Get some kind of an agreement that you can use the old irrigation road, at least in emergencies. You don't need it for regular access but it could come in handy, and anyway you have always used it.

7. Get the payments current on the real estate contract ASAP. Granny counts on that money to make ends meet.

POINTS OF RESOLUTION

Tommie Jones

1. If you can get by with paying $200, and make payments over time, you can live with that. You hope to start a new job next week and could probably pay $25/week.

2. The Smiths need to satisfy you that they are going to be good neighbors and not keep tearing down things which have been there forever (like the old fence) without even talking to you.

3. You must admit that the crummy old adobe and the land that the Smiths bought look pretty nice now.

4. You want to know what the Smiths will do to keep their dogs in, so they stop harassing you. You will admit that since the accident, the dogs have only gotten out once or twice.

5. You think that the Smiths should help with neighborhood projects like maintaining the irrigation ditches. They also should join the neighbors in their fight against the county's proposal to build a satellite jail in the neighborhood, since rich people like the Smiths have more pull than you do.

6. You will agree to limit access to the old road to emergencies or times that you talk to the Smiths first. You want them to take down the fence blocking the road.

7. You are sure Granny will waive late charges and penalties on the withheld payment on the real estate contract if the payments are caught up immediately.

8. You are really sorry that this whole mess happened, but it is hard to admit that to uppity rich people like the Smiths. You are afraid they will just hold it over you and tell the whole neighborhood. To calm Granny and keep her from being upset and worried, however, you will do what it takes to get this settled.

BARNES AND SANCHEZ

II. BARNES AND SANCHEZ

MEDIATOR INFORMATION

This is a private mediation. You are under contract with Webster College to provide mediation services. Your fee is $100/hour and will be paid by Webster. You know that the dispute involves a potential discrimination claim and that a formal grievance has been filed alleging discrimination and harassment.

You have carefully confirmed an understanding with Webster that you will not report or otherwise communicate anything about the matters discussed in the mediation to anyone else in the organization. You will tell the disputants that this understanding will be added to the agreement to mediate. (Agreement to Mediate B in the Forms section)

The disputants' names are Karl(a) Barnes and Louis(a) Sanchez. Since the grievance office referred the case for mediation, you have not had any contact with the disputants and do not know whether they are coming voluntarily.

Keep your actual professional identity.

BACKGROUND INFORMATION

Karl(a) Barnes has been a professor in the Department of Counseling at Webster College for the past five years. S/he has devoted her/himself to building the school's counseling program. When the chairperson of the Counseling Department retired, Karl(a) sought the position. S/he was not hired. Instead, the college brought in Louis(a) Sanchez from a school in Capital City and put her/him in charge.

Louis(a) and Karl(a) did not get along from the moment Louis(a) arrived. Karl(a) was angry because Louis(a) changed areas of the curriculum that Karl(a) had worked hard to develop. Louis(a) was frustrated by Karl(a)'s resistance. Louis(a) began to write negative evaluations in Karl(a)'s personnel file. Karl(a) felt the evaluations were unfair and untrue. Then Louis(a) assigned Karl(a) to supervise student practicums (experiential field placements) as half of her/his teaching load. Karl(a) protested, saying that her/his classroom teaching load and the supervision each constituted a full time job and that Louis(a) was trying to drive her/him out of Webster College. Louis(a) responded that Karl(a) was not managing her/his time efficiently and demanded that s/he submit monthly activity reports, so that s/he could monitor her/him more closely. Karl(a) was outraged by this request, since no one else in the department was required to submit monthly reports on what they were doing. Karl(a) went to the president of the college and complained. The president agreed to talk to Louis(a), but from Karl(a)'s perspective, nothing changed. S/he continued to carry the same workload and s/he continued to be required to submit the monthly reports.

Angry and frustrated, Karl(a) hired a lawyer to represent her/him in a lawsuit against Webster College for discrimination and harassment. The lawyer advised Karl(a) that s/he needed to pursue administrative grievance channels at Webster before going to court. Karl(a) filed a formal grievance which was referred to mediation through a contract which a private mediation office has with Webster College.

CONTRACTING INSTRUCTIONS

Karl(a) Barnes

You are very nervous about being here. You don't understand this process. You told your lawyer that you wanted to go to court to vindicate yourself. Your lawyer said that if you wanted to keep on working at Webster (which you do) you should come to mediation. The lawyer said there would be nothing to lose, but this is costing you time and aggravation, which doesn't seem right. You hope the mediators can get Louis(a) Sanchez to be fair. You do wish something could be worked out to end this torment.

INFORMATION GATHERING

Karl(a) Barnes

Emotional Facts:

You pride yourself on being a good worker and a top professional. To
... you begin your description of the situation with a lot of formality
... lly breaks down as outrage overwhelms you.

... llege you have

3. Your healt
injured your back
physical therapy,
stress have mad

4. You
which has be

5.
succeed a

ISSUES AND AGENDA

Karl(a) Barnes

1. You really want your record cleansed of all the unfair, damaging entries. This is the most important thing to you.

2. You want to stop writing those god-awful monthly reports which are driving you crazy. Or at least have everyone be required to write them.

3. You want a workload that is fair.

4. You want things to change at work so you could look forward to going there again. Right now, all this terrible hassle is making you dread going to the office.

5. If things don't get better, you might even leave, but you will NEVER leave until your name and your record have been cleared.

POINTS OF RESOLUTION

Karl(a) Barnes

1. You are paying your lawyer ($2,500 retainer, $100 an hour) and s/he has predicted this whole thing could drag on for one or two years and cost more than $10,000. You can't afford this potential litigation either emotionally or economically.

2. You believe in Webster College and its counseling program and really would do whatever you could to make things succeed.

3. Your biggest issue is having the negative entries taken out of your personnel file. You won't compromise on this.

4. You also hate being the only one writing monthly reports and think this is unfair, so it is important to you that this be changed, if possible.

5. If the stress of all this pressure and unfair treatment were gone, and you could feel good about going to work, you think you could manage supervising practicums and carrying a full teaching load if you could have some administrative help, i.e., from a work-study student, and if you didn't have to teach the Comparative Psychology course which you absolutely loathe and which is by far the hardest course for you to teach.

CONTRACTING INSTRUCTIONS

Louis(a) Sanchez

You are here because the president of the college told you to come and
very suspicious and reluctant. However, you will go along
trouble at work. Your only hope for mediation
could end all this squabbling and
department.

INFORMATION GATHERING

Louis(a) Sanchez

ISSUES AND AGENDA

Louis(a) Sanchez

1. More than anything, you'd like to end this constant emotional turmoil.

2. You'd like to get rid of Karl(a) Barnes. S/he's a neurotic feather-brain who brings you trouble at every turn.

3. Alternately, you'd like her/him to get on board a team effort to maintain a good counseling program which is cost effective.

4. You want Karl(a) to stop attacking you in faculty meetings and running to the president and stirring up trouble.

5. You want Karl(a) to drop this lawsuit, or whatever it is. This business could absolutely ruin your career. You can't look like a good administrator if your departmental problems end up in court.

POINTS OF RESOLUTION

Louis(a) Sanchez

1. You don't think that the reports you wrote on Karl(a) were all that bad. S/he is really overreacting on this one. Maybe some of the language you used like "hopelessly disorganized" and "fundamentally unreliable" was a little strong. You would be willing to take out all the descriptions, and substitute the word "satisfactory" if that would quiet things down.

2. You are really struggling with budget constraints. There is no way to have someone doing practicum supervision full time. Maybe it would be possible to spread the load by involving more faculty (i.e., four or five professors supervise four or five students each).

3. You don't care if Karl(a) continues to submit monthly reports; they have just been a big hassle, and have not accomplished your goal of helping Karl(a) to perform more efficiently.

4. You need Karl(a) to stop fighting you at every turn, stop complaining, stop making trouble for you, and start supporting your efforts to make the counseling program a success.

WEIR AND THOMPSON

III. WEIR AND THOMPSON

MEDIATOR INFORMATION

This is a small claims court mediation referred by the court's administrative office and you are a volunteer mediator.

The disputants' names are Chris Weir (Plaintiff) and Bobby Thompson (Defendant). The case involves landlord tenant issues. Read the background information which summarizes the allegations in the complaint and counter-claim.

The disputants have received basic information about mediation at an orientation program for disputants and have signed a mediation agreement. (Agreement to Mediate B.)

Keep your actual professional identity.

There is no fee for your services.

BACKGROUND INFORMATION

In mid-March of last year, Chris Weir leased a one-bedroom apartment from Bobby Thompson, owner of a twelve-plex in Nita Valley. The rental period was for six months, beginning April first, last year and ending October first, last year. The rent for the apartment was $370 per month, which did not include utilities. Chris paid a damage deposit of $250 when s/he moved in.

After the lease period expired, Chris stayed on in the apartment with Bobby's consent. On July 3, of this year, Chris told Bobby that s/he would be moving at the end of the month. Chris moved out on August 3, and dropped the key in Bobby's mailbox on that date.

When Chris had not received a refund of the $250 damage deposit after several weeks, s/he went to get her money back from Bobby. Bobby claimed that the apartment cleaning and repairs had cost more than $600, and that Chris also owed another month's additional rent. They had a heated argument.

Chris went to Tenant's Hotline and on their advice, filed suit in small claims court for the return of the damage deposit. Bobby counterclaimed for back rent, interest, late charges, and damages. The case was referred to mediation by the small claims court judge to whom it was assigned. There is no fee to be paid by the parties.

SPECIAL INSTRUCTIONS

Chris Weir

You feel confident you are entitled to a refund of the damage deposit because you have an article which says the landlord must give the tenant an itemized list of deductions in order to keep the deposit, and Bobby never did this.

On the other hand, you feel a little guilty about the state in which the apartment was left. You did have some wild parties and a few dents and holes got knocked in the walls. However, the walls were just cheap sheet rock which only costs a few bucks a panel, so that shouldn't be too big a deal to fix. There were also some stains and cigarette burns on the carpeting, but it was already kind of shabby when you moved in. It wasn't much worse when you left. The glass in the sliding door also got cracked a little bit, but it is in a corner and doesn't really show very much.

You can't imagine why Bobby would think you owe more rent. While you did move in on the first and leave on the third, you had until the fifth before you would owe a late payment on your rent, so this means you had until the fifth to give notice and move. You gave notice on the third and moved exactly 30 days later, so what's the big deal?

You are really sorry you filed this lawsuit. It cost you a $28 filing fee, plus $15 for service of process. All you've done so far is waste your time and money. It really scares you that you are being sued by Bobby for $1,300. You never imagined that could happen. You don't have anywhere near this kind of money. You are just a student who works 20 hours a week on work study.

NITA NEWS

Vol. 1, No. 46   *"In Law We Trust"*

THE PROBLEM BOX
Answering questions about life and law

Q. I rented an apartment on a month-to-month basis, and paid a damage deposit. After I moved out, the landlord refused to give me back my deposit or to answer my calls and explain what is going on. What are my rights in this situation?

A. Under the law an owner who keeps all or a part of a deposit to cover rent owed by or damages caused by a resident must deliver or mail a written itemization of deductions from the deposit within 30 days of termination of the tenancy. The law provides that "if the owner fails to comply, . . . the resident may recover money due him and reasonable attorney fees and costs." (§ 47-8-18) The owner may only use a damage deposit when the resident does not, upon termination of the residency, "place the unit in as clean condition, excepting ordinary wear and tear, as when residency commenced." (§ 47-8-22)

Since you say that you moved out, it may be useful to discuss termination of residency. On a month-to-month tenancy, the owner or the resident may terminate either "by a written notice given to the other at least thirty days prior to the periodic rental date specified in the notice." (§ 47-8-37) A resident who leaves without proper notice may be liable for unpaid rent. The owner must mitigate damages by making reasonable efforts to re-rent the premises, and cannot collect double rent for any period of occupancy.

SPECIAL INSTRUCTIONS

Bobby Thompson

This apartment was left in such a wreck that it looked like a demolition crew had been at work. You got repairs done at bargain prices, and it still cost you $600.

You admit you didn't give Chris written notice on the damages, but that's because you told her/him why you were holding the money when s/he came to ask for the deposit back. Even if this wasn't good enough to allow you to keep the deposit, you can still sue for the damage s/he did to the apartment, which is much more than the deposit. Legal technicalities about notice shouldn't permit her/him to escape from her/his financial obligations.

You think you are entitled to another month's rent because Chris was on a 30 day, month-to-month tenancy. This means s/he had to give notice on the first to be effective. Since s/he didn't give notice until the third of August, that notice wasn't effective until the first of September. Anyway, s/he stayed after the first and that certainly makes her/him responsible for another month's rent. You probably are entitled to September's rent as well.

You did get the apartment fixed up and re-rented by the first of October. The fresh paint, new carpet, etc., made it look so nice you were able to rent it for $450 a month. You are relatively confident about your legal position, but you suspect Chris doesn't have the money. You'd rather have her/him actually pay some of your losses than to have a judgment which is not collectible.

Total Counterclaim:

$ 600.00 damage repair

$ 370.00 August rent

$ 300.00 late charges (at $10 per day for 30 days)

$ 14.80 interest
‾‾‾‾‾‾‾‾‾
$1,284.80 total

HANDY ANDY

RESTORATION & REPAIRS

INVOICE

Bobby Thompson
Nita Valley Apartments
Unit #10

Sheetrock, tape, texture, paint LR walls	$275
Replace LR rug	$250
Replace glass in door	$ 75
	$600

HARPER AND COLE

IV. HARPER AND COLE

MEDIATOR INFORMATION

This is a small claims court mediation referred by the judge and you are a volunteer mediator.

The disputants' names are Denny Harper (Plaintiff) and Mr. and Mrs. Cole (Defendants). One of the Coles will be present at the mediation. The case involves landlord-tenant issues. Read the background information which summarizes the allegations in the complaint and counterclaim.

The disputants have received basic information about mediation at an orientation program for disputants and have signed a mediation agreement. (Agreement to Mediate B.)

Keep your actual professional identity.

There is no fee for your services.

BACKGROUND INFORMATION

Denny Harper rented an apartment at the Mediterranean Gardens Apartment Complex four years ago. Over the years, the property has deteriorated a lot. Eight months ago, Mr. and Mrs. Cole bought the sixteen-unit complex. They met with the tenants, and promised to make repairs and improvements. Since that time, a new furnace and hot water heater have been installed, and a new roof has been put on one of the buildings. Nothing has been done to the interiors of the apartments themselves.

Three months ago, Denny began to withhold his/her rent, stating in a letter to the Coles that his/her apartment was uninhabitable and that s/he would not pay rent until the following work had been done:

— Plastering and painting the entire two-bedroom apartment;

— Replacing broken windows with new storm/screen windows;

— Repairing broken light fixtures;

— Painting and repairing common hallways and entrances in the building.

When the Coles did not respond, Denny bought and installed new storm/screen windows for the apartment, and called an electrician to fix the broken light fixtures. S/he paid the bills, kept the receipts, and sued in small claims court for a total of $647.82. The Coles counterclaimed for $900 in back rent, $450 in late charges ($5.00 per day for 90 days), and $30 in interest. The case was referred to mediation by the small claims court judge to whom it was assigned. There is no fee to be paid by the parties.

ADDITIONAL FACTS

Denny Harper

You are a 30 year old, single parent of a 9 year old son. You are fed up with your living conditions, but cannot afford to leave your $300 per month apartment. You had high hopes for these new owners — who really seemed concerned — but they've turned out to be just like all the rest.

You stopped paying rent, hoping that it would force the Coles to fix your apartment. When that didn't work, you made some of the repairs yourself, using the withheld rent money. You were not extravagant with the repairs, and did only enough to make the apartment habitable and safe. The storm windows were necessary to keep you and your son warm this winter, and you were determined not to live any longer with bare wires hanging from the ceiling. You sued for the amount it cost you. You have receipts for the following expenditures: six storm/screen windows at $87.17 (total $523.02); electrician five hours @ $25.00 (total $125.00)

The rent for the apartment ($300/month) is the most reasonable in the neighborhood by far. Rents in similar buildings run $400 a month and higher. You couldn't afford to pay that much, but you won't be satisfied until you see some action on the rest of the repairs to your apartment.

You tried to get the other tenants interested in a rent strike. They have shown no enthusiasm, and you are tired of carrying the burden of pressing for repairs for the whole complex. Thus, since you filed the complaint, you have become less interested in the common space than in your own apartment, which still needs to be replastered and painted. You are frightened and upset by the countersuit filed by the Coles. You never thought they could escalate the claim to $1,380. You have no money to pay interest and late charges.

ADDITIONAL FACTS

Albert(a) Cole

You and your spouse bought this building as a long-term investment; managing it is your job. The inspection that was done prior to purchase indicated that there were no major problems, but soon you were hit with large and unexpected bills for a new roof, furnace, and multi-unit hot water heater.

You do intend to make the repairs you promised the tenants, but you can't afford to do everything all at once, particularly if the tenants refuse to pay their rent. The rent is too low as it is. The rent for the apartment ($300/month) is the most reasonable in the neighborhood by far. Rents in similar buildings run $450 a month and higher.

You have had no problem with Denny Harper as a tenant. You and your spouse are anxious to quiet her/him down before s/he stirs up the other tenants with talk of rent strikes and self-help. But s/he must understand your financial limitations.

SMITH AND SIFUENTES

V. SMITH AND SIFUENTES

MEDIATOR INFORMATION

This is a private mediation. You know that the dispute involves a commercial lease for the operation of restaurant.

The disputants' names are Terry Smith (the landlord) and Don(na) Sifuentes (tenant/restaurant owner).

The disputants came to mediation because the lease requires them to use the process before litigation and to divide the cost equally.

The disputants have received your extensive mediation information (Client Information) and mediation agreement (Agreement to Mediate B).

Keep your actual professional identity.

Your fee is $120/hour, payable at the end of each session.

BACKGROUND INFORMATION

Terry Smith owns a small commercial building on Palace Avenue in downtown Nita City. The ground floor is an 1,800 square foot restaurant with an attractive garden patio. This space has been leased to Don(na) Sifuentes who operates the Las Comidas restaurant there. Sifuentes leased the premises two years ago on an eight year lease, renewable for five additional years at $18 a square foot, plus an increase determined by the rise in the cost of living index during the first eight years of the lease. Because Sifuentes was doing substantial remodeling and putting in all new fixtures for the restaurant kitchen, initially the space was rented at $14.00 a square foot per year, payable monthly in the amount of $2,100. This was $4.00 a square foot below going market rate for the first five years and it amounted to a rent concession of $36,000. There was no security deposit. Sifuentes has recently decided to leave Nita City and move to California to care for her/his invalid mother. S/he has notified Smith that s/he must give up the restaurant, and has requested either a waiver of the lease's no-sublet clause or an end to the lease, with partial reimbursement of $35,600 for the kitchen fixtures and renovations ($50,000 fixtures and improvements less $14,400 rent concessions to date). Smith has responded by demanding the remaining six years of rent ($25,200 a year for the three discounted years and $32,400 a year for the three full price years for a total of $172,800) based on a clause in the lease that allows the lessor to call due all payments under the lease if s/he has reason to believe that s/he is insecure in lessee's ability to fulfill the lease terms. The parties have come to mediation because the lease requires them to use this process before litigation and to divide the cost equally.

The mediators mailed both of you information (Client Information and Agreement to Mediate B) which you have read and understand.

Summary of Lease Terms

1. Eight year lease with six years remaining.

2. The current monthly rent is $2,100 ($14 per square foot per year multiplied by 1,800 square feet = $25,200 [Annual rent] divided by 12 months = $2,100 [Monthly rent]).

3. Three years remain of discounted initial rent. Then the rent automatically increases to $18 per square foot per year. The discount amounts to $600 a month or $7,200 a year. Increased rent will be $2,700 per month or $32,400 per year.

4. Discount is $4 a square foot ($14 a square foot instead of $18 a square foot.)

5. The lease provides that all fixtures and improvements become the property of the landlord when the lease terminates. The landlord has a duty to sell any equipment to satisfy remaining tenant obligations. The landlord has a lien on all the furniture, fixtures, and equipment.

6. There is a provision in the lease that permits the landlord to accelerate the lease and demand payment in full if there is reasonable cause to believe that the lease is insecure.

SMITH AND SIFUENTES

Special Instructions—Terry Smith

You always had a feeling this deal would go bad. You think Don(na) has more courage than experience, and really got in over her/his head. Actually, the place has done surprisingly well; it's popular, with good food and decent prices, but there seem to be too many employees, too much waste, and too much time when Don(na) is gone and the restaurant is left in the hands of Ramona, the chef/manager. If someone could tighten up the operations and trim the waste, it would turn a nice profit.

You made Don(na) a very fair deal on this lease and it makes you mad to see her/him trying to weasel out of it. You estimate that s/he received rent concessions of $36,000 to cover most of the $50,000 in equipment and remodelling necessary to get the place up and running. This enabled her/him to get into the property with a modest capital outlay of about $14,000. You certainly don't want to pay her/him a cent, and you don't like the idea of a straight sublet because it would give the new tenant too big a rent break given current market conditions.

Real estate values have been escalating in Nita City, and you suspect you could substantially increase the rent with a new tenant. Don(na) signed the lease when the commercial rental market was pretty slow and this property was a bit shabby. Now it is in great shape with first-rate improvements and interior design. However, there are restaurants everywhere in town, so it may be difficult to re-rent this space unless it is remodeled as an art gallery or a retail store. In fact, you recently received a feeler from a prominent business person interested in space for a premier art gallery. You know that the rates on gallery space can go as high as $20-$22 a square foot.

Your lawyer has warned you that litigating this case could take one to two years and cost $15,000-$25,000, not to mention the aggravation. The lawyer asked you what you knew about Don(na's) financial resources and you admitted that s/he did not have a strong personal financial statement. Your attorney raised the possibility that s/he might file bankruptcy, warning you that this could be costly and cause substantial delay. In fact your attorney told you that bankruptcy could tie up the property for months — or even years. What a mess! You can't afford that! She also advised you that you have a legal duty to re-rent the space as soon as possible when a tenant breaks a lease, further reducing the amount of money that Don(na) might owe you for the rental income lost before you find a new tenant, less the amount you can get for the kitchen equipment and other removable fixtures. This is really discouraging.

You and Don(na) spent a lot of time working out this lease, and you see no reason why you should give up your rights under the contract. You can't believe that Don(na) would attempt to soften you up by talking about how much her/his mother needs her/him. Business is business and that's the way the cookie crumbles. You also know that getting the best deal in business negotiations requires taking a hard line initially and making infrequent, small concessions, so you plan to act tough in this mediation although you really do want a settlement. You will ultimately agree to a sublet so long as there is some kind of increase in the rent (say $1 or $2 per square foot . . . $150-$300 per month for the remaining three years of the five year discounted period). If Don(na) wants any cash money, s/he is going to have to get it from her sublessee, not from you. After all, the sublessee is the one who would get the benefit from Don(na)'s investment in the business. If Don(na) will remain liable for the first twelve months of the sublease, you will agree that she can be fully released from liability if all lease payments are current.

SMITH AND SIFUENTES

Special Instructions—Don(na) Sifuentes

You can't believe that Terry is being so hard-nosed and unfair about this. It's not your fault your mother is so ill. Actually, she has Alzheimer's and caring for her will be an incredible nightmare. It's as if Terry places no value whatsoever on family. What if his/her mother was sick and needed care? Wouldn't s/he want business associates to work with him/her?

Terry knows the restaurant hasn't been doing as well as you initially projected. After a difficult first year, losing about $10,000 and exhausting your cash reserves, you broke even in the first quarter of the second year. The last three quarters of the second year have shown a modest total profit of $5,000 (an average of $555 per month). You are pretty confident about your projections for this year indicating a profit margin of about $700 per month. This is in addition to the small salary of $1,500 per month that you take as the restaurant manager. Your biggest expense has been for Ramona Ortiz, your chef. She receives a salary of $2,500 per month. Although this is tough for you to pay in a new restaurant, Ramona's skill and reputation have played an important part in getting your restaurant off the ground in the highly competitive local market.

Ramona has offered to take over the restaurant. You think she'd be great and that this could be a perfect solution. You have already discussed the cost of the furniture ($5,000) which she said she could buy from you over the course of the lease in equal installments. But you also have over $50,000 in restaurant fixtures, equipment, and remodelling improvements which Ramona can't afford to buy, and you deserve to get something back on them. The place was a dump and now it is beautiful! Since Ramona doesn't have any cash on hand to pay you, the only solution you can see is to work out something with Terry. You have already sold your house, and need to get this restaurant mess settled immediately so you can go on out to California. Right now you are really broke, and that's why you need somebody to pay you, not for you to pay somebody else. Actually, your lawyer has suggested that the mention of the possibility of a bankruptcy filing usually softens landlords up since it can tie up a lease for months, maybe even years, and can really drive them nuts. Your lawyer has warned you that there is a small risk you might be responsible for the whole lease amount — that's why she suggested bankruptcy. She also said there were good legal arguments on your side, but that it could take several years and cost many thousands of dollars to fight this out. There is no way you want to be coming back from California to deal with litigation.

You are not a sophisticated businessperson. You were raised to consider the welfare of others and look for ways that everyone comes out okay. This restaurant business was a new adventure for you, and now it seems like it's going to ruin your life unless you can salvage something from it. You are uncomfortable in business negotiations. When you signed the lease, you had your cousin, an experienced real estate agent from California, negotiate with Terry. Unfortunately your cousin is recovering from open-heart surgery and there is no way you can ask for her help at this time.

If you can recover anything at all out of this, even a few thousand dollars, you will settle for that so long as you can be fully released from liability on the lease before the end of the lease. Whatever you and Terry can agree to will have to be run by Ramona for her approval. You know she really looks forward to owning the restaurant and will work with any reasonable arrangement.

DISSOLVING A BUSINESS

VI. DISSOLVING A BUSINESS

MEDIATOR INFORMATION

This is a private mediation. You know that the dispute involves the breakup of a mediation partnership.

The disputants' names are Lou(anne) Peters, Randy Cisneros, Paul(a) Greene, and Stephan(ie) Ritter.

The disputants are totally familiar with the mediation process because all of them are trained, practicing mediators.

The disputants have received your extensive mediation information (Client Information) and mediation agreement (Agreement to Mediate B).

Keep your actual professional identity.

Your fee is $120/hour, payable at the end of each session.

BACKGROUND INFORMATION

Lou(anne) Peters, Randy Cisneros, Paul(a) Greene, and Stephan(ie) Ritter opened a mediation office together a year after finishing the mediation training where they met. Each of them had full-time jobs, and they planned to keep working in their other professions while developing the mediation business. Lou(anne) is an attorney with a predominately family law practice. Randy is an attorney/MBA/CPA who does a lot of corporate work. Paul(a) is an MSW who specializes in family practice within treatment programs. Stephan(ie) is a psychologist who teaches at the University. Their plan was to offer co-mediation by mixed gender, combined professional expertise, teams who would be paired to meet the specific demands of the case.

The four mediators rented a one room office for $450 per month, on a month-to-month lease, which included telephone, xerox, a shared receptionist, and shared kitchen and waiting room facilities. They took out a small ad in the yellow pages for $110 per month, and furnished the office partly with things they each contributed and partly with things they bought. Their purchases were: four chairs @ $75 each, small bookcase $100, antique table $75, computer and printer $1,000, mediation reference books $200, and small filing cabinet $150. They each chipped in $750 to fund the initial costs of starting up their business. There was no written partnership agreement.

The practice was successful, right from the start. Because they were well known in the community and worked hard to publicize their new practice, cases came in quickly. In fact, Paul(a) soon decided to quit her/his family programs job and work in the office full time, supplementing his/her income by taking some solo mediations and custody evaluations. The business charged $125 per hour for co-mediations and $75 an hour for solo mediations or individual mediator work out of sessions. Of this, each mediator received $50 per hour, and the additional $25 went into a fund for paying office overhead and expenses. Paul(a) kept the books and handled the office management, records, and taxes. S/he received $25 an hour for this work.

Although the business was not steady, and seemed to alternate between overly quiet and overly hectic times, the practice was always in the black. In fact, the four mediators were able to pay themselves back their initial individual capital outlays at the end of their first year. After two-and-a-half years together, their problems were relational rather than financial. Stephan(ie) felt like s/he was working two full-time jobs and that her/his teaching and family were suffering, so s/he didn't want to take any more cases. Randy felt like her/his time was worth a lot more than $50 per hour and that if they didn't double their rates, s/he would have to quit. S/he also was continuously annoyed at the way Paul(a) was keeping the books, finding her/his work to be slow and sloppy, and was angry with Stephan(ie) whom s/he found to be unreliable. Paul(a) felt bored and was lonely as the only one in the office full time; s/he wanted to go back to program work. S/he also felt that s/he was expected to do all the menial tasks for the office and was more abused than appreciated. Lou(anne) hated the increasing friction and tension in their weekly office meetings, although s/he was happy with her/his work in the group and wished they could smooth things over and keep the partnership going.

Over the last several months it has become increasingly clear to the four partners that they must dissolve their association. Since everyone knows that feelings have been running high, the group has agreed to bring in outsider mediators to help them work through the terms and mechanics of the dissolution. The big issues seem to be: what to do about the four existing, on-going mediation cases (two staffed by Paul(a) and Lou(anne) and two staffed by Stephan(ie) and Randy), what to do about old clients who might try to contact the office, and what to do about referral calls and new cases. This raises an issue about what to do about the telephone and the yellow-pages ad. There are also the questions of dividing or disposing of the office furniture, clearing out the office and leaving it clean, where to store old files, and winding up the finances for the business.

The parties have agreed to divide the cost of mediation equally.

DISSOLVING A BUSINESS

Special Instructions—Lou(anne)

You just hope you can get through this mediation session without too much pain and turmoil. The breakup feels like a divorce to you, and you are heartbroken to see all the acrimony and nastiness spoiling good friendships and good work associations. After all, the four of you are part of a relatively small professional community and will continue to be thrown together in meetings, committees, and other mediation associations. You loved the business and the close association among the four of you. You wish there was a way to keep the group together, but you can see that this no longer is possible. You know it is important for everyone to express their feelings, but this is so painful and sad. If people start to express strong feelings, you will jump in and either minimize the importance of the issue or try to change the subject.

On the practical side, you feel strongly that the dissolution must be proper and orderly. There must be continued access for old clients, not a disconnect recording on the phone. Files must be maintained, referrals made for new cases, etc. You know these things may be expensive, complex, and difficult, but they must be done. Also, you really want the antique table when the furniture is divided, since it was you who found it on a flea market expedition and spent quite a bit of time stripping and refinishing it. If you had to pay the others for something that you found and salvaged, it would be a real rip-off.

Mediation is very important to you, and you know you will have to find a way to keep it a part of your life, so you don't see the end of the partnership as the end of your mediation career. You are definitely interested in new cases.

To deal with your anxiety, you have prepared an issues list for everyone to use during the mediation. As soon as possible after the session begins, you will hand it out to everyone. You hope that this will make the mediation orderly, calm, and efficient.

DISSOLVING A BUSINESS

Lou(anne)'s Issues Summary

1. The furniture: divide? sell? give away?

2. The phone/yellow pages ad: cost? old client calls? new client calls?

3. Handling existing cases?

4. Storing old client files?

5. Future relationships?

DISSOLVING A BUSINESS

Special Instructions—Paul(a)

You are tired of carrying this business on your shoulders. The other three have the luxury of good-paying jobs. As an MSW, you are lucky to make $30,000 a year. You have found a new job as Director of Family Services at Britenbush Hospital and you are ready for a new life. That doesn't mean you are through with mediation forever, but it's going on the back burner for a while. You could care less about the arrangements for new cases since you will not benefit. Maybe those who benefit from new cases should be available for calls from former clients as well. You are totally unwilling to pay any money to help in closing down the business. That's your clear bottom line.

Since you start your new job next week, you really need someone to agree to take your place mediating your last two cases with Lou(anne). If anyone agrees to do this, you will be in their debt and will want to reciprocate.

The office lease is month-to-month and you've already given them notice starting the first of next month. The office account has enough money in it to pay current bills and that's it. There are no outstanding accounts because all the clients pay per session. There is no extra money at all. You understand the concern about the disconnect recording on the phone, but in order to keep the line, you'd have to keep paying on the yellow pages ad, plus pay a fee to the receptionist, or pay for call forwarding to another number. Even to get a message that says, *This number is no longer in service. Calls are being taken at* . . . costs $55 per month. Of course you'd be the one to know all this, because you've always had to do all the legwork for the office.

Stephan(ie) has been half-hearted about her/his commitment right from the start. No wonder s/he's quitting. You know Lou(anne) feels bad about the breakup, but s/he has a successful law office backing her/him up. And if Randy says one more word about "proper accounting practices" you'll scream. You're not a CPA, never studied bookkeeping or accounting, you just did your best at a job that had to be done. You never saw Randy in the office at night trying to reconcile the checkbook. The accounts are stored in the office filing cabinet and s/he has as much access to them as anyone else. You're through spending time on them. If anyone doesn't trust you and wants to check your work, FINE!!

DISSOLVING A BUSINESS

Special Instructions—Stephan(ie)

You are very glad you had the opportunity to work with the others in the mediation practice. It really helped with your professional development. But you have a career, and a family, and the demands of the mediation practice have just been too much. You think mediation is very important, and want to stay involved with it, but it needs to be in balance with the rest of your life.

You also are a little bored with the endless weekly office meetings that always turn into gripe sessions. They remind you of department faculty meetings. You have mostly co-mediated with Randy who is far too uptight for your taste, always picking at details and pressuring you to get things done. It's time to leave. You are willing to finish up your cases with Randy and then you want to take a break from mediation for a few months. After that, you'll probably be willing to take a couple of cases per year.

You want the business dissolved cleanly and decently. You don't care about money or furniture, you just don't want anyone to ask you to <u>do</u> anything else. Split the furniture, sell it, give it away, you don't care. You understand the client concerns, and hope that Randy or Lou(anne) will find a way to take the calls. As a goodwill gesture you are willing to chip in one-fourth of the cost on the phone for a couple of months. But after that, the person getting the calls should pay, since they are the ones who will get any new cases that come in. If you receive a couple of referrals per year, you are willing to pay an overhead fee to the referring source.

DISSOLVING A BUSINESS

Special Instructions—Randy

You are very disappointed to see this business opportunity fail. Well, not fail exactly, but at least be abandoned without developing its full potential. This practice could have been a gold mine if everyone had just dug in and done their part. But there were always too many distractions.

You want the dissolution to be orderly. You want Paul(a) to produce an inventory and a proper accounting so that appropriate business decisions can be made. If s/he can't or won't, you want her/him to sign a written guarantee that all bills have been paid and all property and money is accounted for. You think the furnishings should be liquidated and the money used to continue the phone service for a brief period of time. You do not think any of you should pay your own money to keep the phone going; that would just be a waste — not cost effective. This practice has already cost you too much time and energy for too little return. You think the files should probably go into Lou(anne)'s office; s/he has the most space and s/he is most likely to keep mediating on a regular basis. You would like to continue to mediate in the future, but only if you can find a way to make the money work out. You bill $150 an hour in your private practice, and although you really enjoy mediating, $50 an hour is ridiculous.

You will finish your ongoing cases, but you aren't interested in new cases unless you can earn at least $100/hour.

D.O.T. MEDIATION

VII. D.O.T. MEDIATION

MEDIATOR INFORMATION

This is a private mediation. You have been hired by the Department of Transportation, Human Resources Division, as outside mediators to handle this case. Your fee is $120/hour and will be paid by D.O.T. You know that the dispute involves a potential discrimination claim, but that no formal complaint has been made.

You have carefully confirmed an understanding with D.O.T. that you will not report or otherwise communicate anything about the matters discussed in the mediation to anyone else in the organization. You will tell the disputants that this understanding will be added to the agreement to mediate. (Agreement to Mediate B)

The disputants' names are Fran Baca, Terry White, Toby Jones, and Bill Jeffers. The mediation program office within the Human Resources Division referred Fran to mediation and notified the other disputants to attend an initial session.

The disputants have received your extensive mediation information (Client Information) and mediation agreement (Agreement to Mediate B) before the initial session with instructions to read them and come to the session with any questions or concerns about mediation.

Keep your actual professional identity.

BACKGROUND INFORMATION

Bill Jeffers, Toby Jones, Terry White, and Fran Baca work at the State Department of Transportation (D.O.T.) in Nita City. Jones, White, and Baca work in the same group. Bill Jeffers is their direct supervisor. Jones is the project leader on a current, major job to which Baca and White are assigned. Therefore, Jones has supervisory authority over much of their daily work. The project involves a new airport for Nita City. The project affects a substantial number of stakeholders, including two Native American tribes and a predominantly Hispanic section of Nita City. It has high public visibility and has been the subject of some controversy.

Baca was recently hired by D.O.T., right after s/he graduated. S/he was chosen for a position as an Engineering-Design Specialist II based on her/his expertise in state-of-the-art engineering techniques in large scale concrete applications such as airports, complex bridges, and highway interchanges. S/he first worked on improvements to the interstate which runs through Nita City. The work was both innovative and practical, and this early success brought Baca praise and recognition at D.O.T. S/he was then assigned to the design team for the new airport. For this project, Baca has been given the designation of Engineering-Public Relations Specialist, spending about 80 percent of her time representing the project in public forums, giving talks, taking visiting dignitaries around the project, and responding to public, congressional, and governmental inquiries. Although D.O.T. personnel regulations specifically authorize this kind of temporary reclassification and job assignment "for the good of the agency," Baca is very frustrated with this work. S/he dislikes public speaking and resents the waste of her/his engineering skills. White is the regular public affairs officer for D.O.T., currently detailed full time to the airport project because of its high profile and political sensitivity. S/he is assigned to assist Baca with PR.

D.O.T. has a new mediation program and has publicized the program within the agency by saying that the mediators are trained to handle concerns that involve race, gender, and cultural differences on the job. Because Baca is unhappy with this assignment and angry about what s/he suspects are the reasons for it, s/he has contacted the mediation program at D.O.T. for help in discussing his/her work and treatment by the project team leader and the public affairs officer. The notes from the intake person indicate that s/he has discrimination concerns. The intake form lists the people involved who need to be present as Bill Jeffers, Toby Jones, and Terry White. No formal charge, grievance, or complaint has been filed.

D.O.T. MEDIATION

Special Instructions—Fran Baca

You are a recent hire at the State Department of Transportation. This is your first professional job after graduate school. Since your arrival at D.O.T. you have been treated as an outsider. This is not new to you. In graduate school you were one of the few Native Americans/Hispanics/African Americans in your class. You are the first member of your family to go to college. You are proud of your skills and your ability to earn advancement on merit. The new airport involves complicated engineering design issues that you would love to work on. However, the project leader seems to want you to spend all of your time at press conferences, talking to legislators, and giving speeches to service groups. You feel that you are being used as an ethnic token by D.O.T. for political purposes and you resent it deeply.

When Jones announced this assignment, you went to talk to him. You told him that you were not comfortable talking to large groups of people and that you thought you were hired for your engineering skills. Jones seemed to dismiss and belittle you, saying, *everybody's got to pull their own weight around here. Buck up, do what you're told, and be happy you've got a job at all.* You left seething inside.

You also have a problem with Terry White. S/he is distant to the point of hostility. At the last public speech you gave, s/he had agreed to back you up if there were tough questions from the audience. At the beginning of the question period, however, Terry walked out of the room. An angry landowner made allegations that the project was a big boondoggle, designed to generate jobs for minority contractors. You were totally taken aback. You did not know how to respond and Terry wasn't there to help you. You are embarrassed and angry about this betrayal.

You are a little intimidated by Bill Jeffers. He is your boss and a big honcho in state politics. He has a lot of power. He could make or break your state government career. He has been influential in state politics for over 20 years, is on a first name basis with the governor, and counts key players in the legislature among his personal friends. You have heard that the current state engineer was Bill's protege and that Bill moved him up the ladder to that position at record speed.

You have felt stymied and miserable in this situation. You keep going back and forth between staying quiet, doing your job the best you can, and playing it safe, or saying what you really think and feel about the racism and injustice you are experiencing. When you heard about a new D.O.T. mediation program you put in a request for a session. If you can't get some relief, there may be no alternative except to quit and look for another job. Several of your friends have advised you to make a complaint with the EEOC and to consult with a lawyer. So far you have not done these things because they seem distasteful to you.

In the mediation session, you are looking for three things: (1) personal respect, (2) acknowledgement of your professional abilities and your value to D.O.T. as an engineer, and (3) some kind of flexibility in or relief from handling your assignment on this airport project.

D.O.T. MEDIATION

Special Instructions--Terry White

You are the public affairs officer for D.O.T. You have 10 years experience at D.O.T. in addition to five years as a TV news reporter. You consider yourself a real pro.

You were excited about this new airport project. It promised to be a lot more interesting than the routine road and bridge work that is D.O.T.'s bread and butter.

You were surprised when Bill Jeffers told you that your assignment would not be as the team leader on public affairs, but as the assistant to an engineer who knows nothing about public affairs and public relations. When you challenged Bill about the reason for the assignment, he told you that he was "under pressure from upstairs to staff more ethnic minorities on visible projects that impact minority communities." He said he wanted Fran Baca up front, so he won't be accused of racial discrimination. He also said that he wants you to make him, Fran, and D.O.T. look good, by taking care of Fran and keeping her from making mistakes. You told him you didn't think this whole situation was fair. You are a professional, not a baby-sitter!

You are frustrated with Bill Jeffers, but you don't know what to do about it. At the most recent public appearance, you walked out just before the question and answer session because you couldn't stand seeing Fran up in front, where you belonged. Later, you felt guilty because you heard that s/he was attacked with some tough questions that you could have helped him/her to handle. What makes it worse is that you promised to back him/her up. You want to apologize, but apologies don't come easy to you. You know Fran hasn't done anything wrong, but you keep feeling that s/he is in your place. Overall, you feel bad that you let Fran down when it was Bill Jeffers you were upset with. From everything you can see, Fran really is a terrific worker and a great addition to D.O.T..

You don't know what to make of the mediation notice. You know Fran initiated the process, but you don't know why. You wonder what will happen and whether s/he will make some allegations against you. You have not talked to Bill or Toby about the upcoming mediation.

D.O.T. MEDIATION

Special Instructions—Toby Jones

You are a retired military officer, a double-dipper. You have only three years until you can retire from your state job with your second pension intact.

Fran was assigned to do the airport PR for your team over your objection. You told Bill Jeffers that Fran is an excellent engineer, and it was a waste not to use his/her talents. In addition to being your boss, Bill Jeffers is a friend. He leveled with you and explained that he didn't have any choice because he had to play a numbers game, and a little "up front color" would look good on the project since there would be a lot of public visibility. You were not totally comfortable with his statement. You pride yourself on being color-blind and looking at talent and merit as the sole basis for assignments. However, as a good soldier and team player you are used to taking orders and carrying them out, even if you don't agree. You also respect your boss and trust his judgment that an assignment of an ethnic minority to the public relations side will be good for the team, the organization, and the project in the long run.

After you assigned Fran to the public relations job, s/he came to you with some sob story about not being comfortable talking to groups and about being mistreated by Terry White. You let her know, in no uncertain terms, that orders are orders. Regardless of the situation, you can't stand complainers and whiners. You were raised to toe the line, pitch in, and say "YES SIR!" when you received an order.

You know that Fran is a talented engineer and you respect his/her skills. In fact you wish that you could use her more on the design and execution of this project. You really need the expertise. You also would like him/her to take the lead on a particularly thorny engineering problem on a new bridge project that you will be starting soon. Given this current behavior, however, you wonder if s/he could handle it.

You were surprised by the request for mediation and don't really understand what it is about. Because you are a team player, you will go and make the best of it. You are loyal to Bill and will defend him if necessary. You tried to reach him to talk about this but since the legislature has been in session, he has been totally unavailable.

D.O.T. MEDIATION

Special Instructions — Bill Jeffers

You are the Division Director for Special Projects at D.O.T. This means you get all of the tough, politically sensitive projects. You are a career state employee, well connected and visible in state politics.

The airport project has generated a lot of pressure to respond to long-standing demands by minority communities in the state for more hiring in real positions of responsibility in state government. Your department is one of the worst offenders, having been historically a white male bastion.

You were pleased to hire Fran Baca. With his/her qualifications and skill, you know that s/he will be an asset to the department. In fact, you think hiring him/her was a real coup, because s/he is so talented and came with great recommendations. The outstanding job s/he did on design of the interstate shows how talented s/he is. And the hire was such great timing. With the airport project coming up, you could put him/her up front to deal with the public, including all of your minority group critics. You thought s/he would be thrilled to have such an important assignment.

You are a little upset with Toby Jones. You thought s/he was savvy enough to handle this project team assignment without making messes for you to clean up. However, you and s/he go back a long way and you will protect her/him if necessary.

Terry White is also in your doghouse. You told her/him to take care of Fran. And then you got a call from a legislator complaining about the poor performance of Fran Baca in answering questions that challenged the integrity of the airport project. You spent 30 minutes on the phone smoothing his ruffled feathers.

Now this mediation request. You don't know what it is all about, except that you know Fran is unhappy. You sure don't want a discrimination complaint by your department spokesperson on the project. That could really mess you up. You need to find a way to calm Fran down and keep the project team intact if at all possible. You see him/her as key to future developments in D.O.T. and you want to make him/her happy. Because the legislature has been in session, you have not been able to sit down and talk to Toby or Terry before the mediation session.

The Art of Mediation